'Priest' as Type of Christ

American University Studies

Series VII
Theology and Religion

Vol. 5

PETER LANG
New York · Berne · Frankfort on the Main · Nancy

John D. Laurance

'Priest' as Type of Christ

The Leader of the Eucharist
in Salvation History
according to Cyprian of Carthage

PETER LANG
New York · Berne · Frankfort on the Main · Nancy

BR
65
.C86
L38
1984

Library of Congress Cataloging in Publication Data

Laurance, John D., 1938–
  «Priest» as type of Christ.

  (American University Studies. Series VII, Theology
and religion; v. 5)
  Revision of thesis (Ph.D.) – University of Notre Dame, 1983.
  Bibliography: p.
  Includes index.
  1. Jesus Christ – Priesthood – History of doctrines –
Early church, ca. 30–600. 2. Priesthood – History of
doctrines – Early church, ca. 30–600. 3. Typology
(Theology) – History of doctrines – Early church, ca. 30–
600. 4. Bible – Criticism, interpretation, etc. – History
– Early church. ca. 30–600. 5. Cyprian, Saint, Bishop
of Carthage. I. Title. II. Series.
  BR65.C86L38 1984   262'.1   84-47539
  ISBN 0-8204-0117-X

CIP-Kurztitelaufnahme der Deutschen Bibliothek

Laurance, John D.:
«Priest» as type of christ: the leader of the
eucharist in salvation history according to
Cyprian of Carthage / John D. Laurance. – New
York; Berne; Frankfort on the Main; Nancy: Lang,
1984
  (American University Studies: Ser. 7,
  Theology and religion; Vol. 5)
  ISBN 0-8204-0117-X

NE: American University Studies / 07

© Peter Lang Publishing, Inc., New York 1984

Printed by Lang Druck, Inc., Liebefeld/Berne (Switzerland)

To my Father and Mother,
my Sisters and Brothers,
my fellow Jesuits

Preface and Acknowledgements

The following pages represent for the most part a
dissertation leading to a doctorate in Liturgical Studies
from the University of Notre Dame, awarded on May 15, 1983.
Some revisions have been made throughout, especially in the
conclusions. For these, as for all else, I assume full
responsibility.

However, I am especially indebted to my advisor, Professor
Edward J. Kilmartin, S. J., who throughout the endeavor was as
seemingly boundless in his generosity and encouragement of me
as he is in theological understanding. I also wish to express
my gratitude to the University of Notre Dame and to the John M.
Max family of Creve Coeur, Missouri, for a share in their memorial
fund, thus helping to make my education possible. Finally, I
gratefully acknowledge the support of my own Jesuit Wisconsin
Province and the interest and caring of my family throughout the
years of study.

John D. Laurance, S.J.
Creighton University
Omaha, Nebraska 68178

TABLE OF CONTENTS

INTRODUCTION

In these pages we propose to study the theology of eucharistic leadership in the works of Cyprian of Carthage.

In the past any number of studies have been made on Church ministry in Cyprian in particular and in the early Church in general. Why then set out on yet another foray into such familiar fields? The fact is, as Karl Rahner puts it, there has also been in our 20th century a "Copernican revolution" in the understanding of sacraments in the Church. Once familiar realities have taken on a whole new meaning. As a result, Church writers, too, such as Cyprian of Carthage, who deal in any way with the sacramental nature of the Church, must be approached now in light of newer perspectives. In the past 20 years, for example, important work has been done on Cyprian's understanding of the nature of the Church. Consequences of this understanding in the areas of Eucharist and Church ministry still remain to be explored. Likewise, although the close relationship of Old Testament priesthood to Office in the Church according to Cyprian has long been a concern for scholars, the relationship of the Bible to the liturgy has only begun to be appreciated. The connection, therefore, in Cyprian's writings between the roles of biblical types and figures of Christ and the role of the one who acts "in the place of Christ" at the eucharistic celebration, i.e. the eucharistic leader, stands now in special need of a fresh investigation.

In the past scholars often approached the text of Cyprian simply by means of word studies and textual analyses limited to his stylistic or lexical capacities. Such studies are of course indispensible as groundwork for any solid theological interpretation of the text. Accordingly, where our present investigation finds previous scholarship of this sort to be still dependable, it does not attempt to re-establish what already has been well-argued and generally accepted. Rather, such scholarship provides us with building blocks in constructing our larger thesis on the meaning of Cyprian's thought in relationship to fundamental biblical understandings on the one hand, and to contemporary theological perspectives on the other.

Where past scholars have relied completely on analyses of individual texts or lexical uses in their theological interpretations of Cyprian, they undoubtably did so only because earlier in the area of sacramental theology the overall horizon of meaning was stable and unquestioned. As a result, the validity of their interpretations were limited, not only by the internal evidence of the writings of Cyprian as a single author, but also by the investigator's own unquestioned theological presuppositions. For example, some earlier Catholic scholars presumed that whenever Cyprian refers to baptism as a "<u>sacramentum,</u>" in that context there is only one meaning that word could have for an orthodox person throughout the history of the Church: namely, one of the seven "sacraments" of the Church. In the same way, because of Cyprian's adamant insistence on hierarchical authority, Protestant writers in the past have automatically attributed to him teachings which for them characterized the sacramental theology of a much later, medieval Rome.

Consequently, in our current investigation of eucharistic leadership
there obviously is need for a broader perspective than merely the
text of Cyprian himself in which to read and interpret his teachings.

In regard, then, to the overall method to be used in dealing with
eucharistic leadership according to Cyprian, the approach to our topic
will follow the manner described by H. de Lubac:

> ...the hypothesis which we propose is born from
> a sufficient number of indications, it brings in
> a logic that is convincing enough from an imposing
> number of texts, it is corroborated in the manner
> of lining up sufficient details from different
> authors for plausibility, and finally it is har-
> monized well enough with what we know to be the
> mentality and language of the Fathers that we are
> well justified in forwarding it.[i]

Absolute certitude may be impossible, so that our aim is to arrive at
the most thorough and internally consistent plausibility-structure
attainable in order to explain the data presented by the writings of
Cyprian. Accordingly, we will first seek to establish the sources of
Cyprian's theology of salvation history in Sacred Scripture itself
(Chapter One), and in second and early third century exegesis (Chapter
Two). In light of the first two chapters we will then investigate
Cyprian's understanding of how the economy of salvation ties together
Old Testament types, Christ and Christian realities (Chapter Three).
Finally, the role of eucharistic leader according to Cyprian will itself
be investigated and analysed against the background of his theology of
salvation history (Chapter Four). A short conclusion will follow.

---

[i]Henri de Lubac, S.J., Corpus Mysticum: L'Eucharistie et l'Eglise
au Moyen Age, 2nd ed. (Paris: Aubier, Editions Montaigne, 1949), p.
352 (my translation).

His Life

Thasius Caecilius Cyprianus was born in Carthage between 200 and 210 C.E. to wealthy pagan parents and became a Christian only in later life, around the year 246. Before his conversion, Cyprian was probably a teacher of rhetoric. He definitely was an influential person in the pagan society of his day. It is clear that the political importance of his becoming Christian did not escape his fellow Christians. Very soon after baptism Cyprian was ordained a presbyter, and in the following year, late 248 or 249, he was made bishop of Carthage. The speed with which he was put in charge of the primatial see of North Africa witnesses both to the force of his personality and to the honor his reputation must have brought to the Carthaginian church, given the marginal status of Christians in the Roman Empire of the time.

Cyprian's episcopal tenure was a stormy one, in which he showed a courageous leadership and administrative prudence. He had to face inner-Church turmoils, including the resentment among long-time presbyters to his becoming their bishop, and also those external onslaughts against the Church known as the Decian (249-251) and Valerian (257-260) persecutions. His willingness to be martyred brought him to his death on September 14, 258.

The major influence on Cyprian's thought, apart from the Bible, was that of his predecessor in the North African church, Tertullian. St. Jerome records the tradition that Cyprian read Tertullian daily and would call for his writings, "Da magistrum" (Give me the 'Master').[ii]

[ii]Hieronymus, Liber de viris illustribus, LIII, Texte und Untersuchungen, XIV, 1, ed. Ernest C. Richardson (Leipzig: Hinrichs, 1896), 31.

However, because Tertullian's adherence to Montanism in his later life would have been tantamount for Cyprian to a definitive rejection of the Church, nowhere does the Carthaginian bishop in the course of his own writings refer to the person of his fellow countryman. At the same time, Tertullian's influence on Cyprian can be felt throughout those same writings. For this reason, one question must constantly be kept in mind throughout this present study: To what extent is Cyprian an original thinker in the theological positions which he takes, and to what extent is he merely reflecting the mind of his "Master?"

Scholars in the past have often characterized Cyprian as a practical, rather than a speculative, theologian.[iii] They point out that he framed theological positions in order to answer the practical problems in Church life caused by Roman persecutions and Church schisms. However, one could also see in this approach an amazing vitality, that Cyprian actually elaborates his theology out of God's ongoing self-revelation in the historical life of the Church. The argument could also be made that, if systematic unity to one's theology is a sign of its speculative maturity, then Cyprian's theology, unified by his overriding concern for the Church,[iv] deserves recognition under this rubric

---

[iii]For example, see H.B. Swete, "Eucharistic Belief in the Second and Third Centuries," The Journal of Theological Studies, III (1902), 174; M.F. Wiles, "The Theological Legacy of St. Cyprian," Journal of Ecclesiastical History, XIV (1963), 139; Pierre-Thomas Camelot, Die Lehre von der Kirche Väterzeit bis ausschliesslich Augustinus, Handbuch der Dogmengeschichte, III, 3b, edd. M. Schmaus et al. (Freiburg: Herder, 1970), 18.

[iv]Fritz Weiss, "Die priesterliche Persönlichkeit Cyprians von Karthago," Schweizerische Kirchenzeitung, XLVI (1958), 562: "Wenn wir Cyprians Charackter betrachten, so fällt uns zuerst eine glühende Liebe zur Kirche auf. ....Hätte er dieser seiner Liebe schöneren Ausdruck

as well for its being profoundly speculative.

His Writings

Thirteen treatises and eighty-one letters have come down to us as rightfully bearing Cyprian's name. The most probable chronological order, together with title abbreviations to be used throughout this study, is the following:[v]

     1. Quod idola dei non sint[vi] (Id)

     2. Ad Donatum (Don)

     3. Testimoniorum libri tres ad Quirinum (Test)

[iv] (cont)geben können als gerade durch seine wichtige Schrift De unitate Ecclesiae? Das ganze Buch ist durchweht von einer grossen Liebe zur Kirche." G.S.M. Walker, The Churchmanship of St. Cyprian, Ecumenical Studies in History IX (Richmond: John Knox Press, 1968), p. 9: "Ardent love for his flock forms the keynote of all that Cyprian did and wrote." For the best analysis on the role of the Church in Cyprian's theology, see Adrien Demoustier, S.J., "L'Ontologie de L'Église selon Saint Cyprien," Recherches de Science Religieuse, LII (1964), 554-588.

[v]With the exception of Quod idola dei non sint, which he omits from the genuine writings of Cyprian, this chronological ordering is that of Michael A. Fahey, S.J., in Cyprian and the Bible: A Study in Third-Century Exegesis, Beiträge zur Geschichte der Biblischen Hermeneutik IX (Tübingen: J.C.B. Mohr, 1971), pp. 18-22. For arguments supporting a more traditional ordering (Don, Test, Vir, Lap, Un, DO, Dem, Mort, Op, Pat, Zel, Fort), see Michael M. Sage, Cyprian, Patristic Monograph Series, I (Cambridge, Mass.: The Philadelphia Patristic Foundation, Ltd., 1975), pp. 377-383.

[vi]Although the authenticity of Quod idola dei non sint had generally been rejected, Johannes Quasten claims that H. Koch sufficiently established its cypriannic character, so that now most scholars accept it into the genuine corpus: Quasten, Patrology, III (Utrecht-Antwerp: Spectrum, 1975), p. 364.

4. De habitu virginum (Vir)

5. De opere et eleemosynis (Op)

6. De dominica oratione (DO)

7. De lapsis (Lap)

8. De ecclesiae catholicae unitate (Un)

9. De zelo et livore (Zel)

10. De mortalitate (Mort)

11. Ad Demetrianum (Dem)

12. Ad Fortunatum (Fort)

13. De bono patientiae (Pat)

Although scholarly opinions on the dates of the treatises vary, for the most part these writings are assigned to the earlier years of Cyprian's life as a Christian. The second last of his works, Ad Fortunatum, was probably composed in 253, leaving only the writing of the De bono patientiae (256) to the remaining five years of his life.[vii]

Cyprian's letters, in contrast, bridge the entire span of his ministry as bishop of Carthage, extending from 248-249 (Epp 1,2,3,4,) to his written resolve in 258 to be martyred in Carthage (Ep 81). Of the eighty-one letters in the corpus, only 65 express his own thought directly. The others are either letters written to him by other people including those by the bishop of Rome (Epp 8; 21; 22; 23; 24; 30; 31; 36; 42; 49; 50; 53, 75; 77; 78 and 80), or are summaries composed by Cyprian of the proceedings of local Church councils at which he pre-

[vii]Fahey, Cyprian and the Bible, pp. 21,22.

sided (Epp 57; 61; 64; 67; 70; 72). Ep 75 is unique among the letters
in its being Cyprian's Latin translation of a Greek letter written to
him by Firmilian, bishop of Caesarea in Cappadocia.

"Priest"

Our study of the eucharistic leader according to Cyprian is entitled,
"PRIEST" AS TYPE OF CHRIST. As will become clear in the course of the
argument, "priest" is used throughout this work as a translation of
Cyprian's Latin word, "sacerdos." Although "sacerdos" contains much
of what the Roman Catholic Church has come through the course of the
centuries to identify with the role of presbyter in the Church (main
celebrant of the Eucharist, vehicle of God's blessings on His people,
ordinary minister of the sacraments, etc.), Cyprian uses this word
almost exclusively of the bishop. At the same time, in a few passages
presbyters are seen to share in the identity of "sacerdos," albeit
in a diminished way, by somehow sharing in the "priestly honor" of
the bishop. Nevertheless, because "sacerdos" refers primarily to
the unique role of bishop in the Church, "priest" in the title of
this work has been included in quotation marks.

CHAPTER I

TYPOLOGY IN SCRIPTURAL TRADITION

Introductory Problematic

    Nowhere in the writings of Cyprian of Carthage is there found a
formal treatise on the nature of the Eucharist. Epistle 63, written
against an abnormal eucharistic practice, is the closest approximation
to such a work. In the course of his argument, Cyprian also includes
reflections on the role of eucharistic leader. One passage from this
letter in particular has been traditionally cited as being key to the
understanding of his teaching on Christian priesthood. For this reason,
and because the approach to salvation history found in this text appears
to be an integral part of his overall Christian vision, we begin our
study with this famous passage.

>   ... Et quod Christus debeat solus audiri,
> pater etiam de caelis contestatur dicens: "Hic est
> filius meus dilectissimus, in quo bene sensi, ipsum
> audite" [Mt 17, 5]. 2 Quare si solus Christus
> audiendus est, non debemus adtendere quid alius
> ante nos faciendum putaverit, sed quid qui ante
> omnes est Christus prior fecerit. Neque enim
> hominis consuetudinem sequi oportet, sed Dei veri-
> tatem... 3 Quod si nec minima de mandatis
> dominicis licet solvere, quanto magis tam magna,
> tam grandia, tam ad ipsum dominicae passionis et
> nostrae redemptionis sacramentum pertinentia fas
> non est infringere aut in aliud quam quod divinitus
> institutum sit humana traditione mutare? 4 Nam
> si Christus Iesus Dominius et Deus noster ipse
> est <u>summus</u> <u>sacerdos</u> Dei patris et sacrificium

2

patri se ipsum primus optulit et hoc fieri in
sui commemoratione praecepit, utique ille
sacerdos vice Christi vere fungitur qui id quod
Christus fecit imitatur et sacrificium verum et
plenum tunc offert in ecclesia Deo patri, si sic
incipiat offerre secundum quod ipsum Christum
videat optulisse (Ep 63, 14, 1-4).
(... And that Christ alone ought to be
obeyed, the Father also witnesses from heaven,
saying: "This is my most beloved son in whom I am
well pleased. Hear him." 2 Therefore, if Christ
alone is to be heeded, we ought not care about what
someone prior to us thought should be done, but what
Christ, who is before all others, was the first to
do. For we ought not at all to follow human custom,
but the true reality of God... 3 But if one may
not dissolve even the least of the Lord's command-
ments, how much more forbidden is it to go against
laws so great, so important, and so related to the
sacramentum of our redemption, or by human tradition
to change what has been divinely established into
something else altogether? 4 For if Christ Jesus
our Lord and God himself is the High Priest of God
the Father and first offered himself as sacrifice
to the Father, and commanded that this take place
in his memory, that priest indeed truly functions
in the place of Christ who imitates that which
Christ did, and consequently offers a true and
complete sacrifice in the Church to God the Father,
if he so begins to offer in accordance with what he
sees that Christ offered.)

Epistle 63 is written against certain Christians who regularly
offered water instead of wine in their morning celebrations of the
Eucharist. They argued that Jesus himself would not have offered
wine at the Last supper if it had taken place in the morning, since no
one drinks or should drink wine at that time of day. In one of his
arguments confronting this practice, Cyprian insists to the contrary on
the importance of the example which Jesus actually did give at the Last
Supper: "ille sacerdos vice Christi vere fungitur qui id quod Christus
fecit imitatur" (That priest truly functions in the place of Christ who

imitates what Christ did: Ep 63, 14). In other words, for Cyprian, the sacrifice of the Eucharist exists only where the one who leads it imitates the Last-Supper actions of Christ in his doing so. According to this argument, if the leader does not act in imitation of Christ, Christ as priest is not present and, as a result, the Eucharist as sacrifice does not take place. A truly life-giving union of the eucharistic sacrifice with the Last Supper therefore depends on an imitation of Christ's historical, saving activity. Since the use of wine is an essential part of the original ritual meal, it is also essential to the Eucharist regardless of when in the day it is offered.

The foundation of Cyprian's argument here is the ontological connection he sees between the imitation of Christ and the presence of Christ. Somehow by virtue of his outward imitation of the Last-Supper actions of Christ the eucharistic leader is engaged in the activity and therefore in the person of Christ himself. Conversely, Christ himself can, through faith, be found and personally encountered in the leader performing a proper offering of the sacrifice. This is the reason, according to Cyprian, why the Eucharist is truly the sacrifice of Christ: Christ is present in the leader to act as priest of the sacrifice.

Here the question arises: How is it, or why is it, that the ritual imitation of Christ effects the presence of Christ? Cyprian does not directly answer this question and, indeed, he gives no evidence that it even occurred to him as a question. However, that very fact -- that the link between imitation and presence would go unquestioned and yet stand as the basis for his argument against his "Aquarian" opponents -- hints that this connection was not the product of his own unique theological thinking. If he wanted to expose the folly of an unorthodox position, Cyprian logically would appeal to the contrary universal Christian tradition on the matter. Such tradition would need no explanation. Even to attempt an explanation would be to call it into question unnecessarily. In the present circumstance, the identity between outward imitation and the presence of Christ appears so central to the argument, and therefore so intimate to Cyprian's faith-content regarding the Eucharist, that it could possibly be part of some commonly-accepted Christian tradition. Furthermore, if this identity does reflect a wider tradition, it would probably occur more than once in the course of his writings. Indeed, without other passages reflecting this identity of imitation and presence and the faith-tradition behind it, we would have no context in which to understand the basic significance of the argument in this passage.

Are there then in the writings of Cyprian further examples of individuals other than the eucharistic leader whose identities are based on their similarity to Christ? If there are such examples, does their imitation of Christ also result in their bearing his presence? If that be so, is the connection between imitation and presence in these examples reflective of some deeper Christian tradition upon which Cyprian also bases the causality of imitation to presence in the relationship between eucharistic leader and Christ?

In the course of his writings there are in fact numerous instances where Cyprian names particular individuals in history as having a unique relationship to Christ. These are those various Old Testament figures in whom the bishop of Carthage finds a predictive value for the coming of Christ because of some personal resemblance that they bear to him.

Cyprian calls these individuals "types of Christ" and in doing so he reflects an early and universal Christian tradition. Indeed, this kind of symbolic interpretation of Old Testament history has roots, as we shall see, even in the Scriptures themselves. Because it was so universal and also combined notions of imitation and presence, we propose to make an initial investigation of the ancient symbolic interpretation of Scripture, including biblical typology, as the possible background tradition out of which Cyprian forms his theology of the relationship of eucharistic leader to Christ.

"Type of Christ" in Cyprian

Cyprian explicitly names four central figures in the Old Testament as "type of Christ:" Isaac (Test I, 20), Joseph (Test I, 20), Samuel (Test I, 20), and Melchisedech (Ep 63, 4, 1). Such individuals are referred to as "types" because either in their personal constitution or in their activities they bear some resemblance to the person and/or activities of the historical Jesus. For example, Cyprian highlights Abel because he imaged the passion of the Lord in his own sacrificial death (DO 24). Noe presents a "figure of the Lord's passion" by his drinking wine as Christ did at the Last Supper (Ep 63, 3). By virtue of his holding his arms outstretched so as to form a cross with his body (in signo ... crucis), Moses was able, like Christ, to overcome the devil, who in turn was prefigured by Amalech (Fort 8).

Biblical typology is applied not only to particular human beings in Old Testament history; it employs the animal and inanimate worlds as well. Thus, for Cyprian the Paschal lamb was slaughtered "as a figure of Christ"

6

(Un 8); the prayer observance by the three youths in the furnace on the third, sixth and ninth hours imaged the mystery of the Trinity (Do 34); and the stone on which Moses sat for support prefigured Christ because it paralleled the strength received from Christ to overcome Amalech (the devil) in battle (Test II, 16). Although certain of these types are original to Cyprian, most of them he owes to earlier Christian authors like Justin, Irenaeus and Tertullian.[1]

Based on these few examples, it is evident that the object of biblical typology is not restricted to Christ. The Trinity and even the devil were seen as prefigured in the Bible. What then were the criteria separating true from false typology? What constituted a legitimate biblical type? Was typology simply a curious invention of overly creative minds? Or is there a basis in Scripture itself that justifies and authenticates this practice in the early Church?

"TUPOS" and Philo's Vertical Typology

K.J. Woollcombe finds that "type" originates from the Greek word, "TUPOS," originally meaning "a blow." Later the word came to have the general meaning of "impression" in the sense of the result given by a blow to a receptive material, as for example, the impression a signet ring gives to warm wax.[2] Because such an impression is necessarily configured to the agent or instrument used in giving it, "type" conveys the

6
6

6

[1] Jean Daniélou, The Origins of Latin Christianity, A History of Early Christian Doctrine Before the Council of Nicaea, vol. III (Philadelphia: Westminster Press, 1977), p. 290.

[2] K.J. Woollcombe, "Le Sens de 'Type' chez les Pères," La Vie Spirituelle, Supplément, V (1951), 85-86.

notion of "image." In addition to being an image, a type is an image whose form is the direct result of the form of the person or object imaged. One might say that the "archetype," the source of the impression, actively conforms the resultant type to itself, and consequently that the form of the archetype "lives on" in the type.

Woollcombe notes that this notion of "type" was used in the interpretation of Scripture as early as the writings of Philo, the Alexandrian Jew of the first century C.E. The world of interacting physical materials offered itself as an apt metaphor for his platonic theory for explaining the deeper meanings of biblical history. To Philo, the ideas of God were archetypes. They were received as types in the human minds of biblical individuals. These types in turn motivated their possessors to bring them into being in the external, historical world.[3]

Although Philo's represents the earliest known use of the word, "TUPOS," in the interpretation of Scripture, his vertical typology between heaven and earth is not the earliest attempt to understand the Bible symbolically. The interest in tracing deeper, more universal meanings in contingent persons, objects and events is found even in the Old Testament writings themselves. As the scriptural corpus expanded through the centuries, its conscious recapitulation of past events by means of symbols became increasingly prevalent.

---

[3]K.J. Woollcombe, "The Biblical Origins and Patristic Development of Typology," in Essays on Typology, edd. G.W.H. Lampe and K.J. Woollcombe (Naperville, Ill.: A.R. Allenson, 1957), p. 54.

The Symbolic Development of the Old Testament

A.G. Hebert highlights this progressive symbolization by dividing the whole of salvation history into three decisive stages of development.[4] He marks each stage with an approximate year: 800 B.C.E., 540 B.C.E. and 50 C.E. In this schema 800 B.C.E. signifies the first redaction of the Pentateuch.[5] The Israelite faithful, he argues, were not recording the events of their history in order to satisfy the antiquarian interests of later generations. They were performing a religious act, a profession of faith that it was Yahweh who led them out of Egypt, Yahweh who made a covenant with them and brought them to the land which he had promised to them. By committing these events and their proper interpretation to parchment, Israel allowed future generations to experience them anew and by them be formed into one continuing people, the people of the covenant.

The second date, 540 B.C.E. represents the great reappraisal of the meaning of history brought on by the Babylonian Captivity.[6] Israel hears and assimilates the word of the prophets from Amos to Ezekiel: Although Yahweh delivered her once from slavery and made a covenant with her, Israel broke the covenant and so was punished. As a nation she may now appear to be dead, but Yahweh will save her again. He will make a "new Covenant" with her, written this time not on stone, but on the tablets of her heart.[7] He will overcome the source of her slavery: her unfaithful-

---

[4]A.G. Hebert, "Imagerie et Doctrine," La Maison-Dieu, 2 2 (1950, 69-84.

[5]Ibid., p. 74.

[6]Ibid., p. 75.

[7]Ibid.

ness, by giving her a share in his own Spirit.

In this second stage, the actions of Yahweh in the past are given as the basis for hope that He will act again as Israel's savior. Thus, the great events surrounding the Exodus, Sinai, Promised Land and Davidic kingship are remembered in a way that makes them convincing symbols of a future and final salvation. As symbols, they not only continue to celebrate and proclaim Yahweh's care in the past, but by doing so they point to a common meaning in all the events of Israel's history: Yahweh is unfolding the plan of his salvation. Sustained, then, by these images, Israel can believe that Yahweh will save her in similar fashion again.

At this point it could be asked: If the Old Testament itself is a witness of faith in God's action in history, must every event presented as historical by the scriptural authors be in fact verifiably historical in order that it be considered a legitimate part of Israel's witness to God's overall action in history? Or is it not rather the case that, if the Old Testament as a whole is based on a series of historical events in the life of Israel, there might be individual episodes within that corpus which were embellished, or even wholly fabricated, in order to express Israel's religious memory of its past?[8] This latter possibility

---

[8] For the contribution and critique of historical-critical scholarship on the Old Testament, see James Barr, "Story and History in Biblical Theology," The Journal of Religion, LVI (1976), 1-17, and his Old and New in Interpretation: A Study of the Two Testaments (London: SCM Press, Ltd., 1966), esp. Ch. IV: "Typology and Allegory," pp. 103-148. Further, for a comparison of approaches to the role of history in the strict sense of the Old Testament narratives, see Martin Noth, The History of Israel, 2nd. ed.; trans. P. Ackroyd (New York: Harper & Row, 1960); and John Bright, A History of Israel, 3rd ed. (Philadelphia: Westminster, 1981).

is precisely the understanding which is presented here. After all, the
mere historicity of past events is unable of itself to explain the
truest meaning of those events within the scope of history. According to
the Old Testament, the ultimate norm for the meaning of history, and
of individual events, is the intention of God as He who expresses himself
within history. In line with this understanding, for the ancient
Israelites history, by virtue of its Origin, is transcendent. Human
events are meaningful only to the extent to which they witness to the
plan of God.[9] Therefore, they are presented in a way that highlights
this common inner mystery. To the biblical writers, the events of
the past are not mere signposts pointing to God, whereas they themselves
are devoid of reality. No, precisely as signs, they are laden with the
presence of the sacred reality to which they refer. Events such as the
Exodus, then, continue to exist far beyond the purely physical and
temporal conditions of their original occurrence.[10]

8(cont) For the ramifications in the area of Old Testament theology,
compare Gerhard von Rad, Old Testament Theology, 2 vols., trans. D.
Stalker (New York: Harper & Row, 1962, 1965), with Walther Eichrodt,
Theology of the Old Testament, 2 vols. trans. J. Baker (Philadelphia:
Westminster, 1961).

[9]Pierre Benoit, O.P., "Prëexistence et Incarnation," Revue
Biblique, LXXVII (1970), 22.

[10]For a fuller treatment of the relation of memory to presence in
Old Testament thought, see B.S. Childs, Memory and Tradition in Israel
(London: SCM Press, Ltd., 1962).

> Anyone who is familiar with the ancient texts
> knows that they are unaware of our modern
> practice of distinguishing, to the point of
> separation, a cause of purely historical origin,
> and a present reality or responsibility, that
> is to say, a present authority.[11]

For the Israelites, the Exodus was never simply a past, verifiable
occurrence. After it took place in history it continued on as a present
part of the overall, unfinished act of history: the act of God. As such,
it also bore an internal resemblance to every other event in the unfolding
of that same, single history, especially to the major turning-points in
that history. Thus, the pattern of the Exodus re-occurred again and
again: the deliverance from the desert into the promised land; the
deliverance of that land into Israel's control through the kingship of
Yahweh; and the deliverance of the exiles from Babylon. Precisely because
this pattern of care for Israel never changed, did it nurture an expectation that Yahweh would always be her savior. In this context, the
original Exodus as a unique historical occurrence became the symbol of
the final, decisive and all-transforming salvation yet to come.[12]

Made conscious of her own sinfulness by her history of failure,
Israel found contrasted in the Exodus the resolute faithfulness of Yahweh,
a faithfulness that would yet free her from her wandering ways. She also
found in past events something of the shape her future salvation would

---

[11]Yves M.J. Congar, O.P., Tradition and Traditions (New York: Mac-
Millan, 1966), p. 12.

[12]Jean Gribomont, O.S.B., "Le lien des deux testaments selon la
théologie de S. Thomas," Ephemerides Theologicae Lovanienses, XXII
(1946), 72.

take. The pattern of history would remain the same since the Yahweh at
work in it is constant in his love for her. Furthermore, since all history forms but one single action of God, insofar as a historical event
manifests this divine action, it is already part of history's final salvation.[13] Thus, the original Exodus and covenant are partial realizations
already of the "new covenant" to come.

The Ontology of New Testament Metaphors

The third state in salvation history, according to Hebert, is the
stage of recognizing in history the effective presence of God's promised
final act of salvation. The year 50 C.E. represents the beginnings of
the New Testament corpus. These writings proclaim Jesus, in his life,
death and resurrection, as the goal of all Old Testament history, and as
its full recapitulation and realization. Once again, they do so by
fashioning symbols out of Old Testament persons, things and events, or
by taking such symbols already elaborated in the Old Testament itself,
and applying them to the person of Christ.[14]

The New Testament presents Jesus as the new Adam (Rom 5, 15), the
new Moses (Mt 5, 1ff: Jn 6, 14), and the new Temple (Jn 2, 19-21). He

---

[13]Paul Tillich, Systematic Theology, vol. I (Chicago: University of
Chicago Press, 1963), pp. 297-427. Tillich in this passage is interpreted by Kelsey, The Uses of Scripture in Recent Theology, p. 85: "An
individual is who he is only as he participatedin a community with which
he shares the symbols that invest life with coherence, meaning, and
vitality. The 'world' is the full range of human experience as ordered
and thematized by communally shared symbols. If the central symbols of
a community are radically changed (e.g. in a revelatory event), that
change transforms both the quality of individuals' existence and the
nature of their 'world.'"

[14]Hebert, "Imagerie," pp. 75ff.

comes, "not to abolish the Law, but to fulfill it" (Mt. 5, 17), and so
these Old Testament realities, not so much live on in him, but are seen
even to have existed originally only because of him (Col 1, 15-20; Jn. 1,
1-18; 8, 56).[15] Corresponding to the metaphor of the Exodus, Jesus is
the true Paschal lamb, given now not only for Israel's salvation, but for
that of the whole world (Jn 1, 35; 19, 36). He is the life-giving
"spiritual" rock which Moses struck in the desert (I Cor 10, 4) and the
true bread from heaven to feed humankind in the wilderness of the world
(Jn 6, 32, 33). At the Last Supper the New Testament depicts Jesus himself as consciously inaugurating the "new Covenant" in his own blood
(I Cor 11, 25; Lk 22, 20).

As can be seen from the nature and extent of this symbolizing process, the New Testament itself constitutes no less than a symbolic
re-interpretation of the Old Testament, where everything has its value
only in terms of its relationship to Jesus Christ.[16] It is a process
which sees Christ already present, although inchoatively, in Old Testament realities because of the saving events of his historical life,
death and resurrection to which those realities point.[17]

---

[15]Benoit, "Préexistence," pp. 21, 22.

[16]Henri de Lubac, S.J., The Sources of Revelation (New York: Herder
and Herder, 1968), p. 31: "...if the fact of Christ had not occurred,
and if it had not been continued in the fact of the Church, all the
exegesis which 'spiritual understanding' or related terms suggest within
Christianity would be pure phantasmagoria."

[17]de Lubac, Sources, p. 40: "When we look for the prefiguration of
Christ in the Bible, we should look less on the subjective level and
more in the objective realm of realities in living development. ...
Christ's presence in the Bible transcends both awareness and men and lies
in the profound logic of idea and event."

14

On the other hand, these New Testament symbols not only affirm an
ontological continuity with the sacred history of the past, they also
announce a discontinuity. Christ is the new Adam, the new Temple -- a
wholly new reality. This disjunction is also reflected in St. Paul's
opposition of "letter" to "spirit" (Rom 2, 29; II Cor 3, 6), "type" to
"the one-to-come" (Rom 5, 14) and "shadow" to "substance" (Col 2, 17).[18]
In other words, God fulfills history according to its own interior
development, but he does so by an event which constitutes history from
its beginning in a wholly transcendent order of being: history participates in the reality of Jesus Christ, God expressing himself (Jn 1, 1-18).
"The world and its history has been designed from the very beginning
with a view to the Word of God become flesh ... Thus the history of the
world is ... the history of God himself."[19]

Behind this disjunction between the New and Old Testaments is a
penetrating awareness of the nature of sacred history. Insofar as the
events of the Old Testament are grasped only in their material and
temporal limitations, as objects of a positivist study of history, metaphors drawn from them would be ultimately meaningless. According to that
view, each event in its particularity remains a totally unique and
unrepeatable happening, and as such can have no existence or significance
beyond itself. The persons or events of the past as possible metaphors
would then be unable to signify some deeper reality at work within history,
or to foster a hope for any future flowering of history into a transcendent salvation. Such metaphors might point out external similarities

[18]Ibid., p. 43.
[19]Karl Rahner, "History of the World and Salvation History," Theological Investigations, V (London: Darton, Longman & Todd, 1966), p. 114.

between persons or events, but they themselves would remain mere empty
shadows. External similarities in events understood as totally unique
are by definition unable to reveal an underlying commonly-shared reality.[20]

This kind of positivist approach to history would simply have been
impossible to the sacred authors. It is true enough that in any case
events such as the Exodus, the Kingship and the Deliverance from Captivity could never have directly signified Christ for the pre-Christian
Israelites. All of the events of history taken together would not constitute that in-breaking of God into time found in the Incarnation of
Christ.[21] It is rather in the experienced _religious value_ common in all
such events that faithful Israelites found a deeper spiritual reality
mysteriously at work in their history, and that the New Testament writers
were further able to identify this reality with their experience of
Christ.

---

[20]Benoit, "Préexistence," pp. 21, 22: "Nous, modernes et cartésiens,
nous sommes portés à considerer les types de la Bible comme des symboles
vides de réalité." L.S. Thornton seems to have just such an understanding
of biblical symbols. See The Form of the Servant, II: The Dominion of
Christ (London; Dacre Press, 1952), p. 15. Kelsey in The Uses of
Scripture in Recent Theology criticizes Thornton for thinking of the
"Bible as a kind of album of pictures" (p. 61).

[21]Hebert, "Imagerie," p. 81: "...toutes les analogies et les
symboles tirés du monde crée sont nécessairement inadéquats à représenter
les réalitiés divines; et la tâche du théologien est d'analyser les
images et d'empêcher qu'on n'en tire de fausses déductions."

> We see that there is a separate milieu between
> the reflex awareness of the image as such --
> the awareness which we possess today of the
> typological character of Israel, and the brute
> awareness of a given object: [This intermediate
> awareness] is the direct, not disengaged, per-
> ception of that which in the object participates
> in the depth of reality.[22]

Sharing in this Old Testament faith-vision that the "depth of reality" is present in key persons, objects and events in Israel's history, the New Testament writers in turn use these same events and persons as metaphors of Christ. Therefore, such metaphors are not based on mere external similarities alone.[23] Rather, they point to a spiritual depth present within the physical, historical world. They develop the Old Testament belief that a divine reality is at work in the movement of history and they announce that this reality was always identical to, and remains co-extensive with, the full mystery of Christ transforming history through his saving life, death and resurrection.

The historical Jesus as Origin of New Testament Metaphors

Y. Congar locates the unity of salvation history in the "divine intention:"

---

[22]Gribomont, "Le lien," p. 76.

[23]de Lubac, Sources, p. 37: "...if the sacrifice of the paschal Lamb really prefigures the redemptive death, the reason for this is not extrinsic resemblance alone, no matter how striking this might be. There is actually an 'inherent continuity' and 'ontological bond' between the two facts, and this is due to the same divine will which is active in both situations and which, from stage to stage, is pursuing a single Design -- the Design which is the real object of the Bible."

> True biblical typology is far more than a
> literary device, the imaginative use of a
> symbolism or of allegories of detail. It
> consists in drawing out the relation between
> the various realities involved in the history
> of salvation at different moments of the un-
> veiling and accomplishment of the plan of God.
> The heart of typology is not just the connec-
> tion in similarity, more or less real, between
> the two things, or simply between two expres-
> sions, but this connection, as it is found
> written in the plan of God, created by and
> founded in the unity of the divine inten-
> tion.[24]

If the "divine intention," at work in all the events of human history, is

the ultimate key to their meaning, that intention must _a fortiori_ be the

decisive factor in the events of Christ's life. Indeed, the New Testa-

ment identifies the source of metaphors interpreting past history in

terms of Christ as Christ himself. In Matthew Christ presents himself

as the fulfillment of Jonah in the whale (Mt 13, 39-41), the eschato-

logical Son of Man (Mt 17, 12), and the Paschal lamb (Mt 26, 28). As

indicated above, in Luke and I Corinthians Christ consciously fulfills

the "new Covenant" of Jeremiah 31, 31 at the Last Supper (Lk 22, 20;

I Cor 11, 25). In the Fourth Gospel Christ likewise links himself to

the serpent in the desert (Jn 3, 14), the manna from heaven (6, 48-58),

the New Jerusalem (7, 38), Moses (6, 32) and Yahweh the Shepherd (10, 14).

Whether or not Christ consciously drew any of these foregoing comparisons

between himself and Old Testament realities during his historical life

on earth, it is clear that New Testament writers deliberately ascribe

the origin of this type of exegesis to the historical Jesus himself.[25]

---

[24] Congar, _Tradition_, p. 69.

[25] _Ibid._, p. 31.

For example, at the outset of his ministry as presented in Luke 4, 21,
the central message of Jesus' preaching is that he fulfills Old Testament
expectations. When the disciples of John want proof of his messiahship,
again Jesus points to himself as the fulfillment of Old Testament scriptures (Lk 7, 22-23). Even after he dies and rises, one of the characteristics by which the disciples of Emmaus recognize the Lord is his exegesis
of the Prophets in terms of himself (Lk 24, 27). In fact, to the degree
that Christ consciously made disciples during his lifetime and commissioned
them to carry on after his death-resurrection, the Good News which he
entrusted to them was the fulfillment of Old Testament scriptures in himself. Finally, the Church itself as founded on the Apostles is the continuation in history of Jesus' own exegesis of Sacred Scripture: "Do
you understand what you are reading?" asks Philip of the Ethiopian eunuch.
"How can I," replies the man, "unless someone guides me?" (Acts 8, 30-
31).[26]

Not only does the intention of Jesus to fulfill Old Testament persons, objects and events standardize the nascent Church's interpretation
of the Scriptures, but that divine-human intention is what gives existence
to those same realities in the first place.[27] Only because Jesus lived,

---

[26]Ibid. See also Damien van den Eynde, Les Normes de l'Enseignement
Chrétien (Paris: Gabalda, 1933), p. 118.

[27]Benoit, "Préexistence," p. 22: "...cette plus-value de signification que nous découvre la révélation du Christ, nous répugnons à la
croire déjà présente dans la préfiguration typique; elle se trouvait tout
au plus dans l'esprit de Dieu, c'est-à-dire sur un mode idéal et non réel.
Encore une fois, les anciens ne pensaient pas ainsi. Pour eux, ces
préparations typiques avaient une vraie réalité en tant que telles, par
leur valeur religieuse, leur existence de signe, réalité plus vraie que
leur contingence matérielle..."

died and rose from the dead in conscious fulfillment of history, is
history, both past and future, in fact fulfilled in him. Therefore the
metaphors of the New Testament not only witness to the underlying unity
of all history in Christ, but they are themselves the medium by which
that history is unified. The metaphors of the Last Supper, for example,
wherein Christ proclaims the "new Covenant" in his saving death-resurrection, is at the same time the vehicle of accomplishing that new
Covenant.[28]

In the view of the New Testament, it is not enough for our salvation
that we ascertain whether Jesus actually did die and rise at a particular
time and place in history. Those events are able to transform human history and us within it, (a) only because the God-Man wills it so, and
(b) only to the extent that we human beings in history receive and accept
the saving intention that they convey. In other words, our salvation
depends on faith, and because the metaphors of the New Testament, espec-

[28]de Lubac, Sources, p. 40: "...the objective continuity of figure
and reality is well-translated, on earth, by continuity of awareness. If
we want the fullness of that awareness, though, the only place to look
for it is in the messianic awareness of Jesus. In that sacred spot,
everything comes together and finds its unity. It is there that the whole
takes on its definitive meaning. .... It is there that the entire
dialectic of the two Testaments is drawn tightly together: the New
Testament in its entirety is brought forth by the Old, while at the same
time the Old Testament in its entirety is interpreted by the New. ....
Jesus is aware that he is fulfilling the religion of Israel, and that it
then becomes completely spiritual in him. He is aware both of fulfilling and of transfiguring, of fulfilling while transfiguring. ....he
lays bare the absolute essence of the great divine Dead which had until
then been totally symbolic -- in point of fact, he fulfills the great
divine Deed in all its reality."

ially the matrix metaphor of Christ himself[29] in his death-resurrection,[30] convey this divine-human saving intention, we can believe[31] that God has saved us in our human history, and only thus do we actually allow those events and their salvation to truly happen.

In summary, then, the metaphors of the New Testament -- Christ as the new Adam, Moses, Paschal lamb, as fulfillment of the Temple and Old Testament feasts and sacrifices, etc. -- accomplish and make present the sacred reality to which they point. They do so because they share in the fundamental metaphor of Christ himself in his death-resurrection as both the expression and the fulfillment in time and space of God's faithful love for his people, thereby establishing all the events of human history in their ultimate existence and religious value. In Christ all history has become the "history of God." Therefore all persons, objects and

---

[29]Gribomont, "Le lien," p. 76: "Cette perception directe du signe en tant que tel n'est possible, évidemment, que pour le signe représentatif, image naturelle, orientant spontanément l'esprit; un example suréminent en serait l'Image parfaite, dont il est dit: 'Qui me voit, voit mon Père' (Jn 14, 9)."

[30]de Lubac, Sources, p. 27: "The 'spiritual meaning' ... interprets the Jewish past solely from the view-point of the Christian present. It is the Old Testament understood in the spirit of the New. Far from having to be wary of an ultimate view, it presupposes such a view, and this is completely legitimate since the ultimate view is based on a definitive Event, which in certain respects is already 'the end of history.' But this ultimate view is of necessity a view in faith."

[31]Hebert, "Imagerie," p. 72: "...cet unique élément d'imagerie, ... ces grands symboles bibliques ... constituent les matériaux avec lequels notre dogme est bâti; ils sont la matière première des formulations de la doctrine théologique. C'est par leur moyen que le croyant, maintenant comme toujours, appréhende la vérité des réalités célestes auxquelles il croit."

events can to a greater or lesser degree be somehow seen as "types of Christ."[32]

Explicit Instances of New Testament Typology

Thus far we have seen that where Philo saw a vertical causality directed downward from heaven to earth and named the impression in the human mind the "TUPOS" of the divine archetype, the thrust found in the symbolic thinking of the Bible itself is totally horizontal, within the realm of history itself. Christ, as it were, is the archetype, and to the extent that persons, objects and events share in his reality are they "types." In fact, in four instances the New Testament uses precisely this word, "TUPOS" in treating of the relationship between:

(1) Adam and Christ (Rom 5, 14)

(2) Events of the Exodus and Christian life (I Cor 10, 6)

(3) Old Testament priesthood and Christ's priesthood (Heb 9, 24)

(4) Noah's ark and Baptism (I Pet 3, 21).[33]

---

[32]According to C.P. Mayer in Die Zeichen in der geistigen Entwicklung und in her Theologie des jungen Augustinus (Würzburg: Augustinus-Verlag, 1969), Augustine expressed this same idea metaphysically: "Die creatio mundi geschah im Prinzip, en archē. Als Prinzip aber ist sie im Geschaffenen gegenwärtig. Die Schöpfung bleibt in den Geschöpfen transparent. So vermag der Gläubige im einselnen das Ganze und im Ganzen den Ursprung zu schauen" (p. 55).

[33]For a more complete list of New Testament types, see Cyprian Vagaggini, O.S.B., Theological Dimensions of the Liturgy (Collegeville: Liturgical Press, 1976), pp. 478-479.

In analysing this New Testament usage of "TUPOS," it is essential
to remember that all analogies limp, and especially so those drawn
between two levels of being. "Symbols drawn from the created world are
necessarily inadequate for representing divine realities."[34] Therefore,
whereas the terms "images," "metaphors," or "types" in our present
discussion affirm an underlying reality commonly shared between two items
in salvation history, they also realize a distinction. Adam is not
Christ. On the other hand, in the New Testament use of Adam as a "type"
of Christ, that decision regarding the salvation of humankind found
defective in the person of Adam can be seen once again in the person of
Christ as fully victorious, so that the solidarity of all human existence
experienced in Adam is both the context and the result of the Christ-
event (Rom 5, 17).

Pauline typology[35] is not restricted to persons only as representa-
tives of Christ. In I Corinthians 10, 4 Paul says that the rock which
gave forth water in the desert "was Christ," in the sense that it was a
"type" of Christ "for us" (I Cor 10, 6). In questioning whether Paul
might be engaging in a purely arbitrary allegorism here, where the mind
predicates reality to verbal or superficial similarities alone, Woollcombe
answers that Pauline typology is based on the real "historical pattern"
of the "Word and Wisdom of God."[36] In the words of T.G. Chifflot:

---

[34]Hebert, "Imagerie," p. 81.

[35]Woollcombe contrasts "Pauline" from "philonic" typology.
"Origins," pp. 52-53.

[36]Ibid., p. 66.

> Petra _autem_ _erat_ Christus [because] the event
> which took place in the desert was itself part
> of the forward movement, driven on by a force
> which surpasses time and for which 'a thousand
> years are as a day,' towards the Easter event,
> and was destined to find, in that event, its
> own true meaning.[37]

Once again, the ultimate validity of typology for New Testament

authors is seen to lie not in the conscious intention of Old Testament

"types" themselves, and therefore, on the basis of their being persons;

nor even in the faith-vision of Old Testament authors who highlight in

events the activity of Yahweh; it lies rather in the purpose and inten-

tion of God Himself at work throughout human history but only accomplished

in, and interpreted by, Christ.[38] Everything that took part in Old

Testament history: persons, physical objects and human events alike, are

theoretically able to be seen as "types" of Christ insofar as they high-

light that divine saving activity in history which is foundationally

accomplished in the death-resurrection of Christ. Clearly, then, "_petra_

autem _erat_ Christus."

The Typological Foundations of the Created World

To some extent it is possible to see in the preaching pattern of

Christ's public life the basis for finding types of Christ in non-human

---

[37]_Water in the Wilderness_ (New York: Herder and Herder, 1967), pp. 56-57. Quoted in de Lubac, _Sources_, p. 37.

[38]Gribomont, "Le lien," p. 75: "...c'est en réalité par la trame même dont il l'a tissu qu'il a fait de l'Ancien Testament une image du Nouveau, et de l'un et l'autre un type de la Gloire."

objects of creation. When Jesus likens the "Kingdom of Heaven" to a

mustard seed, a hidden treasure, or a net thrown into the sea, it may

be said that he is highlighting the mystery-dimension of God's unseen

activity in history by a comparison to everyday "natural mysteries"[39]

of life. However, by means of such comparisons or "parables" he is also

teaching that the Kingdom of Heaven as a supernatural mystery takes

place in and through the natural order of creation itself, that "if it

is by the finger of God that I cast out demons, then the Kingdom of God

has come upon you" (Lk 11, 20). Just as Jesus points to the external

similarities between himself and Old Testament figures as the true

interpretation of a common underlying identity, so too do external

similarities between himself and the patterns found in the created world

point to the self-expression of the one God present in both.[40] "Unless

a grain of wheat falls into the earth and dies, it remains alone; but if

it dies, it bears much fruit: (Jn 12, 24). In fact, it is precisely

through the historical events of the life of Christ that creation is made

to be what it is, and therefore, that the patterns of creation can so

image those of Christ: "He is the image of the invisible God, the first-

born of all creation; for in him all things were created, in heaven or on

---

[39]Birger Gerhardsson, "The Seven Parables in Matthew XIII," New
Testament Studies, XIX (1972), 17.

[40]Henri de Lubac in The Sources of Revelation (New York: Herder and
Herder, 1968) also argues to this underlying unity between the laws of
history and the laws of nature: "No doubt, when [the Israelites] looked
back on the great events of the far-distant Exodus: the deliverance from
Egypt, march in the desert, conquest of the Promised Land, they were conscious of seeing 'real laws of nature' in these events, laws which should
properly have governed the destiny of the chosen people throughout its
history" (p. 38).

earth ..." (Col 1, 15-16).[41] It was only through sin that creation was made to deny its identity with Christ, with the result that now "creation waits with eager longing for the revealing of the sons of God" (Rom 8, 18), and the ways of the unspiritual or natural person can be so opposed to those of the supernaturally reborn in the Spirit (I Cor 2, 14-16).

This awareness, that both creation and the history of the Old Testament are fulfilled by the historical events of Christ's life, death and resurrection, is not only the awareness of the New Testament authors, it is also the fundamental vision common to both the patristic and the middle ages. "There is for them one understanding of God's three books -- each through each -- : the book of creation, the book of the soul, and the book which resumes and explains them both, Scripture."[42] Thus, biblical "typology," as an explicit identification of Christ with a particular reality in the Old Testament, is something of a synecdoche for an overall symbolic interpretation of Scripture and, in fact, of all of life in terms of Christ. Consequently, for New Testament and patristic authors, Scripture is read according to the mind of Christ (I Cor 2, 16), i.e. typologically, not when taken simply as history, but for an understanding of the ultimate structure of the world and the meaning of one's own human life.

Although at various times and by various authors this symbolic inter- pretation has been called the "Allegorical" or "Spiritual" meaning of

---

[41]Benoit, "Préexistence," p. 15.
[42]Congar, Tradition, p. 65.

Scripture,[43] on the basis of the analysis presented here we agree with

Y. Congar that a distinction between the "spiritual" and "literal" mean-

ings of Scripture is often misleading:

> There is only one literary sense, but the facts
> of revelation have a richness of meaning which
> transcends their reality as historic events, and
> consequently their reality as historic events,
> and consequently the texts which present them can
> indicate a content of reality which goes beyond
> what such facts constitute simply as natural
> history.[44]

The Solidarity of the Church with Ancient Israel

According to the New Testament, the Church continues the mystery of

Christ in history in the measure of her faith, hope and charity. Conse-

quently, the Church shares in the same continuity/discontinuity relation-

ship to Old Testament Israel that Christ has, to the point that the

Church, too, is presented as the typological fulfillment of faithful

Israel.

The continuity between Church and Old Testament Israel is what

underlies Paul's comparison of contemporary Jews refusing to believe in

Christ as "the present Jerusalem" to the Church as child of the eschato-

logical "Jerusalem above" (Gal 4, 25-26). His implicit argument is that

---

[43]For a thorough presentation of the structure and changing nomen-
clature of the four-fold sense of Scripture, see Henri de Lubac, S.J.,
Exégèse Médiévale: Les Quatre Sens de L'Ecriture, I (Paris: Aubier, 1959).

[44]Congar, Tradition, p. 65.

the Church alone is the true typological continuation of ancient, faithful Israel: "Jerusalem." Similarly, in Romans 9 Paul refers to this same continuity: "Not all who are descended from Israel belong to Israel" (Rom 9, 7). Here he typologically compares the Church as "children of God" to Jacob, and contemporary unbelieving Jews as "children of the flesh" to Esau. By this comparison Paul argues that, although the Jews of his time continue the ancient religious practices and are in biological unity with the Old Testament community, their fleshly piety no longer contains or expresses the activity of God in history. That work of salvation, begun in the Old Testament, now is to be found in the life of the Church.

The Church's discontinuity with ancient Israel is the emphasis of another Pauline typology. For Paul, the Old Testament discipline on diets and festivals, intending to promote union with God, have been superceded by the Church's integrality with the Christ-event. "These [rules] are only a shadow of what is to come; but the substance belongs to Christ" (Col 3, 16-23). A Christian's union with God is consequently found, not in ancient practices, but in his continued adherence in the Church to Christ, the Head of the body (2, 19), into whose historical death (2, 20) and resurrection (3, 1) he has been immersed.

In this image of baptismal immersion the New Testament finds Church solidarity not only with Christ dying and rising, but also with Old Testament Israel. Through the ritual experience of going through water the Church participates in key formative events in the life of Israel: the crossing of the Red Sea (I Cor 10, 5)[45] and the crossing of the Jordan

---

[45] Jean Daniélou, S.J., The Bible and the Liturgy (Notre Dame: University of Notre Dame Press, 1956), p. 70.

28

(Jn 10, 40).[46] Likewise, in receiving the bread of the Liturgy, the Church feeds at once on the flesh of Christ and on the (true) manna in the desert (Jn 6, 41). Thus, the identity found between the imagery of Church "sacraments" and the Old Testament events is not paranetic; it is in fact ontological: "We have been freed from Egypt."[47] Conversly, these "sacraments" -- whose reality is Christ -- were already present in their biblical prototypes. There is only one "Israel of God," to be found in both Testaments although at two different stages in its salvation history.[48] The imagery used in the "sacraments," as the saving events in the Church's historical life, links that history to the pivotal events of Christ death and resurrection and also proclaims the inner integrity of that history, that the "People of God" are one people in Christ.

Drawing out the implications of biblical typology as it is outlined here, it is clear that no one is saved alone. In uniting Christians in the imagery of the "sacraments" to Christ's saving events, the Church also unites them to the people of God extended throughout history. That is why the Church has always seen the reading of Scripture as God's Word

---

[46]Ibid., p. 102.

[47]Hebert, "Imagerie," p. 77.

[48]de Lubac, Sources, p. 36: "The Church is the 'Israel of God.' The Church is always that people whom God, in his mercy, has chosen for himself. Although national Israel has become universal Church, it is always the same People of God ... For Yahweh, the 'rock of Israel,' is faithful. There is only one same God, who is the Author of two Testaments."

directed to its hearers in the present moment.[49] Through the typology of
the "sacraments" the whole people of God is realized and recognized in
the Church on earth at any given point in history. In the readings
from Scripture the hearers within that Church are therefore made to con-
front their own true selves, and are invited to become more fully what
they already are.[50]

True Christian Living as a Type of Christ

This process of integrating into one's Christian life and behavior
the typology one celebrates in the "sacraments" is not something
extrinsic to their salvific economy. The images the Church enters into
sacramentally are meant for more than mere intellectual or gnostic
enlightenment. They are there to be lived, and only in the living of
them will they and their inner meaning be realized.[51] That is apparently
the reason why, at the end of the exhortation in which he highlights
certain Exodus events as "types" (I Cor 10:6) of the Christian life,
Paul in addition offers his own personal Christian living as an example

---

[49]"... la Bible est la Parole de Dieu, non une parole morte,
emprisonée dans la passé, mais une parole vivante, qui s'adresse
immédiatement à l'homme d'aujourd'hui prenant part à la célébration
liturgique, une parole qui le conçerne, parce que c'est pour lui qu'elle
a été et qu'elle demeure prononcée." Louis Bouyer, "Liturgie et
Exégèse Spirituelle," La Maison-Dieu VII (1946), 30.

[50]de Lubac, Sources, p. 27: "[Salvation history] is [the believer's]
own history, from which he cannot remove himself. This history interests
him personally. It is a mystery which is also his own mystery, identically."
See also James 1, 23: "For if any one is a hearer of the word and not
a doer, he is like a man who observes his natural face in a mirror..."

[51]Ibid., p. 21: "The spiritual meaning of a mystery is the meaning
we discover -- or, rather, into which we penetrate -- by living that
mystery. Still more fundamentally, the entire process of spiritual understanding is, in its principle, identical to the process of conversion."

containing the mystery of Christ: "Be imitators of me just as I am of Christ" (I Cor 11:1).[52] In I and II Timothy we find a Paul who again sees himself in the manner of a personal type of Christ ("hypotyposin" I Tim 1:16; II Tim 1:13).[53] Thus, not only are the images employed by typology ultimately directed to a Christian living of their inner mysteries, but the principle is also established in the New Testament that typology is not finished with the close of the Old Testament. The members of the Church are meant to be living books of the Gospels for each other, especially so the office holdres, such as Paul the Apostle.

Conclusions

The typology employed by Cyprian in his writings where persons are seen as "types" of Christ, in fact reflects not one Christian tradition among others, but Christian Tradition itself.[54] The Gospel, intended by Christ, is that he died and rose "according to the Scriptures" (Rom 16: 1-5). According to Scripture, then, insofar as persons, objects and events prepared his way in Old Testament history and image his saving deeds

---

[52]David M. Stanley, S.J., in "'Become Imitators of Me': The Pauline Conception of Apostolic Tradition," Biblica XL (1959), 859-877; demonstrates that, according to Paul, an apostle was a living type of Christ: "Not only what he says, but how he says it, as well as what he is, have a part to play in the Christian formation of those he evangelizes"(p. 874).

[53]For a discussion of the typological value of the Timothy passages, see K.J. Woollcombe, "Le Sens de 'Type' Chez les Pères," La Vie Spirituelle Supplement V (1951), 89, 90.

[54]Congar, Tradition, pp. 37, 38: "... the whole activity of the early Fathers tends to unite three terms ...: Scripture, Tradition, and Church. Tradition is an interpretation of Scripture, which was originally the Old Testament, ... that interpretation of Scripture which is the interpretation of the Church."

after his resurrection, they in fact are bearers of Christ's presence. It is through this presence of Christ in Old Testament Israel, in the Church, and in creation itself that his salvation is extended to the whole history of the world, that history which has become the "history of God."

It therefore appears possible that the identity made by Cyprian, between the eucharistic leader's imitation of Christ and Christ's presence as priest of the sacrifice, draws from the same well-springs in Christian Tradition as does the typological understanding of salvation history found in the Scriptures themselves. However, any certitude on the matter demands further investigation. We turn next to the writings of Christians of the second and early third centuries to see to what degree the economy of salvation linking Old and New Testaments was seen to continue on in the history of the Church. Is there also a kind of typology operating after the time of Christ which would make Christ present in the time of the Church?

Chapter II

SECOND CENTURY EXEGESIS

The Goal of the Chapter

In Chapter One the attempt was made to find Cyprian's source of
confidence for the unquestioned connection between the eucharistic
leader's imitation of Christ and the resulting presence of Christ (Ep
63,14,3). The conclusion was drawn that the New Testament itself witnesses to a salvation history connection between Old Testament imitation
of Christ and Christ's presence in Old Testament times.

With that background the investigation of Cyprian's leader of the
eucharist continues. The next question can be put this way: According
to Church Tradition, then, is it likewise true that "types of Christ"
making Christ present in salvation history also exist after his death-
resurrection? If so, could the leader of the eucharist according to
Cyprian be an example of this kind of reverse typology? Does the leader,
by acting "as priest in the place of Christ" so as to make him present,
function not as a predictive, but now as a retrospective "type of
Christ?"

Before this question can be answered in regard to Cyprian's
eucharistic leader, it must first be determined whether and to what
degree this imitation-presence economy of salvation, common to both pre-
and post-Incarnational eras of salvation history, exists in the faith-
understanding of the Church (Tradition) and its writers before the time

of Cyprian. For if it does exist, for the reasons which have already been given at the outset of Chapter One, such an economy of salvation history would offer a solid framework within which to interpret Cyprian's theology of eucharistic leadership. Chapter Two will therefore investigate the nature and influence of Christian typology during the post-Apostolic period before Cyprian, especially as found in the works of Tertullian, Cyprian's forebearer in the North African church.

I. Christian Typology and Allegory

Allegorized Typology

As we have seen, New Testament typology is based on the understanding that all historical persons, objects and events, especially
those found in ancient Israel, point to the full in-breaking of God into
history in the person of Jesus Christ. This they do to the extent that
they themselves are part of God's unfolding, yet single, saving action
in history.[55] Conversely, only inasmuch as these realities are part of
God's activity can they be said to "exist" in the first place: "in Him
all things were created, in heaven and on earth, ...and in Him all
things hold together" (Col 1, 16-17). Therefore, true existence is
somehow a participation in Christ.

Out of this faith-understanding of history come two conclusions
important to the later development of Christian typology. First: If
every truly existing person, object and event in history partakes in
the single, overall saving action of God, then to some degree the whole
of that action can already be found "in principle"[56] in every individual
person, object and event.[57] Y. Congar refers to this concept as the
"idea of the part for the whole."[58] A second and corrollary conclusion

---

[55]W. den Boer, "Allegory and History," in: W. den Boer et al. edd.,
Romanitas et Christianitas (Amsterdam: North-Holland, 1973), p. 19.

[56]Cornelius Petrus Mayer, Die Zeichen in der geistigen Entwicklung
und in der Theologie des jungen Augustinus, Cassiciacum XXIV, I (Würzburg: Augustinus, 1969), p. 56.

[57]den Boer, "Allegory," p. 19.

[58]Yves Congar, "L'Ancien Testament, témoin du Christ," La Vie
Intellectuelle, October, 1949, p. 336.

follows: Granted that the material cited in the Old Testament is <u>on</u>

<u>the whole</u> of historical origins -- that it witnesses to the direction of

God's actual working out of salvation in history --, it is not necessary

that <u>every</u> instance of typology be based on historically verifiable per-

sons, objects or events. The truth of any given typological relation-

ship to Christ will be found rather in its reflecting the overall pattern

of God's historical activity. Thus, for example, the fact that the story

of Jonah in the whale is a purely literary creation with no basis in

historical fact does not lessen its typological value (See Matt 12,30).[59]

As a work of literature, such a story rather serves to highlight even

more the sometimes obscure activity of God in those biblical events

-----

[59]Ibid., pp. 340-341, n. 5: "Sans doute n'a-t-on pas toujours
assez remarqué l'abîme qu'il y a réellement (quelle que soit la terminologie qu'on emploie) entre la typologie et l'allégorie. Entre le type
et l'antitype, il y a une correspondance historique, réelle, qui touche
à l'idée principale de l'événement ou de l'institution. Entre l'allégorie
et son application, la correspondance n'existe que dans certains points
arbitrairement choisis pour représenter des faits ou des idées de
différentes sortes. Le type présuppose un propos dans l'histoire qui se
développe et se réalise par étapes, qui s'indique ou s'esquisse d'abord,
puis se précise et se réalise. Dans le type, contrairement à l'allégorie
le rapport est pris du coeur même du sens de la Bible, qui est toute
relative au Christ, à sa mort et à sa résurrection, à l'extension du
mystère de son passage à tous les fidèles pour les faire vivre de vie
éternelle. L'allégorisme, qui construit par l'esprit des rapports
adventices plus ou moins arbitraires, est l'ennemi de la vraie typologie
qu'il entraine indûment dans son descrédit. Il est une fantaisie humaine,
parfois justifiée et bonne d'ailleurs; la typologie retrouve le jeu du
dessein de Dieu lui-même tel que la Bible nous le fait connaître d'un
bout à l'autre."
To the extent that allegory ignores the saving activity of God
uniting all human history is it un-typological and consequently deficient
in conveying the incarnational nature of Christianity. See J.E.L. van
der Geest, <u>Le Christ et l'Ancien Testament chez Tertullien</u>, Latinitas
Christianorum Primaeva, XXII (Nijmegen: Dekker and van de Vegt, 1972),
p. 176.

which are more verifiably historical. Even though the Jonah story is
fictional, its roots are in fact profoundly historical and, consequently,
it is even more available to typology than are those other, "historical"
events in the life of Israel, events which may be too particular in
nature to allow the overall action of God to clearly emerge. Similar
stories, such as Adam and Eve in the garden, the sufferings of Job, and
the Dry Bones vision in Ezekiel, by expressing that deeper theological
view of history, offer a richer identification with the fulness of
salvation found in the historical person of Christ.

These two conclusions point to the theological legitimacy of the
practice of finding ever more types and figures of Christ in Old Testament Scripture in addition to those already named by the New Testament.[60]
They also supply a theoretical basis for extending typology into the
area of allegory, a growing phenomenon in the writings of second century
Christian authors. The very fact that the poetic quality of some Old
Testament passages is so humanly engaging would itself be an invitation
for a Christian to freely interpret the Scriptures in ways which bring
out universally human characteristics of true Christian life.

As has been pointed out earlier, ancient peoples did not place the
same value on the historicity of accounts as we moderns do.[61] That this
is due in part to the predominantly hellenistic modes of thought current

---

[60]According to van der Geest's study, Tertullian's rationale for
determining what aspects of Christ's life are fulfillments of Old Testament prophecies appears haphazard. At any rate, he shows no constraint
to base his typologies on appeals to previous traditions or authorities.
See Le Christ, p. 120.

[61]den Boer, "Allegory," p. 22.

in the second-century Mediterranean world, as some scholars hold,[62] is
highly probable. Indeed, the shift from the Greek cyclic view of history,
in which eternal truths find repetition in historical manifestations,
to the biblical, more developmental view, in which the historical events
themselves and in their succession gradually realize the meaning which
they point to, does not seem to have been fully understood by early
Christian authors.[63] As a result, the distinction between biblical
typology and pagan allegory was somewhat blurred.[64] "Terminology made
no distinction and applied the words TUPOS and ALLEGORIA to both modes
of interpretation."[65]

In the platonic view of history, where the physical world and
historical events are real only to the degree that they image the
invisible world of eternal truths, allegory is a connatural mode of
reaching the essence of things. Granted that allegorical identification

---

[62]W. den Boer, "Hermeneutic Problems in Early Christian Literature,"
Vigiliae Christianae I (1947), 167; James N.S. Alexander, "The Interpretation of Scripture in the Ante-Nicene Period," Interpretation XII
(1958), 279.

[63]den Boer, "Hermeneutic," p. 151.

[64]Ibid., p. 160-161: "The Greek scholars do know symbol, allegory,
and paradigma, but they do not know typology. They are familiar with
the recurrence of historical events and persons. ... But Agamemnon is
not a type of Alexander in the Biblical sense..., he does not fore-
shadow a Greater one, who will accomplish history. ....
"It would be useless to address heathens about this typology,
which is significant of Christianity only. It would be like speaking to
people that have no organ to grasp the meaning of this distinction. It
is therefore quite natural that the struggle about typology should be
fought within the bosom of the Christian Church itself."
See also van der Geest, Le Christ, p. 186.

[65]den Boer, "Hermeneutic," p. 150.

of creatures, events and even words are often highly arbitrary, arbitrariness is a problem only for one who is concerned with particulars; for the platonist at home in the eternal world, real truth can be found only in universals, in those same universals which allegory serves to reveal. Therefore, besides being in tune with the culture of the time, allegory also has the intellectual attractiveness of being able to account for the "true" nature of things. It is no wonder then that, where ancient Hellenists use allegory to find deeper meanings in the stories of Homer (Aphrodite = love, etc.), and Philo does the same thing with the Hebrew scriptures,[66] Pseudo-Barnabas (ca. 135 C.E.?) and Clement of Alexandria (ca. 150-210) look for a fuller Christian significance to the Christian scriptures by allegorizing their history into a timeless tale of every soul's interior journey to God.[67] In addition, then, to recognizing their typological, historical nature, these authors also see Old Testament realities as universal symbols of the moral life (virtues, vices, attitudes) and their interactions as expressions of the cosmic struggle of each Christian with the forces of evil.[68]

---

[66]K.J. Woollcombe, "The Biblican Origins and Patristic Development of Typology," in G.W.H. Lampe & K.J. Woollcombe, edd., Essays on Typology, Studies in Biblical Theology 22, (Naperville: Alec R. Allenson, 1957), p. 52. van der Geest notes that it was especially the Stoics who allegorized Homer to eliminate what was shocking to them: Le Christ, p. 174.

[67]Jean Daniélou, S.J., "Les divers sens de l'écriture dans la tradition chrétienne primitive," Ephemerides Theologicae Lovanienses XXIV (1948), 125.

[68]den Boer, "Hermeneutic," p. 151.

40

The original thrust toward thus allegorizing the Word of God has
been attributed to the Gnostics. Only then as a consequence did Christian
writers adopt it, doing so in order to counteract the growing influence
of gnosticism.[69] Whatever the case, the Christian use of allegory never
wholly lost its typological, historical basis. The denial of historicity
to the Christian message would not only remove any messianic significance
to the person of Christ,[70] it would itself be tantamount to gnosticism.

> While the Apostolic Fathers are on the whole
> more wildly fanciful than the New Testament
> writers, they follow this New Testament exe-
> getical pattern and remain, like St. Paul,
> Christocentric and just to the historical
> sense.[71]

In light of these considerations, when the term "type" is found in
second century writings, its exact meaning can only be determined by a
careful interpretation of the immediate contest. For example, Ignatius
of Antioch's (early 2nd cent.) reference to the bishop as a "type of the
Father,"[72] is an instance neither of simple historical typology, nor of

[69]Woollcombe, "Biblical Origins," p. 69.

[70]den Boer, "Allegory," p. 21.

[71]Alexander, "Interpretation," p. 273.

[72]The typological structure of Ignatius is clearly not a rigid one
since immediately prior to naming the bishop a "type of the Father," he
also presents him as an image of Christ: "Your obedience to your bishop,
as though he were Jesus Christ, shows me plainly enough that yours is no
worldly manner of life, but that of Jesus Christ Himself..." Maxwell
Staniforth, tr., "Trallians" 2 in Early Christian Writings (N.Y.: Penguin,
1968) p. 95. Critical Edition: F.X. Funk, ed., "Ad Trallianos," in
Opera Patrum Apostolicorum I (Tübingen: Laupp, 1897), pp. 203.
204.
Also evident in this passage is a similarly typological sharing in
the reality of Christ on the part of faithful Christians in general.
However, Ignatius does see the various functions of the hierarchy prefigured in a special way: "It is for the rest of you to hold the deacons
in as great respect as Jesus Christ; just as you should also look on the

pure allegory. It rather represents a kind of <u>allegorical typology</u>.
When the analogy implicit in the Ignatian phrase is drawn out, it can
be seen to be legitimate typology -- one based upon salvation history:
'Just as the Father, who is the source of salvation, once sent Christ
into the world, so does each bishop as the distributer of offices in the
community send out his deacons to serve the world beyond the liturgical
assembly.'[73] On the other hand, "type of the Father" can also be called
"allegorical" since it was only in Jesus, and not in his own person,
that the Father acted in history. Indeed, in the Ignatian example, it
is more properly the deacons, and not the bishop, who act in the place
of Christ and so are the true "types," making His mystery present in
later human history. Comparing the bishop's position in the community to
the Father's is actually an analogy drawn, not between two agents within
history, but between an earthly, temporal being and a heavenly, eternal
one -- the characteristic pattern of allegory. Although it may be true
that Ignatius actually understands the Father to act through the bishop,
in accordance with traditional Christian doctrine the Father would only
do so through the mediation of Christ. At the same time, what is most
important about this example is that we have in it a very early instance
of "reverse typology," where agents in salvation history after the time
of Christ are connected typologically to His saving events.

72(cont)bishop as a type of the Father, and the clergy as the
Apostolic circle forming His council; for without these three orders
no church has any right to the name." Staniforth, "Trallians," 3,
pp. 95-96; Funk I, III, 1, p. 205.
[73]Woollcombe, "Biblical Origins," p. 70.

42

This interpretation of Ignatius can be corroborated by a further example of reverse typology found in the later second-century account of the martyrdom of Polycarp (155-6 C.E.):

> The circumstances that the traitors were men of [Polycarp's] own household, and that the Police Commissioner -- to whom chance had even given the actual name of Herod -- was resolved on bringing him into the arena, manifestly meant that he was to fulfil his destiny by sharing the experiences of Christ, and that his betrayers would likewise be doomed to the punishment of Judas.[74]

In other words, by his own death Polycarp typologically witnesses to the historical death of Christ and, in fact, he even undergoes ("sharing") that very same death. Moreover, in the prayer Polycarp offers at his burning he uses the language of a eucharistic liturgy, suggesting in addition that he is a type of Christ by virtue of his full living out of the eucharistic mysteries. If one substitutes the pronoun "I" with the plural "we" the liturgical character of the passage becomes more evident:

> I (we) bless thee for granting me (us) ... to share the cup of thine Anointed and to rise again unto life everlasting, both in body and soul, in the immortality of the Holy Spirit. May I (we) be received ... a sacrifice rich and acceptable ... For this, and for all else besides, I (we) praise thee, I (we) bless thee, I (we) glorify thee; through our eternal High Priest in heaven, thy beloved Son Jesus Christ, by whom and with whom be glory to thee and the Holy Spirit, now and for all ages to come. Amen.[75]

---

[74] Maxwell Staniforth, tr., "The Martyrdom of Polycarp" 6, in Early Christian Writings (New York: Penguin Books, 1968), p. 157.

[75] Staniforth, "The Martyrdom of Polycarp" 14, pp. 160-161. See Cyril C. Richardson, Early Christian Fathers (New York: Macmillan, 1970), p. 148, for a select bibliography on this prayer of Polycarp.

Consequently, in spite of clear allegorizing tendencies in second century authors, we have not only definite evidence that appreciation for the historical nature of the Christ-event continued after the time of the New Testament, but that persons in the Christian era of salvation history were even seen to be identified typologically with the historical Christ. Furthermore, in the passages from the Martyrdom of Polycarp we find that this typology is intimately related to the liturgical celebration of the Christian community. This fact will be of no little importance in our later dealing with the question of how the bishop-priest at the eucharist can be said by Cyprian to "act in the place of Christ."

"Matthean Exegesis"

Not all of the Christian authors in the second century were attracted toward allegory. J. Daniélou has found another development in Christian typology which, instead of emphasizing universal truths, concentrates on those concrete, historical correspondances between salvation history events. He names this kind of exegesis "Matthean," owing to the pattern in the first gospel of finding the external circumstances of Christ's historical life on earth, from his birth through his passion and death, already predicted by analogous circumstances in Old Testament narratives.[76] For example, Matthew presents Christ as the fulfillment of the Old Law by comparing the events of his life with those of Moses. Just as Moses

---

[76]Daniélou, "les divers," p. 121.

gave God's law from a mountain, Christ is described as doing the same (Matt 5,1).

There are, however, certain dangers to this heavy emphasis on a correspondance of descriptive details.[77] By concentrating on circumstances one runs the risk of totally historicizing the mystery of Christ, that is, of confining his reality in history simply to the events of his life on earth.[78] Doing so would effectively deny any true presence of Christ to the ongoing life of the Church. Furthermore, it can be readily seen how a "crude typology,"[79] arguing solely from similar exterior circumstances to a common intrinsic salvation, could also lead to a magic mentality, wherein the mere performance of an archetypal action is enough to insure its saving efficacy. Such a possibility could be an important consideration in our later examination of Cyprian's dictum, "he truly acts as priest in the place of Christ who imitates what Christ did." We must accordingly be aware whether or not Cyprian falls prey to just such an overemphasis on detail, whether he attributes power to the mere physical repetition of Christ's historical actions so that he loses all need for Christ's personal agency in the Church through his

---

[77]Daniélou notes that one result of this emphasis on external correspondances has been millenialism: the expectation that the end of the world will exactly fulfill the detailed descriptions of apocalyptic events found in Scripture: "Les divers," p. 125.

[78]For a contemporary discussion of historicism as a phenomenon in Christian Tradition see Robert Taft, S.J., "Historicisme: une conception à revoir," La Maison-Dieu CXLVII (1981), 61-83.

[79]Henri du Lubac, S.J., The Sources of Revelation, trans. Luke O'Neill, (New York: Herder and Herder, 1968), pp. 47-48.

presence in the Spirit. However, any analysis of this question must await our full presentation of Cyprian's overall understanding of typology.

In the second century the same Church writers who indulged in allegory, such as Pseudo-Barnabas and Justin Martyr (ca. 110-165 C.E.), were also attracted to this kind of "Matthean" exegesis. They used it as a kind of apologetics, appealing to the correspondences between Old Testament passages and the events of Christ's life to prove the truths of the orthodox Christian faith.[80] In arguing with opponents who also accepted the authority of the Bible, they used typology to prove the tenets of the Church's faith. This practice so formed the Christian mentality of the age that, for Tertullian and his contemporaries at the end of the century, "to believe" carried with it the additional meaning of "to be right."[81] However, where earlier authors in their appeal to historical identities lost some appreciation for the newness in history of God's action in Christ, Tertullian was always careful to maintain it.[82]

> The Apostolic Fathers and Justin held on to the historicity of the hidden allusions to Christ. ... However, they no longer sought out the concordances in the fundamental chrarcteristics of the actions of God. They emphasized rather the

---

[80]J.E.L. van der Geest, Le Christ et L'Ancien Testament chez Tertullien, Latinitas Christianorum Primaeva 22 (Nijmegen: Dekker & van der Vegt, 1972), p. 76

[81]Ibid., p. 121.

[82]Ibid., p. 63.

> exterior concordances, the analogies, which
> made them lose sight of the enrichment. Thus
> typology lost a characteristic element. In
> the post-apostolic epoque the subtle sense of
> the connection and distinction of time is lost.
> It is not blurred to the point that the his-
> toric reality of the type is lost, but one no
> longer pays much attention to it. ... More and
> more one sees the hidden allusions of the Old
> Testament as camouflaged descriptions of sal-
> vation revealed in Christ. Ps. Barnabas and
> Justin find in the Old Testament "not only
> prophetic images of Christianity, but the
> reality itself of Christianity's fundamental
> teachings."[83]

Throughout most of the second century, therefore, the modes of

exegeting sacred Scripture never fully escape a universalist,

platonic vision of reality. We have already seen that such is the case

where Church authors tended toward allegory. In regard to "Matthean

exegesis" in this period, even though it represents an attempt to find

God's salvation in the particularity of individual events, there remains

the same inability to do justice to the historical development of sal-

vation history. Consequently, the newness of God's action in Christ

and the discontinuity between Old and New Testaments are lost in the

philosophical confusion. Like a platonic prototype projecting its

reality into lower levels of being, the foundational events of Christ's

life, death and resurrection are seen to image themselves uniformly both

backward into Old Testament types and figures and forward into the

historical life of the Church.[84] It then becomes difficult in such a

---

[83] Ibid., pp. 158-159.

[84] Alexander Gerken, _Theologie der Eucharistie_ (München: Kösel,
1973), pp. 76-79.

world-view to give a theoretical basis to the need for co-workers
with Christ in the work of salvation. The realities of history are seen
as mere static witnesses to God's full activity found only in the events
of Christ's life on earth. All other persons and events share in that
activity, not as agents further realizing a project begun and substantially accomplished in the earthly Christ, but as sacred ikons sharing
in a Christ-reality of which they themselves are so many images. However,
the flow of history would not allow this predominance of platonism to
continue forever. Even as the second century nears its close the pressure
from gnostic doctrines forced Church thinkers into a greater appreciation
for the uniqueness of historical events and for the internal development
of God's salvation in history.

II. Salvation History in Tertullian

Scripture as Proof of Faith

Tertullian (ca. 150-220 C.E.), the great master of the North
African church, thought and wrote continually in a polemical context.[85]
Against the Marcionites who taught a separate god behind each of the
Testaments, thereby denying continuity between the two epochs,
Tertullian is forced to use allegory in order to give meaning to those
Old Testament passages which on the literal level appear to contradict
Christian faith. He appeals to Paul's use of allegory to justify his
own.[86] However, when he turns his guns toward the gnostic docetists
who wanted to spiritualize everything in the Scriptures, Tertullian
absolutely refuses to allegorize.[87]

> Not always nor in regard to everything is the
> form of prophetic utterance an allegorical one,
> but only now and then and in certain instances.[88]

---

[85]T.P. O'Malley, Tertullian and the Bible: Language - Imagery -
Exegesis, Latinitas Christianorum Primaeva 21 (Nijmegen: Dekker & van
de Vegt, 1967), p. 149: "In Tertullian the context of the argument at
hand is necessary for an evaluation of his expressions."

[86]Aem. Kroymann, ed., "Adversus Marcionem" in: Quinti Septimi
Florentis Tertulliani Opera, Pars I: Opera Catholica Adversus Marcionem,
Corpus Christianorum, Series Latina I (Turnholt: Brepols, 1954), III,
5, 4, pp. 513-514, quoted in van der Geest, Le Christ, pp. 182-184.

[87]van der Geest, Le Christ, p. 184.

[88]J.G. Borleffs, ed., "De Resurrectione Mortuorum," in: Quinti
Septimi Florentis Tertulliani Opera, Pars II: Opera Montanistica,
Corpus Christianorum, Series Latina II (Turnholt: Brepols, 1954), XX,
9, p. 946.

50

As one of the earliest Church writers in the West, Tertullian already shows that characteristic Western interest more in the ethical and concrete dimensions of religion than in its speculative, universalist side.[89] As such, although he is constitutionally opposed to allegory, he nevertheless makes use of it where otherwise the sense of Scripture could not be saved.[90] As we have seen, in the theoretical confusion regarding the hellenistic and biblical visions of history, allegory cannot yet be fully distinguishable from typology.[91] As a result, oftentimes "the only Christian option with regard to the Old Testament was 'allegorize or abandon.'"[92]

For Tertullian, the operative criterion in deciding when to allegorize is whether or not the direct, literal sense of a passage precluded conformity to an overall Old Testament prefigurement of Christ.[93] If it did, it was "empty," vanus, and demanded an allegorical reading.[94] However, when Scripture is viewed from the perspective of the Church, Tertullian sees Tradition as its fundamental criterion for interpretation. To the question, to whom does Scripture belong?, he answers, "Only the churches which stand in the succession of the apostles

---

[89]Gerken, Theologie der Eucharistie, p. 84.

[90]van der Geest, Le Christ, p. 188.

[91]Ibid., p. 186.

[92]James N.S. Alexander, "The Interpretation of Scripture in the Ante-Nicene Period," Interpretation XII (1958), p. 280, quoted in: van der Geest, Le Christ, p. 188.

[93]van der Geest, Le Christ, p. 163.

[94]Tertullian, Adv. Marc. III, 18, 5, quoted in van der Geest, Le Christ, p. 189.

possess the teaching of Christ."[95] There is therefore a norm outside of Scripture itself to guide its interpretation, that is, the Church, whose faith is found expressed in it. Here we see that Tertullian affirms what was discovered in Chapter One, namely that Christ's own understanding of the Old Testament handed on to his disciples, the earliest "church," has in turn become expressed in the New Testament. Thus, the faith of the Church is the content of Scripture in both its Old and New Testaments. Furthermore, faithfulness to that interpretation demands continual explanation and protection by the Church, particularly by those in the Church who are successively commissioned since the Apostles for this very purpose. Without this consistency of interpretation, the Church itself would soon lose its identity and purpose. Consequently, a particular Old Testament passage is "vanus" and needs allegorizing when it cannot be harmonized with the interpretation handed on by Christ and continued in the teaching of the Church.

That Scripture for Tertullian is meant to serve the faith of the Church is evident from one of the names that he gives to it. Eighty-seven times in the course of his writings he calls the Old Testament "instrumentum," which in juridical language meant "a means of proving."[96]

---

[95]R.F. Refoulé, ed., "De Praescriptione Haereticorum," in Quinti Septimi Florentis Tertulliani Opera, Pars I: Opera Catholica Adversus Marcionem, Corpus Christianorum, Series Latina, I (Turnholt: Brepols, 1954), XXff, pp. 201ff., cited in Alexander, "Interpretation," p. 275.

[96]van der Geest, Le Christ, p. 16.

The Law and the Prophets therefore prove that Christ is the savior.[97]
Tertullian looks upon the Old Testament as a source of proofs that the
faith of the Church is true.[98] It is not that believers need rational
demonstrations in order to receive the gift of faith in the first place.
Rather, the Scripture as "instrumentum" serves to awaken that faith
once it is given and, just as importantly, gives it a form.[99]

Order: The Key Characteristic of Salvation History

Form is crucial for Tertullian. To his Western, practical mind
form and the order it gives comprise the primary characteristic of
divine activity. Above all God is a God of order.[100] Consequently,
when Tertullian considers the Scriptures, he stresses their unity in
Christ. For example, where I Corinthians 10-11 reads, "Those things
happened to them (in the Old Testament) in a figurative way,"
Tertullian changes "those things" to "everything:" "Everything happened to the people in a figurative way."[101] By doing so, he presents

---

[97]Ibid., p. 122. Implicit in this reasoning is the ontological
interdependence between the historical person of Christ and other
historical beings which somehow contain and manifest his presence so as
to act as proofs of his saving reality. This interdependence, as we
shall see, is the ultimate significance of Tertullian's use of the word,
sacramentum.

[98]Ibid., p. 121.

[99]Ibid.

[100]Ibid., p. 128,

[101]A. Reifferscheid et G. Wissowa, edd., "De Idololatria," in:
Quinti Septimi Florentis Tertulliani Opera, Pars II: Opera Montanistica,
Corpus Christianorum, Series Latina II (Turnholt: Brepols, 1954), V, 4,
p. 1105: "apostolus affirmet omnia tunc figurate populo accidisse."
Cited in van der Geest, Le Christ, pp. 163-164.

his vision of the whole Old Testament as <u>ordered</u> around the person of Christ. Similarly, in a passage where Tertullian tries to view all human history from God's perspective, he says that whereas human beings see time in terms of past and future, for God there is no past and future; there is only "one time:"[102] the present. It is in their eternal presence to Him that all things are immediately <u>ordered</u> by God in their relationship to Christ. This is also the reason why Christ can already be present in those "past" Old Testament realities which as types prepare for his coming.

Another way of speaking of this formal unity of salvation history is found in St. Paul's use of the word, <u>MUSTERION</u>. The Apostle takes this term from Jewish wisdom and apocalyptic writings[103] to refer to "the sacred plan of God from the unfolding of the history of the world."[104]

---

[102]E. Dekkers, ed., "Apologeticum," in: <u>Quinti Septimi Florentis Tertulliani Opera</u>, Pars I: <u>Opera Catholica</u> Adversus Marcionem, Corpus Christianorum, Series Latina I (Turnholt: Brepols, 1954), XX, 5, p. 122. See van der Geest, <u>Le Christ</u>, p. 101.

[103]Christine Mohrmann, "Sacramentum dans les plus anciens textes chrétiens," <u>Harvard Theological Review</u> XLVII (1954), 141: "Il apparaît toujours plus clairement que l'évolution la plus ancienne de <u>musterion</u> dans le grec des chrétiens, et notamment chez saint Paul, ne devrait pas être séparée de l'usage des Septante, lequel remonte à son tour à celui de la langue courante et commune, et non pas -- à mon avis -- à un usage technique des mystères païens."

[104]Louis Bouyer, "Mysterion," <u>La Vie Spirituelle</u>, Supplement 6 (1952), 400.

> God, the true Sage, has a plan for the salvation
> of the world, a plan completely contrary to what
> professional sages are able to imagine. For this
> plan is a great "mystery," the great secret of
> divine Wisdom, until the last day when it will
> please God to reveal it. This day has arrived:
> in Christ, in his cross, a scandal for the Jews
> and folly for the Greeks, and the mystery-key of
> the divine plan is proclaimed by the very ful-
> filling of it.[105]

For St. Paul, the accomplishment of God's plan for salvation is not

confined to the historical life of Jesus, but it extends throughout

salvation history:

> More profoundly still, the "mystery" is Christ
> himself, but Christ including in himself his
> whole body, the Church, as his proper fulness
> (Eph 1-23). Accordingly, the mystery is the
> recapitulation of human and cosmic history in
> that of Christ, the reconciliation of humanity
> among its members and with God in the Body of
> his Son.[106]

Similarly, in addition to its being carried on by the Church after

Christ's historical life on earth, MUSTERION in St. Paul is seen also

---

[105]Ibid.: "Dieu, le seul vrai Sage, a un plan pour le salut du
monde, plan tout au rebours de ce que pouvaient imaginer les sages pro-
fessionnels. Car ce plan est le grand "mystère", le grand secret de la
divine Sagesse, jusqu'au jour ultime où il plaît à Dieu de le révéler.
Ce jour est arrivé: dans le Christ, dans sa Croix, scandale pour les
Juifs et folie pour les Grecs, le mystère-clé du plan divin est proclamé
par sa mise en oeuvre elle-même ..."

[106]Ibid., p. 402: "Plus profondément encore le 'mystère', c'est
le Christ lui-même, mais le Christ incluant en lui tout son Corps,
l'Église, comme sa propre plénitude (Eph 1-23). Et par là, le mystère
est la récapitulation de l'histoire humaine et cosmique dans celle du
Christ, la réconciliation de l'humanité entre elle et avec Dieu dans le
Corps de son Fils."

to be present and active in the shadowy prefigurements of the Old Testament.[107] As a result, by this single word St. Paul denotes salvation in its unity and fulness, but especially as an _order_ given to world history by the mind of God.

Sacramentum Tertullianeum: Scholarly Findings

When it comes to translating this crucial Pauline word, scholars generally agree that Tertullian continues the practice of second century Latin communities in using, not the Latin cognate of MUSTERION, i.e. mysterium, but rather the classical Latin sacramentum.[108] Because the pagan mystery religions are called mysteria, even contemporary Latin translations of the Bible are careful to avoid any form of the word.[109] However, no single word ever fully translates another. There is always some difference in their verbal histories and connotations. The translating of MUSTERION by sacramentum is no exception.

Scholars throughout this century have found at least two basic meanings that Tertullian gives to the word, sacramentum, but they are divided over which of the two is more fundamental.[110] Analysing the

[107]Ibid.: "A travers tout cela, enfin, le 'mystere' du Nouveau Testament garde sa double implication de révélation du sens des figures anciennes (celles de l'Ancien Testament) et de figure encore des réalités ultimes toujours attendues."

[108]Réné Braun, Deus Christianorum: Recherches sur le Vocabulaire Doctrinal de Tertullien. Publications de la Faculté des Lettres et Sciences Humaines d'Alger XLI (Paris: Presses Universitaires de France, 1962), p. 436.

[109]Ibid., pp. 436-437.

[110]Emile de Backer, "Tertullien," in: J. de Ghellinck, S.J., ed., Pour L'Histoire du Mot "Sacramentum," (Louvain: Spicilegium Sacrum Lovaniense, 1924), p. 61.

56

134 occurrences of _sacramentum_ in Tertullian, E. de Backer (1924)
finds that 84 are based on the classical Roman meaning of "oath,"
whereas the remaining 50 center on the meaning of "mystery."[111]
Arguing from the usage by classical Latin authors, de Backer sums up
earlier scholarly consensus by stating that _sacramentum_ originally
meant an "oath," especially that oath which is taken upon entrance
into military service.[112] Because in taking an oath one engages in a
formal relationship with God, the mysterious One, de Backer reasons
that _sacramentum_ comes to take on the meaning of 'something mysterious,'
and that Tertullian in turn uses it to signify Christian doctrine as
mystery.[113]

More recently, D. Michaélidès (1970) has written a whole volume
in order to show that "oath" is ultimately the sole meaning of _sacra-
mentum_ in the writings of Tertullian.[114] Where de Backer details a
loose constellation of meanings in Tertullian's use of the word --
"oath," "rite of initiation," "religion," "truth," "doctrine,"
"sacrament," "sign," "symbol," "figure," "_mysterium_," "plan," and
"prophecy"[115] --, Michaelides attempts to show passage by passage from
Tertullian that every use by the North African is tied directly to the
single meaning of "oath." In doing so he has not escaped very severe

_____

[111]_Ibid._, pp. 143, 144.
[112]_Ibid._, p. 70.
[113]_Ibid._, p. 149.
[114]Dimitri Michaélidès, _Sacramentum chez Tertullien_ (Paris: Études Augustiniennes, 1970).
[115]de Backer, "Tertullien," pp. 143-144.

criticism, to the effect that he forces Tertullian's sacramentum onto

an a priori procrustean bed of his own making.[116]

A. Kolping (1948) also analyses sacramentum in Tertullian, finding

two separate roots to the Latin word: (1) an active one: (sacr-) 'that

which consecrates,' and (2) a passive one: (-mentum) 'that which is

consecrated.'[117] According to Kolping, the first corresponds to the

classical Latin use for "oath," and the second to the notion of

"mystery," or "holy object." Furthermore, in contrast to de Backer,

Kolping does not understand Tertullian's use of sacramentum as "mystery"

solely in the folk usage as 'something mysterious,' but predominately

in the pauline, biblical meaning of MUSTERION: 'God's plan for sal-

vation accomplished in Christ.' Consequently, Kolping sees Tertullian

as more dependent in his use of sacramentum on the ecclesial environ-

ment of the time than on the heritage of classical Latinity. He argues

that the very unreflectiveness with which Tertullian uses sacramentum

to translate MUSTERION in biblical citations[118] shows, not only that

he was not the first to coin the Christian use of the word, but that in

his writings "oath" is neither its original nor its exclusive meaning.[119]

---

[116]van der Geest, Le Christ, p. 143: "Nous serions victime de nos propres systématisations si nous voulions ici marquer des limites rigoureuses."

[117]Adolf Kolping, Sacramentum Tertullianeum: Erster Teil: Untersuchungen über die Anfänge des christlichen Gebrauches der Vokabel sacramentum, (Regensberg-Münster: Postberg, 1948), p. 98.

[118]Kolping, Sacramentum Tertullianeum, p. 47; Tertullian translates a biblical musterion by sacramentum nineteen times. See also C. Mohrmann, "Quelques observations sur 'sacramentum' chez Tertullien," in: W. den Boer et al. edd., Romanitas et Christianitas, (Amsterdam: North-Holland, 1973), p. 240.

[119]Kolping, Sacramentum Tertullianeum, p. 101, n. 17.

If one agrees with Kolping that Tertullian simply appropriates
without comment the translation of MUSTERION by sacramentum in Latin
Bibles of his time, the question remains how to explain his frequent
use of sacramentum as "oath." Both Kolping and C. Mohrmann (1952)
admit the difficulty in clearly defining lines of dependency between
these two basic meanings of the word.[120] However, Mohrmann proposes
that Tertullian employs sacramentum as "oath" only in a derivative and
figurative way.[121] She does so because she sees the original sense of
the word in classical Latin, not as an "oath," but as a "religious
engagement" which in some circumstances expressed itself by an oath.[122]
Sacramentum, then, could be used to translate the pauline notion of
MUSTERION without necessarily or primarily having also to signify an
oath. At the same time, knowing the classical use of the word to denote
a military oath, Tertullian uses sacramentum in that sense as a metaphor for Baptism and Eucharist just as he frequently uses other military
words[123] to highlight the committment and struggle of Christian life,

---

[120]"il est difficile d'en déceler la structure sémasiologique,"
Mohrmann, "Quelques observations," p. 233. See also Kolping, Sacramentum
Tertullianeum, p. 98.

[121]Mohrmann, "Sacramentum dans les plus anciens textes chrétiens,"
p. 150.

[122]Ibid., p. 145.

[123]"Les allusions faites par Tertullien à la vie militaire sont
nombreuses. Le Chrétien est assimilé à un soldat dont Dieu est le chef,
l'Eglise à une armée, la communauté chrétienne à une commilitio, la croix
à un étendard, etc. Il s'agit là de métaphores qui, en premier lieu,
étaient inspirées par certaines tournures et images pauliniennes, mais
qui pouvaient avoir aussi des liens avec certaines conceptions religieuses
païennes du monde contemporain," Mohrmann, "Quelques observations," p.
239.

the militia Dei: 'Just as pagan Latins express their religious committment by an oath, especially on their entering into military service, so
too do Christians engage themselves with God in Baptism by promises
spelling out the faith contained in that sacramentum.'

Michaélidès rejects this Kolping-Mohrmann explanation of
Tertullian's use of sacramentum:

(1) First of all, Michaélidès accounts for the unreflective way
that Tertullian renders the biblical MUSTERION by "sacramentum,"
theorizing that "the principal meanings of the word (sacramentum)
appeared almost simultaneously under the pen of Tertullian,"[124] so that
he owes nothing to any previous Christian use of that word. Mohrmann
remarks, "There indeed is a bold thesis, one not easy to accept."[125]
For her, the very fact that there are a multiplicity of related meanings
in Tertullian's writings would be strong evidence that he continues a
previous evolution in the Christian use of sacramentum.[126]

(2) Secondly, as mentioned earlier, Michaélidès re-states the
older scholarly consensus that 'military oath' is the basic meaning of
Tertullian's sacramentum. In Roman Law, in a dispute between two
parties wherein both bound themselves by oaths to the rightness of their
claim, those parties also put down a surety or monetary bond which the
loser in the trial would have to forfeit.[127] Michaélidès' basic theory

---

[124]Dimitri Michaélidès, Sacramentum chez Tertullien, (Paris:
Études Augustiniennes, 1970), p. 344.

[125]Mohrmann, "Quelques observations," p. 236.

[126]Ibid.

[127]Michaélidès, Sacramentum, pp. 33-35.

60

is that Tertullian's every use of _sacramentum_ should be understood according to this Roman concept of _oath_ and the _bond_ that is connected with it. At one point in his rebuttal to this thesis, van der Geest denies the particular contention of Michaélidès that Tertullian understands every promise of God in salvation history (_sacramentum_) as a pledge (bond) backed by an oath.[128] For van der Geest, it is evident from examples like this that Michaélidès' effort to give such rigorous limits to the meaning of Tertullian's _sacramentum_ has made him a victim of his own systemization.[129]

   (3) Next, Michaélidès claims that when Tertullian uses _sacramentum_, he does not mean to translate but rather to interpret the biblical MUSTERION.[130] As we stated already, no single word ever fully translates another and to some extent the translating word always represents an interpretation added to the original. However, to state that Tertullian consciously meant to change the meaning of a word in Scripture by giving it an interpretation which the Church did not already find there demands some further explanation. It is Tertulliam himself who argues that the only true meaning of Scripture is the one given to it by the Church.[131]

   (4) Finally, Michaélidès strongly objects to Mohrmann's reducing the identification of _sacramentum_ with "oath" to a mere "literary turn-

---

[128]van der Geest, _Le Christ_, p. 108.
[129]_Ibid._, p. 143.
[130]Michaélidès, _Sacramentum_, p. 19.
[131]See footnote #95.

of-phrase."[132] He believes that by doing so one denies to Tertullian
"any depth of vision on the central theme of his work, fides."[133]
However, Michaélidès' insightful theological analysis of the inter-
relationships of the many meanings of sacramentum in Tertullian in
terms of fides -- lived Christian faith -- is really independent of
whether Tertullian used the word literally or metaphorically. Even if
Tertullian extended the Christian meaning of sacramentum by metaphor
to mean "oath," verbally comparing the demands of the pauline MUSTERION
on Christian living to those on a soldier by the oath of initiation
(sacramentum) into military life, he nevertheless did so in a very
serious way,[134] as is witnessed by the frequency and variety of ways
in which he applies this metaphor.[135] Consequently, one can as surely
discern a coherent theology behind Tertullian's use of sacramentum as
metaphor as he might if "oath" were in fact the literal, root meaning of
the word in Tertullian's vocabulary. The herculean effort to logically

---

[132]"La rapprochement de sacramentum chrétien et de 'serment
militaire,' là où il s'agit de la formule baptismale, est un artifice
littéraire ...", Mohrmann, "Sacramentum," p. 150; Michaélidès, Sacramentum, p. 340.

[133]Michaélidès, Sacramentum, p. 340.

[134]Mohrmann, "Quelques Observations," p. 239: "Les rapprochements
qu'il établit entre sacramentum-serment militaire et sacramentum-baptême,
ont, pour lui, une signification qui dépasse le simple jeu verbal et
permettent, grâce à ce jeu, d'exprimer quelque chose de profond et
d'essentiel; mais ils ne sont pas pour autant une manière d'expliquer
l'origine de l'usage chrétien de sacramentum."

[135]Ibid., pp. 239-240. "Ce precédè de rapprochement de termes
chrétiens et de termes militaires est assez usuel chez Tertullien: je
renvoie, entre autres, à l'usage de statio." See also Mohrmann, "Statio,"
Vigiliae Christianae VII (1953), 221 ff.

62

relate all uses of <u>sacramentum</u> in the North African's writings to "oath"
or "bond" is actually as unnecessary as it is unconvincing.

In her critique of Michaélides, C. Mohrmann (1973) gives R. Braun's
(1962)[136] summary as an apt statement of what she considers to be the
best scholarship on <u>sacramentum</u> in Tertullian.[137] The main points of
this summary are the following:

(1) Tertullian left his personal stamp on the Christian meaning
of <u>sacramentum</u>, but for the most part the new meanings of that word were
elaborated during the period of latinization of Western, especially
North African, Christian communities.[138]

(2) In these communities <u>sacramentum</u> appropriated, first, all the
meanings of the biblical and ecclesiastical <u>MUSTERION</u>, especially its
notion of "hidden truth or plan of God mysteriously revealed," and then
it acquired the concrete meaning of a "sacred sign." <u>Sacramentum</u> in
the sense of "oath" played no part in this development.[139]

(3) In translating the Christian word, <u>MUSTERION</u>, <u>sacramentum</u>
emphasizes more the sacredness (<u>sacr-</u>) of the "Mystery" than it does its
obscurity or hiddenness.[140]

---

[136]Réné Braun, <u>Deus Christianorum: Recherches sur le Vocabulaire
Doctrinal de Tertullien.</u> Publications de la Faculté des Lettres et
Sciences Humaines d'Alger XLI, (Paris: Presses Universitaires de France,
1962), pp. 435-443.
[137]Mohrmann, "Quelques Observations," pp. 234-235.
[138]Braun, <u>Deus Christianorum</u>, p. 436.
[139]Ibid., pp. 436-438.
[140]Ibid., pp. 438-439.

(4) Tertullian, as a learned man, aligns the classical Latin
meanings of sacramentum as "religious engagement" and particularly as
"oath" with those of his Christian background. Although he seriously
compares baptism to a military oath in order to stress that one's service
to Christ demands the committment of one's whole being, it would be
erroneous to see in this expression the semantic basis for all of his
other Christian uses of the word.[141]

"Sacramentum:" Code word for "Salvation History"

Tertullian, as we have seen, has a passion for order. To him, God
is first of all a God of order. Consequently, in his translating the
word St. Paul uses to catch up and unify the whole of God's saving
activity, MUSTERION, Tertullian might be expected to give to sacramentum
the same fundamental theological perspective given by St. Paul. C.P.
Mayer repeats A. Kolping's observation that just such a synthesis is at
work in Tertullian's sacramentum:

> The verbal convention found in the New Testament,
> especially as presented by Paul, of designating
> messianic salvation as MUSTERION is the spiritual
> clasp which holds together the myriad uses of
> sacramentum in Tertullian.[142]

---

[141]Ibid., pp. 439-440.

[142]"Die im Neuen Testament, besonders 'bei Paulus vorliegende
Sprachgewohnheit, das messianische Heil als musterion zu bezeichnen, ist
die geistige Klammer, die die vielfältige Anwendung für sacramentum bei
Tertullian hält,'" Cornelius Petrus Mayer, Die Zeichen in der geistigen
Entwicklung und in der Theologie des jungen Augustinus, (Würzburg:
Augustinus, 1969), p. 290, quoting A. Kolping, Sacramentum Tertullianeum.
p. 48.

Mayer shows that Tertullian calls the overall <u>organization</u> of salvation,

arising out of the Trinity, the "<u>oikonomiae sacramentum</u>,"[143] which in

turn can be seen in God's saving deeds of the Old Testament: "<u>Creator</u>

<u>autem tam ipse notus quam et sacramenta eius</u>" ('One can recognize the

Creator in his holy actions in history').[144] However, these <u>sacramenta</u>

were obscure and hidden until the fulness of time.[145]

Mayer then argues that Tertullian's use of <u>sacramentum</u> to mean

"sacred doctrine" develops out of God's saving events in history

(<u>sacramenta</u>) as the <u>truth</u> about God which they contain: "<u>praedicatio</u>

<u>totius sacramenti</u>."[146] Furthermore, the particular items of teaching

making up this doctrinal <u>sacramentum</u>, such as belief in the Resurrection,

are in their turn also called "<u>sacramenta</u>."[147] Finally, in regard to

Tertullian's use of <u>sacramentum</u> for Baptism and Eucharist, Mayer reasons

that it represents "the concretizing of the teaching content of the

<u>sacramenta</u>," giving that content "effective ritual power."[148] In other

words, according to Mayer, God's obscure activity in salvation history

in types and figures (<u>sacramenta</u>) becomes the object of the Church's

teaching (<u>sacramentum</u>) in its many articles of faith (<u>sacramenta</u>); in

---

[143]Aem. Kroymann et Ern. Evans, edd., "Adversus Praxean," in <u>Quinti</u>
<u>Septimi Florentis Tertulliani Opera</u>, Pars II: Opera Montanistica.
Corpus Christianorum, Series Latina II. (Turnholt: Brepols, 1954), II,
4, p. 1162.

[144]Kroymann, ed., "Adversus Marcionem," V, 6, 2; CCSL I, 678.13-14.

[145]<u>Ibid</u>., 678:14-17; referred to by C.P. Mayer, <u>Die Zeichen</u>, p. 291.

[146]J.G.Ph. Borleffs, ed., "De Resurrectione Mortuorum," LXIII, 9;
CCSL II, 1012.44.

[147]<u>Ibid</u>., XXII, 8; CCSL II, 948.41 & XXVI,3; 953.14. Cited by
Mayer, <u>Die Zeichen</u>, p. 291.

[148]Mayer, <u>Die Zeichen</u>, p. 291: "Die Konkretisierung des Lehrgehaltes
der sacramenta wird zum rituellen Vollzug."

turn, the essence of that teaching is ritualized (Baptism & Eucharist = sacramenta) in order to convey more powerfully the truth about God that it contains.

The obvious difficulty with this analysis is its underlying reduction of salvation to a conceptual message from God to his people, instead of its being an existential engagement of each in the life of the other, the emphasis which is so clear in Tertullian's use of sacramentum as "oath" in the context of Baptism. It therefore seems much more reasonable to assume that, if Tertullian, together with Paul and with his own Christian community in North Africa, found God in the events of history, he would as surely find Him in Christ's saving events as they are realized in the rites of the Church. Instead of their being concrete, ritual means of conveying abstract truths, Baptism and Eucharist are better understood as sacramenta directly in the pauline MUSTERION sense: God's saving deeds in human history (in the midst of the Christian assembly) through Jesus Christ. Mayer himself remarks: "What is most striking about Tertullian's concept of sacramentum is his strong dependence on the presentation of salvation history."[149]

---

[149] Ibid., p. 293: "Zusammenfassend können wir sagen: Was an Tertullians sacramentum-Begriff am meisten auffällt, ist seine starke Anlehnung an die Darstellung der Heilsgeschichte."

Sacramentum as Ordered in Christ

As noted earlier, Tertullian understands the whole Old Testament
as a prefigurement of Christ,[150] that Jesus "fulfills everything that
had been predicted of him."[151]   At the same time, the types and figures
of the Old Testament not only point to a Christ to come,[152] but to
some degree they already make him present,[153] so that Tertullian names
them "sacramenta." In our consideration of salvation history according
to Tertullian, therefore, a sacramentum can be seen to be any person,
event or object (-mentum) which, by imaging[154] Christ is the holy

---

[150] See above, footnote #101

[151] "Adimplens omnia, quae super ipso fuerant praedicta," "Adversus
Marcionem," IV, 29, 15; CCSL I, 627.27, quoted in van der Geest, Le
Christ, p. 111.

[152] E.g. Tertullian sees the brazen serpent as "crucis istius
(Christ) sacramentum," "Adversus Iudeos," X, 10; CCSL II, 1377.80.
See also de Backer, Tertullian, p. 103.

[153] "La prophétie le rendait déjà présent, mais pas dans toute sa
réalité," van der Geest, Le Christ, p. 114.

[154] van der Geest notes that T.P. O'Malley, Tertullian and the
Bible, (Nijmegen: Dekker, 1972), p. 161 ff., and Michaélidès,
Sacramentum, pp. 191 ff., agree that Tertullian associates the word,
"figura", with "sacramentum," Le Christ, p. 162. O'Malley also finds
that "figura" bears the weight of "typus," since Tertullian uses that
Grecism only 3 times in all his writings. Thus, "figura" and "typus,"
imagery language, are in close conjunction with "sacramentum." Furthermore, Tertullian associates the word, "imago," with the metaphysics
that is basic to "sacramentum," arguing against the allegorists that
'first there must be a reality that exists before there can be an
image that symbolizes that reality:' "Nam etsi figmentum veritatis
in imagine est, imago ipsa in veritate est sui: necesse est esse
prius sibi id quod alii configuretur," "De Resurrectione Carnis," XXX,
5; CCSL II, 959.23-25, quoted in van der Geest, Le Christ, p. 190.

(sacr-) medium of God's presence in faith[155] to people throughout history. Consequently, in this single word Tertullian expresses the ordering of all salvation history in and through the person and work of Jesus Christ.

Figura Corporis

If sacramentum denotes a historical reality that points to Christ and makes Him present, then Tertullian's naming Baptism and Eucharist "sacramenta" would indicate that he in fact understands a "reverse typology" to be at work in the liturgical activity of the Church, that a "sacramental" economy exists after the historical life of Christ which acts similarly to types and figures of the Old Testament in imaging Christ and thereby making him present. A further indication that this is indeed the case is the scholarly discussion in this century around Tertullian's celebrated references to the Eucharistic bread as the "figura corporis" ('type of the body') of the Lord:

---

[155] Michaélidès,' analysis of the faith-dimension of Tertullian's "sacramentum" remains valid in our estimation in spite of the other drawbacks of his study. See especially his "Conclusion générale," Sacramentum chez Tertullien, pp. 335-345. For an excellent systematic treatment of the relation of faith to the presence of Christ in contemporary terms, see E.J. Kilmartin, S.J., "Apostolic Office," Theological Studies XXXVI (1975), 246-264.

68

>Having taken the bread and given it to
>his disciples, he made it his body, saying:
>'This is my body,' that is, a figure of my
>body."[156]

H. de Lubac (1949) argues that most commentators understand a

platonist typology behind this use of "figura corporis," that the

eucharistic bread is the "exemplarist" presence of the static, non-

temporal body of the Lord.[157] As a result, the phrase, "figure of the

body," unnecessarily raises the question whether Tertullian holds to

the "real presence" of Christ in the Eucharist.[158] However, de Lubac

continues, if the relationship between bread and body in these passages

is understood in terms of Christian typology, that is, as involving

---

[156]"Acceptum panem et distributum discipulis, corpus suum illum
fecit, Hoc est corpus meum dicendo, id est figura corporis mei,"
"Adversus Marcionem," IV, 40, 3; CCSL I, 656.24-26. See also Adv. Marc.
III, 19; CCSL I, 532:16-22.
    For a discussion among 20th century scholars around Tertullian's
"figura corporis" see: H.B. Swete, "Eucharistic Belief in the Second
and Third Centuries," Journal of Theological Studies III (1902), 173-
174; A. d'Alès, La Théologie de Tertullien, (Paris: Beauchesne, 1905),
p. 360; C.H. Turner, "'Figura Corporis Mei' in Tertullian," Journal of
Theological Studies VI (1906), 595-597; Henri de Lubac, S.J., Corpus
Mysticum: l'Eucharistie et l'Eglise au Moyen Age, 2nd ed., (Paris:
Aubier, Editions Montaigne, 1949), "Note B: Sur l'Eucharistie 'antitype,'" pp. 351-357; C.W. Dugmore, "Sacrament and Sacrifice in the
Early Fathers," Journal of Ecclesiastical History II (1951), 24-37;
Victor Saxer, "Figura Corporis et Sanguinis Domini: Une Formule
Eucharistique des Premiers Siècles Chez Tertullien, Hippolyte et
Ambroise," Rivista di Archeologia Cristiana XLVII (1971), 65-89.
[157]de Lubac, Corpus Mysticum, p. 252.
[158]"Real Presence" is thus a concept arising out of the question
whether the body of Christ existing now in heaven exists also in or
through the eucharistic bread and wine. This concept does not, however, admit of the distinction between "type" and "antitype" so fundamental to the tradition of Christian typology or of the historicity of
Christ's death and resurrection constantly held as indispensible for our
salvation.

two historical realities, then it becomes obvious that the true intent
of the author is to underline "the correspondance of the entire
Eucharist (action and reality, rite and matter, sensible exterior and
mystical reality) to the body of Christ sacrificed on the cross."[159]
Therefore, in de Lubac's estimation, the Eucharist "represents" and
"refigures" the saving events which Old Testament sacrifices "presented"
and "prefigured."[160] de Lubac's conclusions are independently affirmed
in a later study on Tertullian's "figura corporis" by V. Saxer (1971):
"By employing the word 'figura' in regard to the Eucharist, the Fathers
(including Tertullian) meant to set it in relation to the death of
Christ."[161]

Saxer argues convincingly for another thesis (which had actually
been placed by C.H. Turner in 1906) that Tertullian's use of figura
corporis as a gloss on 'hoc est enim corpus meum' represents the text
of a common first century eucharistic prayer.[162] This fact, together
with other instances where "figura corporis" or its Greek equivalent is
applied to eucharistic elements by Hippolytus, Serapion, Cyril of

---

[159] de Lubac, Corpus Mysticum, p. 355. According to J. Daniélou,
S.J., "corpus" for Tertullian means any given thing to the degree that
it exists: "nihil est incorporale nisi quod non est (de Carne Christi,
XI, 4, CCSL II, 895.23-24)," J. Daniélou, S.J., The Origins of Latin
Christianity, (Philadelphia: Westminster, 1977), p. 347. Therefore,
"corpus" in this present discussion does not necessarily refer to a
static or physical reality as over against the relational being of a
type or figure.

[160] de Lubac, Corpus Mysticum, p. 156.

[161] Saxer, "Figura Corporis," p. 87.

[162] C.H. Turner, op. cit.

Jerusalem and Ambrose,[163] demonstrates that the early Church (Tertullian included) understood its ritual "sacraments" so fundamentally as salvation history events, in a manner similar to types and figures of the Old Testament, that it did not even hesitate to amend the biblical words of Christ in order to bring out that truth.

To the question originally posed, whether "reverse typology" is operative in the thinking of the immediate predecessors of Cyprian, the answer is clearly affirmative. With this background investigation we are now in a position to study the writings of Cyprian for his own proper understanding of the place of typology in the economy of Christian "sacramental" life in general, and in the eucharistic celebration in particular.

---

[163]See Saxer, "Figura Corporis," pp. 72-84 and de Lubac, Corpus Mysticum, p. 353.

Chapter III

SALVATION HISTORY IN CYPRIAN

Introduction

At the outset of our study we noted Cyprian's belief that the eucharistic leader's imitation of Christ's Last-Supper actions is in fact the work of Christ making himself present and effective through the leader. We then set out in search of the source for Cyprian's confidence that such imitation is in fact the dynamic presence of Christ. Beginning with the Scriptures themselves, we found that the New Testament represents the fundamental faith of the Church, namely that Christ, who fulfills the Old Testament by his life, death and resurrection, was already present in Old Testament history through the shadowy imitations by types and figures of those saving deeds (Chapter One). Next, investigating the writings of second and early third century Christian authors, we discovered an understanding of salvation history involving a "reverse typology." Holy persons living after the time of Christ are seen to participate in Christ and make him in his saving events present in subsequent history (Chapter Two). Against this background, the task of the present chapter is to investigate to what degree Cyprian himself reflects this "reverse typology," to what degree he sees an imitation-presence relationship at work between Christ and historical figures living before as well as historical figures living after the time of Christ.

In order to provide a response to this question, Chapter Three studies the fundamental words behind Cyprian's theology of salvation history. Section One deals with his use of "sacramentum" and its two componants, "imago" and "veritas." Scholars traditionally have recognized "sacramentum" as the key to Cyprian's understanding of Christ's presence in the workings of the Church. However, this word is especially valuable for our topic by the fact that Cyprian uses it for Old Testament as well as New Testament realities.

Section Two is devoted to a study of "portare," "adunare" and "repraesentare," as words which convey to the fullest degree Cyprian's underlying theology of salvation history.

It may be noted at the outset that Cyprian nowhere in his writings uses the terms "typus" or "figura" for anyone in the Church. In his restricting these words to Old Testament realities, he is faithful to the example of his "Master," Tertullian.[164]

---

[164] J.E.L. van der Geest, Le Christ et L'Ancien Testament chez Tertullien, Latinitas Christianorum Primaeva XXII (Nijmegen: Dekker & van de Vegt, 1972), pp. 175, 176.

I. <u>Sacramentum</u> - <u>Imago</u> - <u>Veritas</u>

<u>Sacramentum</u>

The word, <u>sacramentum</u>,[165] continues to be as important to Cyprian's theology of salvation history as it was to Tertullian's. In a much smaller corpus of writings than his predecessor, Cyprian uses <u>sacramentum</u> no less than sixty-four times.[166] For the most part, scholars have understood his use of the word according to their understanding of its meanings in Tertullian's works. In fact, J.B. Poukens deliberately groups the sixty-four instances into two large categories of meaning, 'MUSTERION' and 'oath,' the same two categories which E. de Backer used in his study of <u>sacramentum</u> in Tertullian.[167] In a manner also similar

---

[165]B. Renaud states that further study is needed on the precise meanings of <u>sacramentum</u> and of <u>portare</u> in the writings of Cyprian. L'Eglise comme assemblée liturgique selon saint Cyprien," <u>Recherches de Theologie annienne et médiévale</u> XXXVIII (1971), 23. The goal of this chapter involves us in just such a study.

[166]A. d'Alès presents an excellent schema of Cyprian's sixty-four uses of <u>sacramentum</u>: <u>La Théologie de Saint Cyprien</u> (Paris: Gabriel Beauchesne, 1922), pp. 86-88. Although he records sixty-four, he fails to note the occurrence of the word in Test II, 14: "sacramenta <u>Dei</u>," but cites Test II, 15: "sacramento <u>passionis</u>" in its place. Thus, there are at least sixty-five instances of <u>sacramentum</u> in Cyprian's writings.

[167]E. de Backer, "Tertullien," and J.B. Poukens, "Cyprien et ses contemporaines," in <u>Pour l'histoire du mot</u> 'Sacramentum'. I. <u>Les Antenicéens</u>. J. de Ghellinck, E. de Backer, J. Poukens, G. Lebacqz, edd. (Louvain: "Spicilegium Sacrum Lovaniense," 1924), pp. 59-152.

to the practice of de Backer, these scholars sort out Cyprian's uses of
sacramentum into further subdivisions of meaning: A. d'Alès (1922) --
(1) Sacred Reality (mystery, doctrine, precept) twenty-three uses, (2)
Typological twenty-six uses, (3) Christian Sacrament nine uses, (4)
Military Oath six uses;[168] J.B. Poukens (1924) -- (1) Oath seven, (2)
MUSTERION (mystery, symbol, revelation, precept) forty-two, (3) Doubtful
(Christian Sacrament) fifteen;[169] J.C. Navickas (1924) -- (1) Classical
(oath) five, (2) Doctrinal (profession of faith, a doctrine, prophecy,
testimony) twenty-three, (4) 'Sacrament' ten.[170]

A cursory examination of the above divisions reveals the heavy use
Cyprian makes of sacramentum in order to signify a salvation-history
type or figure. Although, as we have noted, Poukens is constrained by
the categories of de Backer ('oath' and 'MUSTERION'), d'Ales and
Navickas classify twenty-six out of the sixty-four uses as "typological"
or "figurative." This would suggest that Cyprian continues the fundamental salvation-history significance which we found in Tertullian's use
of the word. Nevertheless, none of the three scholars, d'Ales, Poukens
or Navickas, is able to argue back to any single basic meaning behind
all the instances of sacramentum in Cyprian's writings.

A. Demoustier (1964) claims that, in the final analysis, Cyprian's
sacramentum must have a single, common underlying significance. There

---

[168] A. d'Ales, op. cit.
[169] J.B. Poukens, op. cit.
[170] John Cyprian Navickas, The Doctrine of St. Cyprian on the
Sacraments (Würzburg: C.J. Becker, 1924).

must ultimately be one fundamental meaning to the word behind the many
and varied uses found in his writings, "the reason for the univocity in
the analogy."[171] Accordingly, Demoustier sets out to find the common
demoninator in all the uses of sacramentum by Cyprian that allows the
martyr-bishop to use the same word in such a seeming variety of meanings.
In doing so Demoustier arrives at the following characteristics common
to all sixty-four acknowledged instances in Cyprian's writings:

(1) Perceptible Reality: In search of that univocal meaning,
Demoustier discovers that the "majority of uses correspond to a context
where particular perceptible realities are being dealt with (e.g.
Scriptural types, rites)."[172] The fact is, however, all instances
without exception involve a created element in time and space which in
turn allows some kind of this-worldly human experience, as is evident in
Demoustier's second characteristic of sacramentum.[173]

---

[171]A. Demoustier, S.J., "L'Ontologie de l'Eglise selon saint
Cyprien," Recherches de Science Religieuse LII (1964), 557, 558: "Il
faudrait trouver au delà des nuances multiples un facteur commun, une
raison d'univocité dans l'analogie."

[172]Ibid., p. 558. "... la plupart des emplois correspond à un
context où il s'agit de réalités preceptibles bien déterminées (figures
de l'Ecritures, rites...)."

[173]J.B. Poukens states that, although "sacramentum" in Tertullian's
one-hundred and thirty uses of that word signifies the theological
notion of "an abstract mystery" seven times, only once is it so used in
Cyprian's writings: "Sacramentum fidei non esse profanandum" (Test III,
50) (Pour l'Histoire, p. 171). However, Cyprian considers the concrete
words of the profession of faith during baptism to be a sacramentum of
the Trinity: Ep 73, 5, 2. Such, then, is most likely the meaning of
"sacramentum fidei" in Test III, 50 as well, and not that of "an abstract
mystery."

On the other hand, M. Fahey re-states E. W. Watson's contention
that "mysterium" is used once by Cyprian as an equivalent for "sacramentum" in Test II, 19: "Hujus rei mysterium ostensum est apud Iesum
Nave" (Watson, "The Style and Language of St. Cyprian," Studia Biblica
et Ecclesiastica IV [Oxford: Clarendon, 1896], 253: Fahey, Cyprian

(2) <u>Divine Action</u>: Next, Demoustier observes that some of the
"perceptible realities" found in Cyprian's <u>sacramenta</u> are not as tangibly
material as are others, such as, for example, the individual Scriptural
formulas which comprise the text of the Lord's Prayer,[174] or the solidarity of Christians around their bishop and of bishops with each other
("<u>sacramentum unitatis</u>").[175] Cyprian nevertheless names these phenomena
<u>sacramenta</u>. According to Demoustier, the reason he does so lies in the
fact that:

> the religious mentality of the Ancients expressed
> itself in a language called "symbolic:" words,
> gestures, actions that translate an experience [of]
> a person of this world relating [him or her] in a
> synthetic way to the Beyond, to the sacred.[176]

That is to say, for Cyprian a <u>sacramentum</u> is not dependent for its value
or efficacy on its objectified holiness (<u>res sacra</u>), but rather on the

---

173 (cont) <u>and the Bible: a Study in Third-Century Exegesis</u>
[Tübingen: J.C.B. Mohr, 1971], p. 614). Elsewhere Fahey highlights the
typological nature of "<u>ostendere</u>," that it signals in Cyprian's vocabulary the explanation of a type (p. 615). Here, however, "<u>mysterium</u>" is
not the subject of a typological action as a cypriannic <u>sacramentum</u>
would be, but rather the direct object. "mysterium" is the reality
being pointed to or typified: "<u>ostensum est.</u>" Instead of its being a
synonym for "<u>sacramentum</u>" here, "<u>mysterium</u>" more probably signifies the
spiritual presence of a reality which is witnessed to and effected by a
<u>sacramentum</u>. Thus, Test II, 19 would be translated, "The mysterious
presence of this reality is pointed to in the form of [the <u>sacramentum</u>],
Jesus (Joshua) Nave."

[174]Demoustier, "L'Ontologie," p. 558, n. 21.

[175]See our Treatment of "<u>sacramentum unitatis</u>" in section II of
this chapter.

[176]Ibid., p. 558: "D'une facon générale, la mentalité religieuse
des anciens s'exprime dans un language dit "symbolique": paroles,
gestes, actions qui traduisent une expérience reliant sur un mode
synthétique l'homme de ce monde-ci à l'au-dela, au sacré."

action of God communicating Himself through it (symbolic).[177] A

sacramentum, therefore, can be any genre of perceptible reality found in

our world: be it a person, object, Scriptural formula, inter-personal

relationship or event, but only to the extent that it is the locus and

vehicle for the divine initiative into human and Christian life.

(3) Christological: In a study of the three following texts

Demoustier points to the fundamentally christocentric nature of Cyprian's

sacramentum:

> (a) Item libellus alius continet Christi sacramentum,
> quod idem venerit qui secundum scripturas adnuntiatus est,
> et gesserit ac perfecerit universa, quibus intellegi et
> cognosci posse praedictus est ... (Intro, Test I).
> (Moreover, the second book contains the sacramentum
> of Christ, namely that he would come who is announced
> according to the Scriptures, and that he would carry out
> and bring to completion everything by which he is foretold
> as able to be known and recognized ...)

> (b) Vinum ... quod Christi sanguis ostenditur qui
> scripturarum omnium sacramento et testimonio praedicetur.
> Invenimus enim et in Genesi circa sacramentum Noe hoe idem
> praecucurrisse et figuram dominicae passionis illic extitisse
> ... et sic (Noe) imaginem dominicae passionis expresserit.
> (Ep 63, 2 & 3).
> (Wine ... prefigures the blood of Christ which is
> proclaimed by the sacramentum and testimony of all the
> Scriptures. For we find even in Genesis as a sacramentum
> that Noe anticipated the same thing and stood out as a
> figure of the Lord's passion in that he drank wine ... and
> thus he expressed an image of the Lord's passion.)

> (c) Item in sacerdote Melchisedech sacrificii dominici
> sacramentum praefiguratum videmus secundum quod scriptura
> divina testatur et dicit: "Et Melchisedech rex Salem
> protulit panem et vinum, fuit autem sacerdos Dei summi et
> benedixit Abraham" (Gen 14, 18). Quod autem Melchisedech
> typum Christi portaret declarat in Psalmis Spiritus Sanctus
> ....ergo in Genesi ...
> praecedit ante imago sacrificii in pane et vino scilicet

---

[177]Ibid.

78

constituta: quam rem perficiens et adimplens Dominus
panem et calicem mixtum vino obtulit, et qui est
plenitudo veritatem praefiguratae imaginis adimplevit
(Ep 63, 4, 1 & 3).
(Moreover, we see prefigured in the priest, Melchisedech,
a sacramentum of the Lord's sacrifice as divine Scripture
testifies and states: "And Melchisedech, king of Salem,
offered forth bread and wine, for he was a priest of the
high God, and he blessed Abraham" (Gen 14, 18). But that
Melchisedech bore the type of Christ the Holy Spirit
declares in the Psalms..................................
....
therefore in Genesis ... the image of sacrifice clearly
constituted in bread and wine is already present proleptically (ante). Fulfilling and completing this reality,
the Lord offered bread and the cup mixed with wine, and he
who is the Fulness brought to completion the truth of the
prefigured image.)[178]

In the Introduction to the Testimonies, text (a), Cyprian states

that its second book "contains the sacramentum of Christ." By this he

means that the collection of biblical types of the second book form one

single announcement of Christ insofar as the mystery of Christ makes

itself known in them.[179] Demoustier also notes that sacramentum can

refer to any single biblical figure to the extent that it images the

historical Christ. Here he offers text (b) and (c) as examples. He

states that in text (c) sacramentum signifies bread and wine, the bread

and wine offered by Melchisedech and that offered by Christ, since both

instances point to Christ. Demoustier is correct here to emphasize

that sacramentum for Cyprian always refers to Christ. There is no

sacramentum that is not a sacramentum of Christ. However, as will

_____

[178] The quotation from Cyprian represented by text (c) has been
expanded over that made by Demoustier in order to give sufficient context for our analysis.

[179] Demoustier, "L'Ontologie," pp. 559-561.

become evident in the analysis of Demoustier's next basic characteristic
of sacramentum, that word is never used to refer to the Last Supper
offering itself.

(4) A-temporal: Demoustier argues from Cyprian's discussion of
wine in Ep 63 that sacramentum does not of itself signify "temporal
anteriority" to the historical Christ. That is to say, it is used to
signify not only past, Old Testament types and figures, but also some
realities found after the time of Christ.

> Sacramentum by itself does not signify temporal
> anteriority since it denotes in the third text
> (c) bread and wine as signifying Christ as much
> in the sacrifice of Melchisedech, the image, as
> in its truth, the [Last] Supper.180

By his drawing this conclusion, although Demoustier argues convincingly
for the a-temporal character of Cyprian's sacramentum, it is evident that
he has mis-read the text in regard to another important characteristic
of that word. In Ep 63,4, the word sacramentum is actually applied, not
to wine, but to the person of Melchisedech in his action of offering
wine. In other words, in this passage it is the offering event as a
whole, not simply wine, that is called "sacramentum praefiguratum." For
immediately after this phrase Cyprian continues to speak, not of wine,
but of the "king of Salem," a "priest of the high God," one who

---

180Demoustier, "L'Ontologie," p. 561: "Sacramentum ne signifie pas
par lui-même l'antériorité temporelle puisqu'il désigne dans le troisi-
ème textele pain et le vin comme signifiant le Christ aussi bien dans le
sacrifice de Melchisédèch, l'image, que dans sa vérité: la Cène."

"bore the type of Christ." In text (c) the "reality" (rem) which the
Lord fulfills at the Lst Supper grammatically refers, not to the
objective substance, wine, but rather to the priest, Melchisedech, in
his "sacrifice" (sacrificii) of bread and wine. Consequently, neither
does sacramentum here refer to the wine of the Last Supper. The fact
is that only once does Cyprian name an item associated with the earthly
Jesus or with his historical activity a "sacramentum:" his seemless
robe.[181] For Cyprian, Christ in his historical, saving activity constitutes the very reality (veritas) to which all sacramenta as such refer.[182]

---

[181]Un 7: "Hoc unitatis sacramentum, hoc vinculum concordiae
inseparabiliter cohaerentis ostenditur quando in evangelio tunica Domini
Iesu christi non dividitur omnino nec scinditur ... Unitatem ille portabat de superiore parte venientem ... sacramento vestis et signo declaravit
ecclesiae unitatem." Jesus effected the unity of the Trinity in his
humanity by his sacred passio, a unity binding humanity to him and humans
to one another in his Church in a concrete visible way (unitatis sacramentum). The seemless robe he whore is an exterior sign (signo) occurring
within the historical accomplishment of his passio: "Signum" recalls the
cross for Cyprian (Dem 22; 26; Fort 8). More profoundly, it points to
the unity with the Trinity achieved through the cross, and it becomes a
sacramentum to us who receive its witness (See Demoustier, "L'Ontologie,"
pp. 582-3). For a fuller treatment of the Church's union with Christ and
among its members, see Section II of this chapter, pp. 107-147.
    Cyprian is not the first to place typological value on clothing.
Tertullian finds predictions of Christ in the vestments of Old Testament
priests as they are described in Zechariah 3 (Adv. Marc. III, 7, 6). See
also Section I of Chapter IV below: "Induere Christum," pp. 156-162.

[182]Baptism in Ep 73,5,2 is called a sacramentum of the Trinity by
virtue of the triple statement of belief and triple immersion: "insinuat
trinitatem, cuius sacramento gentes tinguerentur." However, Christ's life
is the sole source of knowledge of the Trinity, since in the events of
his life, death and resurrection, the effective power and presence of the
Trinity is realized in history: "Unitatem ille portabat de superiore
parte venientem, id est de caelo et a Patre venientem" (Un 7). Thus,
the Old Testament practice of prayer at the 3rd, 6th, and 9th hours is
also a sacramentum, not however of the Trinity abstracted from history,
but of the realization of the Trinity in human history during the crucial
hours of Christ's death, resurrection and subsequent sending of the
Spirit: "horam tertiam sextam nonam sacramento scilicet trinitatis quae
in novissimis temporibus manifestari habebat" (DO 34).

It is especially instructive that in this passage, Ep 63, 4,
Cyprian names a priest (sacerdos) in the act of offering a "sacrifice"
of bread and wine at a given point in salvation history a "sacramentum,"
explaining that by such an offering that priest bears the type of Christ.
Here once again Cyprian's principle is relevant: "That priest truly acts
in the place of Christ who imitates what Christ did" (Ep 63, 14). His
constant naming the bishop "sacerdos" suggests that Cyprian might also
have concluded his discussion of Melchisedech by calling the bishop or
presbyter offering the Eucharist, itself a sacrifice in bread and wine,
both "sacramentum" and "type of Christ." The fact that he does not do
so anywhere in his writings is not proof that the martyr-bishop does
not understand the Christian "priest" to be truly a "sacramentum" and
"type of Christ." One possible reason for not following out the salvation-
history parallel of Melchisedech to eucharistic leader to the point of
using the name "sacramentum" might be the over-sacralizing of a living
person which such a word could suggest.

Although we have to disagree with Demoustier's reading of Ep 63, 4,
the "a-temporality" of the word sacramentum is obvious from the fact
that Cyprian uses the word both for Old Testament phenomena like circumcision (before the time of Christ) and for Christian "sacraments,"
especially baptism (after the time of Christ):

> Sacramentum est in umbra adque imagine
> ante praemissum, sed veniente Christo veritate
> completum (Ep 64, 4).

> The _sacramentum_ is sent in shadow and image
> beforehand in anticipation, but with the coming
> of Christ it is filled with [his] reality.

According to Demoustier's analysis, the basic univocal meaning of
sacramentum for Cyprian includes an understanding of an economy of
salvation common to all of history. That economy is the same as was
found to be operative between the Old and New Testaments (Chapter One)
and in the typological vision shared more or less by Christian authors,
including Tertullian, throughout the second and early third centuries
(Chapter Two), namely, that the imitation of the historical Christ by
types and figures points to his active presence in their own historical
activities. In other words, for Cyprian Christian sacraments are
redemptive events ontologically ordered to the historical Christ in much
the same way as are Old Testament types. But in regard to our present
investigation, what is even more important is that this fact also holds
true for the leader of the Eucharist. Insofar as the performance of
his liturgical role is a representation of the central activity of
Christ's passion, the self-offering in bread and wine, this typological
identification points to the inner presence of Christ in his historical,
saving activity.

In a single paragraph Demoustier summarizes the findings of his
search for the univocal meaning at the basis of all of Cyprian's uses of
sacramentum. In presenting this passage we emphasize and number the four
fundamental characteristics of the word _sacramentum_ that emerge for us

from Demoustier's investigation:

> ... <u>Sacramentum</u> looks to the action of Christ
> which makes itself present and known by means
> of a <u>perceptible reality</u> (1). This latter
> varies, which is the reason for equivocity.
> But the relationship between the <u>action of God</u>
> (2) and the human action is always the same.
> The image (<u>typum</u>, <u>imago</u>) becomes <u>sacramentum</u>
> because in it <u>Christ makes himself known as he
> who accomplishes it</u> (3). <u>Sacramentum</u> disting-
> uishes itself very clearly then from an image
> or a sign. It is the affirmation through
> this image or that sign of the divine revealing
> and santifying action for which they serve as
> the underpinnings. That is why the word is not
> confined to the interpretation of Scripture.
> <u>Every act of</u> God (4) revealing itself by means
> of a <u>reality of</u> our world can be called a <u>sac-
> ramentum</u>.[183]

Imago and Veritas

Although Demoustier argues convincingly for a single basic meaning

to all the uses of <u>sacramentum</u> in Cyprian's writings, in his dealing with

the passage quoted above from Ep 64, 4, he seems to allow for a funda-

---

[183]Demoustier, "L'Ontologie," pp. 561-562: "... <u>Sacramentum</u> renvoie
à l'action du Christ qui se présente et se fait reconnaître par le moyen
d'une réalité perceptible. Cette dernière varie, c'est la raison
d'équivocité. Mais le rapport entre un agir de Dieu et un agir humain
est toujours la même. L'image (<u>typum</u>, <u>imago</u>) devient <u>Sacramentum</u> parce
qu'en elle, le Christ se fait reconnaître comme celui qui l'accomplit.
<u>Sacramentum</u> se distingue donc très nettement de l'image ou du signe. Il
est l'affirmation à travers cette image ou ce signe de l'action divine
révélatrice et sanctificatrice dont ceux-ci sont les supports. C'est
pouquoi le mot n'est pas réservé à l'intérpretation des Écritures. Tout
acte de Dieu se révélant par le moyen d'une réalité de notre monde peut
être appelé ainsi."

mental distinction in Cyprian's thinking between a pre-figurative and

a Christian sacramentum. The passage, once again, is the following,

> Sacramentum est in umbra adque imagine
> ante praemissum, sed veniente Christo veritate
> completum (Ep 64, 4).
> (The sacramentum is sent in shadow and image
> beforehand in anticipation, but with the coming
> of Christ it is filled with [his] reality.)[184]

Demoustier remarks on this passage: "Circumcision on the eighth day is

sacramentum of the resurrection in image. Baptism is sacramentum in

truth" [emph. mine].[185] C.P. Mayer also implies the same distinction for

Cyprian between pre-figurative and Christian sacramenta:

> Alongside the sacramenta of teaching and figural
> prophecy Cyprian knew "salutaria sacramenta"
> (Test., Intro.; Ep 69, 12, 2) and counted bap-
> tism among them with its laying on of hands, and
> the Eucharist.[186]

Granted that Cyprian clearly makes a distinction between Old Testament

and Christian sacramenta, the question remains: Does his use of imago

---

[184]See also Dem 22: "Quod ante occiso agno praecedit in imagine
impletur in Christo secuta postmodum veritate;" and Zel 17: "De sacramento crucis et cibum sumis et potum, lignum quod aput Merrham profecit
in imagine ad saporis dulcedinem tibi in veritate proficiat ad mulcendi
pectoris lenitatem ..."

[185]Demoustier, "L'Ontologice," p. 561: "La circoncision le
huitième jour est sacramentum de la résurrection en image. Le baptême
l'est en vérité."

[186]C.P. Mayer, Die Zeichen in der geistigen Entwicklung und in der
Theologie des jungen Augustinus. Cassiciacum XXXV, I (Würzburg:
Augustinus-Verlag, 1969), pp. 296-297: "Neben den sacramenta der Lehre
und der Figuralprophetie kennt Cyprian die salutaria sacramenta und
rechnet dazu die Taufe, die damit verbundene Handauflegung und die
Eucharistie."

in contract to _veritas_ signify a total lack of the saving presence of
Christ in Old Testament, prefigurative _sacramenta_ so that only the
Christian _sacramenta_ bestow saving power (_salutaria sacramenta_)?

In his commentary on the same two words, _imago_ and _veritas_, as
found in the writings of Tertullian, J. Finkenzeller observes:

> _Figura_ (imago) and _veritas_ correspond to one
> another. A phantasm to which no intelligible
> reality is proper cannot naturally enter into
> an image; for image is more than an indicating
> symbol. It is also somehow an entrance-to-
> manifestation of the intelligible reality.
> Bread in the use of figural prophecy just as
> eucharistic bread are called, as indication
> of the body of the Lord, _sacramentum_.[187]

In other words, Tertullian's contrast of _imago_ (or _figura_) and _veritas_
point, not to an essential difference between those _sacramenta_ occurring
before and those occurring after the time of Christ, but rather to the
two basic elements that are intrinsic to every _sacramentum_ wherever it
may be found in salvation history: (1) the perceptible space-time
phenomenon: the _imago_, and (2) the reality of God's saving action in

---

[187] J. Finkenzeller, _Die Lehre von den Sakramenten im allgemeinen von
der Schrift bis zur Scholastik_. Handbuch der Dogmengeschichte, edd. M.
Schmaus et al., IV, la (Freiburg: Herder, 1980), p. 29. "Figura (imago)
und veritas entsprechen sich. Ein Phantasma, dem keine, intelligible
Wirklichkeit (veritas) eigen ist, kann naturgemäß nicht in ein Bild
eingehen; denn Bild is mehr als bloß andeutendes Symbol. Es ist auch
irgenwie In-Erscheinung-Treten der intelligiblen Wirklichkeit. Das Brot
in der Anwendung der Figuralprophetie wie auch das eucharistische Brot
heissen als Andeutung des Herrenleibes sacramentum."

Christ's sacrifice realized once again in history, but this time in the participatory[188] and unique way of each new _imago_: the _veritas_.[189] In any true _sacramentum_ the one cannot exist without the other.

If one allows, in line with the great debt in theological matters owed to his North African predecessor, that Cyprian shares in Tertullian's vision of _sacramentum_,[190] he could as well be expected to agree with his "Master" on the _imago-veritas_ composition of every _sacramentum_. Why then does he clearly differentiate an Old Testament type as a "_sacramentum in umbra adque imagine_" from baptism as a "_sacramentum ... veritate com-pletum?_"[191]

Before we attempt an answer to this pivotal question, we must first determine the meaning Cyprian attaches to "_passio_," a word that will be central to our discussion of _imago-veritas_.

Passio

The full meaning of "_passio_" in Cyprian's writings is not immediately evident to the 20th century reader. It is more specific and much more

---

[188]For a concise presentation of the neo-platonic underpinnings of patristic theology, see A. Gerken, _Theologie der Eucharistie_ (München: Kösel-Verlag, 1973), pp. 61-86.

[189]For an overview of the Christian use of "_veritas_" before Cyprian, see R. Braun, _Deus Christianorum_: _Recherches sur le vocabulaire doc-trinal de Tertullian_ (Paris: Presses Universitaires de France, 1962), pp. 445-446. Tertullian uses the phrase "_veritas nostra_" in the same sense as "_fides nostra, sacramentum nostrum:_" p. 446.

[190]Finkenzeller, _Die Lehre_, p. 32.

[191]Ep 64, 4.

exact than our present-day motion of the "passion" of Christ or of the

martyrs. In our estimation the best interpretation of Cyprian's "passio"

is that given by B. Renaud. His reading can be briefly summarized:

'Passio refers to the self-sacrifice of Christ that is fully achieved on

Calvary but which is also fully present ("in solidum") beforehand in the

ritual expression of his sacrificial intention at the Last Supper.'[192]

With this understanding, Cyprian continues the theological awareness

of the New Testament concluded to in Chapter One of this present study,

namely that, because Christ is divine, his conscious intention to fulfill

human history by his life, death and resurrection is the reason why it is

in fact fulfilled in him. Therefore, Cyprian also sees in Christ's

intention, articulated in the ritual self-offering of the Last Supper,

the full presence of Calvary itself where that offering is consummated.

It is apparently clear to Cyprian that Calvary without the full inner

---

[192]B. Renaud, "Eucharistie et culte eucharistique selon Saint
Cyprien" (Université Catholique de Louvain: Unpublished Dissertation,
1967), p. 242. In this excellent work Renaud cites other studies of
Cyprian's "passio:" p. 39, n. 77; p. 240, n. 24; p. 241, nn. 25-27.
See also M. Reveillaud, Saint Cyprien: L'Oraison Dominicale (Paris:
Presses Universitaires de France, 1964), p. 151: "La passio du Christ
est sa dernière journee, qui commence avec l'institution de la Cène dans
la chambre haute."
     Cyprian refers to the sufferings of the martyrs also with "passio,"
because Christ in his passio is present in their martyrdom: Epp 31, 3;
58, 2; 66, 7; DO 24; Fort 11. The identification of the martyr's passio
with the saving deeds of Christ is not unique to Cyprian. Peter Brown
observes that in general "the passio [of the martyr] abolished time.
The deeds of the martyr or of the confessor had brought the mighty deeds
of God in the Old Testament and the gospels into his or her own time:"
The Cult of the Saints: Its Rise and Function in Latin Christianity
(Chicago: University of Chicago Press, 1981), p. 81.

88

offering of Christ would be a worthless happening with no power at all
to save humankind.

One example of how Cyprian sees an unbreakable bond between the
inner offering and the enacted sacrifice is his discussion of the offering of Abel. Although both Cain and Abel offer sacrifices to the Lord,
only Abel's is acceptable because it expresses an inner sacrifice of the
heart. It was truly fitting, then, that Abel was allowed to give his
life in martyrdom. Because he possessed the interior dispositions of the
Lord, his sacrificial death was truly a participation in the _passio_ of
Christ.[193] Therefore, for Cyprian, "_passio_" signifies above all the
Lord's inner intention of self-offering, which in turn expresses itself
in his physical sacrifice. This is the reason why Cyprian can designate
the Last Supper as the "_passio_" without any explicit mention of the
Calvary death.[194]

Veritas

The question can now be resumed: 'Why does Cyprian differentiate
Old Testament _sacramenta_ as being "_in imagine_" from baptism, a Christian
sacramentum, as being "_in veritate?_" Until now, part of the difficulty
in understanding Cyprian's distinction between _imago_ and _veritas_ has been

---

[193]"merito ille dum in sacrificio Dei talis est, ipse postmodum
sacrificium Deo factus est, ut martyrium primus ostendens initiaret
sanguinis sui gloria dominicam passionem qui et iustitiam Domini habuerat
et pacem" (DO 24).
[194]Ten of the thirteen occurrences of _passio_ in Ep 63 are predicated
solely of the Last Supper: B. Renaud, "Eucharistie," p. 242. See also
M. Réveillaud, _Saint Cyprien_, p. 151.

a misunderstanding of his use of <u>veritas</u>. One example of this misunderstanding was noted earlier: A. Demoustier's reading of Ep 63, 4. In that
text Demoustier presumes that Cyprian understands the wine used by the Lord
at the Last Supper as a <u>sacramentum</u>.[195] However, the <u>passio</u> of Christ (the
saving activity of his earthly life including the Last Supper) constitutes
not a <u>sacramentum</u>, but the full reality, the <u>veritas</u> itself, to which every
<u>sacramentum</u> in history gives witness. That this is Cyprian's understanding
is evident from a passage found further on in Ep 63, 4, 3:

> ... per Melchisedech sacerdotem ... praecedit
> ante imago sacrificii in pane et vino scilicet con-
> stituta: quam rem perficiens et adimplens Dominus
> panem et calicem mixtum vino optulit, et qui est
> plenitudo veritatem praefiguratae imaginiis adim-
> plevit.
> (The image of the sacrifice in bread and wine
> clearly set forth already took place through the
> priest Melchisedech: Fulfilling and completing this
> reality the Lord offered bread and the cup mixed with
> wine, and he who is the Fulness fulfilled the <u>veritas</u>
> of the prefigured image.)

If Christ is Fulness (Col 1, 19: "<u>plenitudo</u>") in such a way as to bring
<u>veritas</u> to completion, then He is logically the fulness of <u>veritas</u>.[196]

---

[195] Demoustier, L'Ontologie," p. 561. "Sacramentum ... désigne ...
le pain et le vin comme signifiant le Christ aussi bien dans le sacrifice
de Melchisedech, l'image, que dans sa vérité: la Cène."

[196] Cyprian identifies <u>veritas</u> with Christ on the basis of Jn 14, 6:
"'Ego sum veritas,' Propter quod si in Christo sumus et Christum in nobis
habeamus et si manemus in veritate et veritas in nobis manet, ea quae
sunt vera teneamus" (Ep 74, 9, 2). Furthermore, <u>veritas</u> and God's action
in Christian lives are identical: "gratia et veritas una est"
(Ep 71, 1, 3).

It is also clear from this passage that the reality (veritatem) of
the Lord's "passio" is already, although partially, present in the "prefigured image," that is, in the sacrifice of Melchisedech. Three
reflections on Ep 63, 4, 3 bear out this conclusion:

(1) Cyprian asserts in this text, not that the Lord 'first
established' or 'originated' the veritas in the historical, saving
activity at the Last Supper, but that he 'brought it to completion:'
adimplevit. However, one cannot 'bring to completion' that which does
not in some way already exist.

(2) The word "res" as it is found in this passage (quam rem),
according to M. Fahey, is one in a number of its uses by Cyprian as a
synonym for veritas.[197] At the same time, quam rem here logically
refers back to Melchisedech's sacrifice as its antecedent. Consequently,
the historical, saving Christ, the res-veritas, already exists to some
degree in the "prefigured image" of Melchisedech offering bread and
wine.

(3) Cyprian clearly understands that Christ 'fulfills' the image
by constituting through his saving deeds (the Last Supper offering) the
reality (veritatem) to which the image gives witness, i.e. 'prefigures.'
According to Cyprian, the image could only give such witness by virtue
of the reality's already, although in a 'shadowy' (umbra), incomplete
way, working through it (quam rem perficiens et adimplens). There is
therefore no doubt that for Cyprian veritas is present in Old Testament
sacramenta.

---

[197]M.A. Fahey, Cyprian and the Bible: a Study in Third-Century
Exegesis (Tübingen: J.C.B. Mohr, 1971), pp. 616-617.

"sacramentum in image"?

As to the question, then, why does Cyprian characterize an Old Testament type, circumcision, as "sacramentum in image" and Christian baptism as "sacramentum in truth,"[198] the first response must be that, strictly speaking, he does not do so. Let us consider again the passage quoted by Demoustier from Ep 64, 4, 3:

> Sacramentum est in umbra adque imagine
> ante praemissum, sed veniente Christo veritate
> conpletum.
> (The sacramentum is sent in shadow and
> image beforehand in anticipation, but with the
> coming of Christ it is filled with [his]
> reality.)

Cyprian does not speak about two essentially different kinds of sacramenta. He states that a sacramentum as it occurred in Old Testament history differs from one found after the time of Christ only in the clarity (umbra) and depth (imagine) of its veritas, that is, in the relative degree to which the historically saving Christ is present and active in each. In contrast to Old Testament types, Christian sacramenta are "filled" (conpletum) with the veritas. Neither sacramentum, Old Testament or Christian, is absolutely identified with the veritas as "sacramentum in truth" over against the other as "sacramentum in image." More accurately, the Christian sacramentum of baptism in its image-dimension is characterized as being as totally filled as an image can be (conpletum) with the reality to which it gives witness (veritate). Because baptism is celebrated after the time of Christ by those who know

---

[198]Demoustier, "L'Ontologie," p. 561.

92

of Christ's historical sacrifice and are mandated to its celebration, the fulness of meaning to which the baptismal rite refers, the death-resurrection of the Lord, is unmistakeable. As a result, it is more powerfully active in that sacramentum than it could ever have been to one who first witnessed the salvific quality (veritas) of circumcision in the ancient Israelite community.[199]

A. Demoustier argues further for the contrast of "sacramentum in image" from "sacramentum in truth" by quoting a phrase also found in Ep 64, 4: "Quae imago cessavit ..." (This image has ceased). However, in its full context this phrase actually lends more support to the argument presented here.[200] In Ep 64, 4 Cyprian explains why the baptism of infants need not imitate Jewish circumcision by being deferred until the eighth day: Because Christ rose on the eighth day, giving us the spiritual circumcision of baptism, there is no further need of Jewish circumcision as a pre-figurative sacramentum (quae imago cessavit),

---

[199] For a fuller discussion of the Israelite's direct experience of the Sacred in the created world, see Chapter One. See also J. Gribomont, "Le lien des deux testaments, selon la théologie de s. Thomas," Ephemerides Theologicae Lovanienses XXII (1946), 70-89, esp. 76: "On voit qu'il y a un milieu entre la connaissance réflexe de l'image comme telle, la connaissance que nous possédons aujourd'hui du caractère typique d'Israël, et la connaissance brute de la res: c'est la perception directe, dégagée, de ce qui, dans la chose, fait sa valeur de signe, de ce qu'elle participe de la réalité profonde."

[200] "Nam quod in Iudaica circumcisione carnali octavus dies observabatur, sacramentum est in umbra adque imagine ante praemissum, sed veniente Christo veritate conpletum. Nam quia octavus dies, id est post sabbatum primus, dies futurus erat quo Dominus resurgeret et nos vivificaret et circumcisionem nobis spiritalem daret, hic dies octavus, id est post sabbatum primus et dominicus, praecessit in imagine. Quae imago cessavit, superveniente postmodum veritate et data nobis spiritali circumcisione" (Ep 64, 4, 3).

including its eight-day delay. "That image has ceased once the overriding reality (_veritate_) took place and its spiritual circumcision
(baptism) was given to us." In this passage, _quae imago cessavit_ in no
way states that Old Testament _sacramenta_ were mere images in their
occurrence in Old Testament times, or that the _veritas_ of Christ has
saving effects only after the time of its foundational realization in the
"passion" - resurrection of the Lord. Cyprian's argument is rather that,
as a _sacramentum_, Jewish circumcision with its eight-day delay belongs
strictly to its own proper time in history. Now, however, there is no
further need for any such pre-figurative _sacramentum_ (_quae imago cessavit_),
since the reality to which it would witness has itself entered into
history fulfilling the figure in its own external form and structure:
Christ rose _on the eighth day_. Baptism, on the other hand, as a _sacra-
mentum_ shaped to point to that Fulness as having already arrived
(_sacramentum ... veritate conpletum_), carries with it access to all those
spiritual benefits (_spiritali circumcisione_) which once were realized by
Old Testament circumcision, but at the time only in a very incomplete way.
Consequently, the _imago_-function of the Old Testament _sacramentum_ has
been taken over (_quae imago cessavit_) by its fulfillment in the external
details of Christ's historical life: "on the eighth day;" and its
salvific _veritas_-function as _sacramentum_ is taken over by the Christian
sacramentum of baptism: "spiritual circumcision."[201]

---

[201] The explanation given here in regard to Ep 64, 4, 3 holds, _ceteris
paribus_, for other examples from Cyprian's writings where the contrast of
"imago" with "veritas" might also be misunderstood as an opposition of an
empty image to the saving reality: "... quod ante occiso agno praecedit
in imagine impletur in Christo secuta postmodum veritate" (Dem 22); "... de
sacramento crucis et cibum sumis et potum, lignum quod aput Merrham profecit in imagine ad saporis dulcidinem tibi in veritate proficiat ad
mulcendi pectoris lenitatem ..." (Zel 17).

94

"veritas" Christ in history

Further mis-interpretation of Cyprian's veritas occurs where scholars
understand Christian sacramenta in his writings as the full reality
directly pre-figured by various Old Testament sacramenta. M. Fahey gives
three examples of this view:

> (1) ... the inebriating cup of wine itself only a
> symbol found fulfillment in the Eucharist cup which
> is the antitype: "cuius rei sacramentum" (Ep 63,
> 11); (2) and "cum sacramentum quoque rei" (Ep 63,
> 12). The Jews lacking grace needed water turned into
> wine as at Cana, but the Church which is God's fullest
> creation is the real wine. (3) Finally, speaking of
> the origin of "canonical hours" Cyprian concludes:
> "Subsequently the antitype was revealed for which
> previously there were only figures (Manifestata post-
> modum res est sacramenta olim fuisse, quod ante
> iusti precabantur)" (DO 34) [numbering mine].[202]

In order to interpret these passages cited from Cyprian more faithfully, it will be helpful to place them in their larger contexts. We
begin with the first citation:

> (1) ... quibusdam in locis aqua offeratur in
> dominico calice, quae sola Christi sanguinem non
> possit exprimere. 2 Cuius rei sacramentum nec in
> Psalmis tacet Spiritus Sanctus faciens mentionem
> dominici calicis et dicens: 'Calix tuus inebrians
> perquam optimus" (Ps 22, 6) (Ep 63, 11, 1-2).
> (... in certain places water is offered in the
> Lord's cup, which by itself cannot express the blood
> of Christ. As a sacramentum of this reality neither
> is the holy Spirit silent in the Psalms, referring
> to the Lord's cup when he says: 'Your inebriating
> cup is by far the best.')

---

[202] Fahey, Cyprian and the Bible, p. 617.

The actual antecedent to "cuius rei" in this passage is not the
Eucharist cup as such, but rather the dominico calice: that original
linking of wine to the passion, found in the Eucharist cup but foundationally realized at the Last Supper. Cyprian states that the Holy Spirit
predicted in Ps 22, 6 that the Lord would use wine in his cup.   This
fact is then an overwhelming argument for him that wine be used at the
Eucharist precisely because such a prediction is a "sacramentum," that
is, it already contains to some degree the reality to which it points.
(It is not, as Fahey contends, "only a symbol.") Consequently, just as
an Old Testament sacramentum carries the Lord's saving presence by means
of a proleptic imitation of his saving activity on earth, it also serves
as a witness of what in the Lord's life must be imitated in order to make
Him active and present in the life of the Church.   The Eucharist, then,
must likewise imitate the Lord's offering of wine at the Last Supper if
it is truly to be the Lord's cup and convey his saving presence.   Therefore, although the Eucharist participates deeply in the veritas of the
Last Supper (dominico calice), it does so only to the extent that it is
a sacramentum, an image in history of that reality.

For the sake of clarity the third of Fahey's three citations, taken
from DO 34, will be considered here before the second. In this passage
Fahey finds the Christian liturgical practice of prayer at the 3rd, 6th,
and 9th hours to be the "antitype" (res-veritas) of the Old Testament
sacramenta of prayers at the same three hours, exemplified by the young
men praying in the furnace. However, the larger context presents a
different picture.

(3) In orationibus vero celebrandis invenimus
observasse cum Daniele tres pueros in fide fortes et
in captivitate victores horam tertiam sextam nonam
sacramento scilicet trinitatis quae in novissimis
temporibus manifestari habetat....................
quae horarum spatia iam pridem spiritaliter deter-
minantes adoratores Dei statutis et legitimis ad
precem temporibus serviebant. et manifestata postmodum res est sacramenta olim fuisse, quod ante sic
iusti precabantur. nam super discipulos hora ter-
tia descendit Spiritus sanctus qui gratiam dominicae
promissionis inplevit. item Petrus hora sexta in
textum superius ascendens signo pariter et voce Dei
monentis instructus est, ut omnes ad gratiam salutis
admitteret, cum de emundandis gentibus ante dubitaret.
et Dominus hora sexta crucifixus ad nonam peccata
nostra sanguine suo abluit et ut redimere et vivi-
ficare nos posset, tunc victoriam sua passione
perfecit (DO 34).

(In regard to celebrating the obliged prayers,
we find that the three youths with Daniel, stout in
faith and victorious in captivity, observed the third,
sixth [and] ninth hours clearly as a <u>sacramentum</u> of
the Trinity, which in the last times makes itself
manifest...
These intervals of hours, spiritually identifying
from of old the adorers of God, were set down in
statutes and as legal times for prayer. And afterwards the reality was revealed, [showing] that those
once were <u>sacramenta</u>: the fact that beforehand the
holy ones prayed in such a manner (at the 3rd, 6th,
and 9th hours). For on the disciples at the third
hour descended the holy Spirit in order to instill
the grace of the Lord's promise. Again, at the sixth
hour Peter went up on the roof and was instructed
both with a sign [given] and a voice [spoken] by a
correcting God, to the effect that he should admit
all to the grace of salvation, whereas beforehand
he doubted that the gentiles should be cleansed
(baptized). Furthermore, the Lord, crucified at the
sixth until the ninth hour, washed away our sins with
his blood and, so that he might redeem and bring us
to life, he then brought the victory to completion
with his <u>passio.</u>)

From the context it is evident that the <u>res</u> or "antitype" of the Old

Testament practice of prayer at the 3rd, 6th, and 9th hours (<u>sacramenta</u>)

in this passage is not the Christian canonical hours as such, but rather

the saving mystery of the Trinity made manifest (manifestata) in the
unfolding hours of Christ's passio and the subsequent sending of the
Spirit. Much of the difficulty here arises out of Fahey's mistranslation
of the text: "Manifestata postmodum res est sacramenta olim, quod ante
sic iusti precabantur." Instead of his rendition: "Subsequently the
antitype was revealed for which previously there were only figures," the
sentence is more correctly translated: "Afterwards the reality was
revealed, [showing] that those once were sacramenta: the fact that beforehand the holy ones prayed in such a manner." One can nevertheless agree
with Fahey that the concept of res-veritas ("antitype") in this passage
does include events which occur after the historical life of Christ on
earth: the outpouring of the Spirit at Pentecost and Peter's prayer on
the roof. It can therefore be argued that for Cyprian the res-veritas
is not fully accomplished within the time period of Christ's life on
earth, but by design (gratiam dominicae promissionis) it demands the
mediation of the Holy Spirit and reception by the Apostles. Furthermore,
it is through this mediation and this ongoing reception in the later
life of the Church, as we shall see, that Christ by means of sacramenta
continues his veritas-work in history: a fact which emerges more clearly
in the second of Fahey's three quotations from Cyprian.

In this second passage, Ep63, 12, contrary to Fahey's contention,
Cyprian does not look upon the Church as the "real wine," whereas Israel
was only an empty image of wine. Once again, it is not a question here
of the Church and its sacraments as being sacramenta in veritate over
against Old Testament realities as sacramenta in imagine.

98

    (2) Quam vero perversum est quamque contrarium,
ut cum Dominus in nuptiis de aqua vinum fecerit, nos
de vino aquam faciamus, cum sacramentum quoque rei
illius admonere et instruere nos debeat, ut in
sacrificiis dominicis vinum potium offeramus. Nam
quia apud Iudaeos defecerat gratia spiritalis, defecit
et vinum: vinea enim Domini sabaoth domus Israel est.
Christus autem docens et ostendens gentium populum
succedere et in locum quem Iudaei perdiderant nos postmodum merito fidei pervenire, de aqua vinum fecit, id
est quod ad nuptias Christi et ecclesiae Iudaeis cess-
antibus plebs magis gentium conflueret et conveniret
ostendit. Aquas namque populos significari in Apocalupsi
Scriptura divina declarat dicens: "Aquae quas vidisti,
super quas sedet meretrix illa, populi et turba et
gentes ethnicorum sunt et linguae" (Apoc. 17, 15). Quod
scilicet perspicimus et sacramento calicis contineri
(Ep 63, 12).
    (How truly perverse and how at odds it is that,
when the Lord at the wedding made wine from water, we
would make water out of wine, especially when the sacramentum of that reality ought to be a warning and
instruction for us that in the Lord's sacrifices we
should rather offer wine. "For the vineyard of the
Lord of hosts is the house of Israel" (Isaiah 5, 7).
Christ, however, made wine out of water, showing and
teaching that the people of the gentiles, we ourselves,
on the basis of faith, succeeded to and arrived at the
position which the Jews had lost (Mt 21, 33-41); that
is to say, that at the wedding of Christ and the Church,
he illustrates that with the departure of the Jews it
was rather a people of the gentiles that flowed together
and gathered into one. For in the Apocalypse divine
Scripture declares that the waters signify the people,
saying: "The waters that you saw, upon which sits that
harlot, are the peoples and multitude and nations and
languages of the ethnic tribes." This is precisely what
we see contained by the sacramentum of the cup.)

"sacramentum" in the phrase "sacramentum quoque rei illius" refers

to the parable of the empty vineyard in Isaiah (5, 1-7) which Cyprian

uses to re-inforce (quoque) his appeal to the miracle of Cana in order

to show that wine ought to be offered at the Eucharist (in sacrificiis

dominicis) instead of plain water. The logic of the passage is a diffi-

cult one. Cyprian cites the Isaian parable as a sacramentum of the Cana

miracle (rei illius) which itself is something of a sign (ostendens)
pointing to the deeper meaning in Christ's saving death. The vineyard of
the Lord, Israel, is found to be lacking in grapes (wine), that is, in a
faithful response to God. Christ therefore changes water into wine in
order to signify the opening of the way for gentiles (water) to possess
the relationship to the Lord which Israel once had but then forfeited.
Cyprian implies but does not express the missing link in this chain of
thought: In his offering of wine mixed with water at the Last Supper
Christ actually offers us (gentiles) along with himself in his passio,
just as water and wine become one when mixed together, so that in our
eucharistic repetitions of that sacrifice (sacrificiis dominicis) we in
effect celebrate the "marriage" of Christ and his Church (nuptias Christi
et ecclesiae). Consequently, for Cyprian the water-to-wine transformation
at the Cana marriage participates in the veritas of the passio since it
expresses already the inner intention of the Lord to offer us, his faithful ones, in union (marriage) with himself in his passio. Likewise,
only when the Eucharist cup contains wine (Christ) mixed with water
(gentiles) is it a true sacramentum of the passio of Christ (sacramento
calicis).

In line with this reasoning, it is clear that if we already are
being offered by the Lord at the time of his passio, then we in fact form
part of the veritas, and our ratification and reception of the passio-
offering at every Eucharist constitutes a deeper realization of that
veritas in history. That is obviously why Cyprian can say in another
place: "The Lord's passion is the sacrifice we offer" (Ep 63, 17, 1).[203]

---

[203]"passio est enim Domini sacrificium quod offerimus."

The "we" who offer the Eucharist are, of course, the Church: those members of humanity who, living after the time of Christ and accepting the apostolic preaching in faith, consciously ratify through sacramenta in their own lives the union which Christ effects with them in his passio. Furthermore, because the sacramenta of the Church do express that consciousness, they contain in a special way and in a special intensity the passio to which they witness. In the passio, as we have seen, Christ in his self-offering to the Father unites himself to all humanity, not only in his physical sufferings, but also in his conscious intention (Last Supper). In a parallel fashion and in contrast to Old Testament sacramenta, the Church not only physically images, but also by its sacramenta consciously intends that same unity which is willed and effected by Christ in his passio.[204] This conscious intention accounts for a depth of veritas to a Church sacramentum ("veritate conpletum") that is obviously not possible to an Old Testament sacramentum ("in umbra adque in imagine" [Ep 64, 4, 3]). The mutual intention of Christ and his Church so unites the two in his passio that Cyprian can point to certain Old Testament realities, such as Rahab's house (Un 8),[205] the houses of the Israelites during the Passover killing of the first-born

---

[204] The bishop of Carthage never lost sight of the determining role of one's inner intention for the ultimate value of his or her outer actions: "[Cyprien] rappelle avec force que, sans l'entente et sans la charité, sans la practique habituelle des vertus chrétiennes, le martyre n'a aucune valeur (Un 14); tandis qu'inversement, la pratique de ces vertus, à elle seule, confère la couronne du vainqueur (Ep 14, 2, 2; 10, 5, 2; etc.):" S. Deléani, Christum Sequi: Étude d'un thème dans l'oeuvre de saint Cyprien (Paris: Etudes Augustiniennes, 1979), p. 91.

[205] For an exposition of Cyprian's ecclesiology involved in his Rahab typology, see J. Daniélou, "Rahab, figure de l'Eglise," Irénikon XXII (1949), 26-45, esp. 36-37.

(Ep 69, 4) and Anna at prayer in I Kings 1, 13 (DO 5) as sacramenta

directly prefiguring, not Christ, but the Church.[206] He can do so, how-

ever, only because through sacramenta in which the Church consciously

offers itself in Christ does Christ in his passio become so intensely

present and active in the Church, and does the Church so share in his

veritas, that it can even be said to be pre-figured by Old Testament

sacramenta. In other words, the full mystery of Christ in history,

predicted by Old Testament types, must include an ongoing conscious

reception and ratification among human beings (the mixing of water and

wine) if Christ's once-and-for-all self-offering is truly to be effective

for the salvation of the world.

"veritas:" the inner value of all history

It is likewise clear from Cyprian's writings that Christ does not

offer along with himself in his passio only those who live after his own

---

[206]Cyprian sees the Church to be so vitally incorporated into the
veritas of Christ that, for him, the Jews in the Exodus constitute the
"shadow" and "image" of the Church (the reality): "In exodo Iudaicus
populus ad umbram nostri et imaginem praefiguratus ..." (Fort 7). In
fact, because the veritas of Christ is meaningless without its tropologi-
cal interpretation, that is, apart from an estimation of its presence
and activity in the life of the Church, for Cyprian all Old Testament
types and figures are somehow prefigurements of the Church's present
life in Christ: "'Haec autem omnia figurae nostrae fuerunt'" (Ep 69, 15,
1). The translation of I Cor 10, 6 used here by Cyprian matches more
closely the Greek "TYPOI HEMON" than does the Vulgate's "in figura facta
sunt nostri." In context, Cyprian cites this Pauline statement in order
to support his argument that the Red Sea prefigures Christian baptism.
    See also Walter Simonis, Ecclesia Visibilis et Invisibilis
(Frankfurt: Josef Knecht, 1970), p. 16, n. 97: "'Wahrheit' ist für
Cyprian ein eminent kirchlicher Begriff."

life on earth. In fact, the very first death to be recorded in salvation history participates in the <u>passio</u> of Christ:

> Abel pacificus et iustus, dum Deo sacrificat
> innocenter, docuit et ceteros, quando ad altare
> munus offerunt, sic venire cum Dei timore, cum
> simplici corde, cum lege iustitiae, cum concordiae
> pace. merito ille dum in sacrificio Dei talis est,
> ipse postmodum sacrificium Deo factus est, ut
> martyrium primus ostendens initiaret sanguinis
> sui gloria dominicam passionem qui et iustitiam
> Domini habuerat et pacem (DO 24).[207]
> (Abel, the peaceful and holy one, as he was
> innocently sacrificing to God, taught others in
> doing so that when they offer a gift at the altar,
> this is how they are to come forward: with the
> fear of God, with a simple heart, with requisite
> holiness, with the peace of fraternal love (<u>con-
> cordiae</u>). It is fitting that he, showing himself
> just such a person in offering God's sacrifice, a
> short time later himself became a sacrifice to God,
> so that as the first to show witness, he ushered
> in the Lord's <u>passio</u> by the glory of his own blood,
> as one who possessed both the holiness of the Lord
> and his peace.)

Abel is understood here as one in and through whom the Lord in his <u>passio</u> is already made present in human history from its very beginnings. His holiness and peace are said to be actually those of Christ himself. In fact, it is Abel who ushered (<u>initiaret</u>) Christ's self-sacrifice (<u>passionem</u>) into history through his own self-offering. Thus, through the human agency of Abel Christ himself was acting. It is furthermore clear that for Cyprian Abel in his death is not a mere empty image of Christ. Rather, because Christ offers all human beings throughout history along with himself in his sacred <u>passio</u>, and because Abel in

---

[207] See also Pat 10; Fort 11; Ep 58, 5, 1.

effect ratifies his being offered by Christ by his own inner sacrifice, his death at the hand of Cain constitutes the initiation into history of the saving passio of Christ.

Other signs that the passio of Christ is present and active in Old Testament types are scattered throughout the writings of Cyprian. By holding his arms out, in the posture of Christ on the cross (in signo et sacramento crucis), Moses was able to overcome the armies of Amalech, who bore the type of the devil (Fort 8). David, the physical forefather of Christ, already possesses the patience of Christ spiritually (christiana patientia) in his dealings with Saul (Pat 10). By their sufferings the Maccabees show that they are united (in passione) to Christ as sons of God (se Dei filios) to the Son of God (Fort 11).[208] In fact, the third Maccabee son is consciously happy (multum beatus) to be able to stretch out his arms in prayer and have his hands cut off because, by imaging the cross with his body, he imitates the form of the Lord's passion (passionis dominicae instar imitari) (Fort 11).

Cyprian's remark that the third Maccabee son was happy (multum beatus) to image the passio of Christ raises the question whether he seriously thought that Old Testament types had a foreknowledge of Christ in any way. In light of his reflections that sacramenta before Christ occur in umbra adque imagine (Ep 64, 4, 3), and that only after Christ appeared, the Fulness of the veritas, did Old Testament types truly stand out as sacramenta (DO 34), it is clear that, to Cyprian, a thematic

---

[208]Ep 58, 6: "Filius Dei passus est ut nos filios Dei faceret ..." (Also, Op 1).

knowledge of Christ was unavailable to those who came before Christ. A much more plausible explanation is that the martyr-bishop rhetorically attributes a consciousness of solidarity with Christ to Old Testament types in order to highlight his faith-conviction that God acts in human history only through the *passio* of Christ. The unthematic Christian experience, even in suffering, or inner peace and integrity in doing God's will is obviously Cyprian's justification for attributing that same happiness to God's Old Testament faithful. He thereby teaches that the mysterious happiness found in a suffering obedience to God is explained by the fact that such obedience is *and* *always* *has* *been* a personal sharing in Christ in his suffering *passio*.

In a survey of the evidence on Cyprian's understanding of *imago* and *veritas* within the *sacramentum* the following conclusions emerge:

(1) Every *sacramentum*, whether occurring before or after the historical life of Christ, is a manifestation and an additional realization in history of Christ's *passio*.

(2) The *passio* of Christ is his self-offering foundationally accomplished by his life on earth, especially at the Last Supper and the sacrificial death. Inasmuch as in his *passio* Christ also offers all humankind in union with himself, to the extent that others in history express that same attitude of self-sacrifice to God, they do so only in virtue of the offering of Christ and, consequently, they participate in and further realize the saving *passio* of Christ. Since these expressions share in the one reality that sanctifies all others, the *passio*, they are called "*sacramenta*."

(3) Veritas refers to the salvific content of the passio (a)
primarily as it is originally realized in the historical life of Christ,
and (b) secondarily as it is actively present in each individual sacramentum.

(4) Because the full veritas includes our self-offering in that
of Christ's, although in principle that dual offering was accomplished
in the intention (esp. Last Supper) and in the flesh and blood (esp.
Calvary) of the historical Christ, the saving power of the veritas remains
ineffective for human-kind without both (a) the mediation of the Holy
Spirit and (b) the ratifying reception by human beings throughout human
history. "Sacramentum" is the name Cyprian gives to conspicuous manifestations of this veritas-work of Christ, whether achieved proleptically
in Old Testament times or in full self-awareness in the life of the
Church.

(5) The material dimension of the sacramentum is that which
separates it off as one event among a plurality of events in this world.
This materiality is also the substratum supporting the sign-value or
imago of the sacramentum. Moreover, since the veritas expresses and
realizes itself only in and through this sign-value, the very element
which is the principle of individuation in the sacramentum is also the
medium of its identity with the passio of Christ. That is to say, the
veritas, Christ in his saving deeds, is realized in the sacramentum only
in and through the material uniqueness of the imago and not in any trans-
historical, once-and-for-all way. Consequently, Christ's salvation is
only as available to any given time and place in history as sacramenta
physically indigenous to that historical locale make it available. All

sacramenta, therefore, are similar to one another in their witness to the one and the same passio, but individually unique to their own particular time and place in history. Conversely, the passio has saving power for historical human situations beyond that of Christ's own life on earth only insofar as in its sacramenta it actually enters into the time-space constitution of those situations. Sacramenta do not transpose people forward or back into the history of Christ's life on earth. Although they do point to or recall that life, they themselves are events in the present moment which, by means of their imago-witness to the passio, reveal and actualize the ultimately true value (veritas) of the present human situation. They do so, of course, only through the power and mediation of the Holy Spirit.

II. Portare - Adunare - Repraesentare

Portare

Perhaps the single most important word for the understanding of
Cyprian's theology of salvation history is the word portare. Apart
from a few instances where portare exhibits only the basic meaning of
"bearing" or "carrying" some physical object,[209] the remaining examples
denote, as we shall see, an inner participation on the part of one
reality in the being of another.

L. Bayard points out that Cyprian finds forms of portare in two
passages of the Latin Bible available to him:[210]

(1) Isaiah 53, 4: "Hic peccata nostra portat et
    pro nobis dolet ..."
    (He carries our sins and he sorrows on our
    behalf ...)

(2) I Corinthians 15, 47-49: "Primus homo e terrae
    limo, secundus e caelo: qualis ille e limo,
    tales et qui de limo, qualis caelestis, tales et
    caelestes. Quomodo portavimus imaginem eius qui
    de limo est portemus et imaginem eius qui de caelo
    est."
    (The first man is from the mud of the earth, the
    second from heaven: like him who is from the mud,

---

[209]Un 17; Ep 4, 1; Mort 8; 12; Lap 30; and Pat 12. Although cited
by B. Renaud as further examples, "portavi" in Fort 11 occurs in a quote
from II Macc 7, 27, and "portare" in Ep 22, 2, 1 is found in a letter not
authored by Cyprian: Renaud, Eucharistie, p. 252, n. 52.

[210]L. Bayard, Le Latin de Saint Cyprien (Paris: Hachett, 1902), pp.
90-92. See also E.W. Watson, "The Style and Language of St. Cyprian," in
Studia Biblica et Ecclesiastica IV (Oxford: Clarendon, 1896), pp. 248-
254; M. Réveillaud, Saint Cyprien: L'Oraison Dominicale (Paris: Presses
Universitaires de France, 1964), pp. 137, 170, 179-180; and B. Renaud,
Eucharistie, pp. 252-254.

> so are they who come from mud, and like the
> heavenly one, so are the heavenly ones. Just
> as we bore his image who is from mud, let us
> also bear the image of him who is from heaven.)

The Corinthians text speaks of a solidarity between prototypes
(Adam, Christ) and those who bear their respective images. Those who
bear the images do so in such a way that they share in the nature of the
prototype (qualis ... tales). That this idea is important to Cyprian
is evident from his quoting I Cor 15, 47-49 no less than four times in
his writings.[211] The Isaian text, on the other hand, directly states
only that the Servant (Christ) bears our sins. It says nothing about
our possibly sharing in his nature. However, the use in Sacred Scripture
of the verb portare in two separate writings, both of which deal with
the same subject matter, appears to be sufficient cause for Cyprian also
to read into Isaiah 53, 4 the Corinthians idea of a commonly shared
reality: "nos omnes portabat Christus qui et peccata nostra portabat"[212]
(Christ bore us all, to the point of even bearing our sins). With the
double use of portare in this phrase Cyprian stresses here what he states
even more clearly elsewhere, that not only does Christ carry our sins,
but his one reality carries with it that of all other human beings ("in
uno omnes ipse portavit"[213]), especially the reality of the members of

---

[211]Test II, 10; Test III, 11; Vir 23; Zel 14. Tertullian sees a
human being's two-fold nature stemming from his two-fold origin: Adam
and Christ (de Anima 40, 1; de Mon. 5, 5): J. Daniélou, The Origins of
Latin Christianity (Philadelphia: Westminster, 1977, pp. 248-249.

[212]Ep 63, 13, 1.

[213]DO 8.

his Church ("<u>populum</u> <u>nostrum</u> <u>quem</u> <u>portabat</u>"[214]).

To the <u>Corinthians</u> teaching that, as our earthly nature stems from Adam, so from Christ comes a heavenly nature, Cyprian adds the further awareness, suggested by <u>Isaiah</u>, that Christ also shares together with us in a humanity weakened by sin: "<u>infirmitatem</u> <u>hominis</u> <u>quem</u> <u>portabat</u>."[215] Furthermore, because we are truly present and realized in Christ even in our sinfulness (<u>nos</u> <u>omnes</u> <u>portabat</u> ... <u>peccata</u> <u>nostra</u> <u>portabat</u>), to the degree that we accept his salvation (<u>portemus</u> <u>et</u> <u>imaginem</u> <u>eius</u>) are we likewise already transformed and taken up into his own divine, Trinitarian life: "<u>unitatem</u> <u>ille</u> <u>portabat</u> <u>de</u> <u>superiore</u> <u>parte</u> <u>venientem</u>, <u>id</u> <u>est</u>, <u>de</u> <u>caelo</u> <u>et</u> <u>a</u> <u>Patre</u> <u>venientem</u>."[216]

Although it is true that the sins that Christ bore were not his own ("<u>aliena</u> <u>peccata</u> <u>portare</u>"),[217] nevertheless, the human nature which he bore, made infirm by our sins, was truly his own. This is clear from a discussion dealing with the heretic, Marcion, where Cyprian asks the question:

> Eundem novit filium Christum de virgine
> Maria natum, qui sermo caro factus sit, qui
> peccata nostra <u>portaverit</u>, qui mortem moriendo
> vicerit, qui resurrectionem carnis per semetipsum
> primus carne resurrexisset ostendit (Ep 73, 5, 2)?

---

[214]Ep 69, 4, 2.

[215]DO 14.

[216]Un 7. In commenting on this text, Demoustier concludes, "... le Christ portait Dieu et ... nous portons le Christ. Nous vivons de l'humanité du Christ qui, elle, vit de la vie divine" ("L'Ontologie," p. 582).

[217]Pat 6. Also, Ep 11, 5, 2: "cum peccator ipse non esset, sed nostra peccata <u>portaret</u>."

> (Did he (Marcion) acknowledge the same Son,
> Christ born of the virgin Mary, the Word who was
> made flesh, who carried our sins, who conquered
> death by [his] dying, who in his own self was the
> first to inaugurate the resurrection of the flesh,
> and [who then] displayed to his disciples that he
> had risen in the same flesh?)

Cyprian's emphasis on the fact that Christ rose from the dead in the same flesh (in eadem carne) into which he had been born (caro factus est), with which he is to be identified (per semetipsum), and which bore our sins (peccata nostra portaverit), demonstrates that the martyr-bishop sees our salvation accomplished by a transformation in Christ's flesh of our sinful humanity. Since Christ never ceased to be the Son (filium) and the Word (sermo), the events of his life, death and resurrection ushered his sin-weakened humanity into the life of the Trinity.[218] As the first to rise from the dead, Christ in his humanity already

---

[218]Cyprian's consciousness of the decisive importance of Christ's divinity in his assuming and saving human nature is even more explicit in his earlier Quod idola dei non sint (Id): "... Sermo et Filius Dei mittitur, ... in Virginem delabitur, Deus cum homine miscetur. Hic Deus noster, hic Christus est, qui mediator duorum hominem induit, quem perducat ad Patrem. Quod homo est, esse Christus voluit, ut et homo possit esse quod Christus est" (Id 9). In regard to this text, H.M. Diepen remarks: "L'Homme dont le Christ notre Dieu se revêt, c'est l'humanité à laquelle il veut communiquer le salut en la présentant au Père" ("L'Assumptus Homo' patristique," **Revue Thomiste** LXIII [1963], 243). In effect, the basic elements of Cyprian's portare theology are already present in his earliest treatise. By personally appropriating human nature, the Word "leads" it (perducat), that is "bears" it, to the Father. Furthermore, the use of "miscetur" suggests that, because God and humans are effectively united in Christ's passio, the union of water and wine at the Eucharist is able to unite us to Christ: "Nam quia nos omnes portabat Christus ... Quando autem in calice vino aqua miscetur, Christo populus adunatur ..." (Ep 63, 13, 1).

(<u>primus</u>) carries us with him into Trinitarian life. Consequently, wherever Cyprian states that Christ "bore our sins" (<u>peccata nostra portabat</u>) he actually includes within that simple phrase the doctrine that Christ is Lord and Savior by carrying and redeeming in his own humanity that of all other human beings.

The emphasis here once again is on Christ, Christ in his saving life, death and resurrection: his <u>passio</u>. He first carried us (<u>nos omnes portabat</u>), we did not carry him. Although our physical humanity is held in common with Adam, its intrinsic value apart from Christ is that of the mud of the earth (<u>e terrae limo</u>), such is what we are (<u>tales et qui de limo</u>). By assuming this humanity, weakened further by our sins, and introducing it into Trinitarian life by the events of his <u>passio</u>, Christ establishes in his own self the prototype of true humanity: the <u>veritas</u>. As a result, just as Christ originally carried us in our worthlessness, we are to follow the inujnction of St. Paul and carry him in his <u>veritas</u>: "<u>portate Deum in corpore vestro</u>" (I Cor 6, 20).[219]

As noted already, in light of <u>Isaiah</u> 53, 4 Cyprian understands the parallelism of I Cor 15, 47-49 between the <u>qualis</u> ... <u>tales</u> relationship of prototype to types on the one hand, and the phraseology "<u>portare imaginem</u>" on the other, as two ways of saying the same thing. To bear

---

[219]Cyprian quotes this exhortation no less than five times: Test III, 11 & 63; Vir 2; DO 11; Fort 6. This is in addition to the four citations of I Cor 15, 47-49 already mentioned where Paul exhorts, "<u>portemus imaginem eius qui de caelo est</u>" (Test II, 10; Test III, 11; Vir 23; Zel 14). On the reciprocal "bearing" between Christ and the Christian, see B. Renaud, "Eucharistie et culte eucharistique selon Saint Cyprien" (Université Catholique de Louvain: Unpublished Dissertation, 1967), p. 254.

someone's image is to partake in that person's reality.[220] This equation

is clear also from Cyprian's explanation of the <u>Corinthians</u> (I Cor 15,

47-49) passage:

>Imaginem autem caelestem portare non possumus,
>nisi in eo quod esse nunc coepimus Christi simili-
>tudinem praebeamus (Zel 14).
>(However, we cannot bear the heavenly image
>unless we show forth the likeness of Christ in
>what we have now begun to be.)

The presupposition underlying the argument of this text is that one

'carries the image of Christ' precisely in the living out of his or her

own proper existence as a Christian (<u>esse</u>).

There is furthermore no substantial change in meaning where <u>typum</u>

or <u>figuram</u> is substituted for <u>imaginem</u> in the cypriannic phrase "<u>portare</u>

---

[220]That Moses' external actions are similar to those of the
historical Christ Cyprian attributes to the actual participation of
each in the existence of the other. He also sees in Amalech an inner
participation in the being of the devil because of Amalech's engagement
in an effort to thwart God's salvation through Moses just as the devil
always attempts to do in regard to the work of Christ: "Moyses ad
superandum Amalech qui figuram <u>portabat</u> diaboli in signo et sacramento
crucis adlevabat supinas manus ..." (Fort 8).
   That '<u>portare figuram</u>' points to the participation of one being
in that of another is seen where Cyprian discusses Egypt and its
Pharoah in terms parallel to those condemning Amalech in the text just
quoted. In that passage, however, he does not use <u>portare</u>. Rather,
he states categorically that the Pharoah <u>was</u> the presence of the devil,
and Egypt <u>was</u> in fact a form of the servitude to the world (<u>id est</u>)
which it represents: "Iudaicus populus ... evasisset Pharaonis adque
Aegypti, id est, diaboli et saeculi, durissimam servitutem ..." (Fort 7).
For the typological force of the phrase "id est" see M. Fahey, <u>Cyprian</u>
<u>and the Bible: a Study in Third-Century Exegesis</u> (Tübingen: J.C.B.
Mohr, 1971), pp. 621, 622.

imaginem:"[221]

> Invenimus denique et patriarchas et prophetas
> et iustos omnes qui figuram Christi imagine praeeunte
> portabant ... (Pat 10).
> (Accordingly, we find that the patriarchs and
> prophets and all the just, those who were bearing
> the figure of Christ with a prevenient image ...)

In other words, Old Testament individuals "bore the figure of Christ" to the extent that they imaged beforehand (*imagine praeeunte*) the historical Christ.[222] In this connection *figura* and *imago* as direct objects of *portare* are synonymous terms.

The inclusive adjective, *iustos*, is crucial to an adequate interpretation of the use of *figura* and *imago* in the above-cited passage. It is because of their holiness (*iustos*) that the patriarchs and prophets "bore the figure of Christ" even before (*praeeunte*) Christ lived his historical life on earth. They are like Christ primarily because of

---

[221]"*Imago* and *typus* have exactly the same meaning as *figura* in Cyprian's writings. There seems to be no alteration of meaning throughout the short span of years that separates Cyprian's various treatises and letters:" Fahey, *op. cit.*, p. 617. J.E.L. van der Geest points to an identical equivalence of *typus* and *figura* in the works of Tertullian: *Le Christ et L'Ancien Testament chez Tertullien* (Nijmegen: Dekker & van de Vegt, 1972), p. 160.

Similarly, "*portare*" in these phrases is not such a *terminus technicus* that substitution for it cannot be made. Asserting that Elijah bore the type of Christ, Cyprian writes: "Helieas itaque typum Christi *gerens* ..." By his use of *gerens* instead of *portans* he holds *portare* open as a metaphor to as many connotations as possible around the notion of "carry." As a result, where *portare* is used it is able to bear an even fuller weight of meaning and is more able to suggest the mystery-content of Christian participation in Christ.

[222]This use of *figuram Christi ... portabant* in regard to the patriarchs and prophets has substantially the same meaning of *fuit typus Christi*: "Isaac, qui fuit typus Christi ... Joseph, qui et ipse fuit typus Christi ... Samuel typus fuit Christi" (Test I, 20).

their holiness, not because of a conscious patterning of his outward

behavior. After all, they lived their lives before Christ's incarnation,

and so they were not yet able either to see or to hear about him.[223]

Indeed, for Cyprian, inner holiness always results in outward expressions

that are analogous to those of the historical Christ, even in those who

_____

[223]Holiness is likewise for Christians the source of their similarity
to Christ: "Potest et sic intellegi, fratres dilectissimi, ut quoniam
mandat et monet Dominus etiam inimicos diligere et pro his quoque qui
nos persecuntur orare, petamus et pro illis qui adhuc terra sunt et
necdum caelestes esse coeperunt, ut et circa illos voluntas Dei fiat quam
Christus hominem conservando et redintegrando perfecit. nam cum dis-
cipuli ab eo iam non terra appellentur sed sal terrae et apostolus primum
hominem vodet de terrae limo, secundum vero de caelo, merito et nos qui
esse debemus patri Deo similes, qui solem suum oriri facit super bonos
et malos et pluit super iustos et iniustos, sic Christo monente oramus
et petimus, ut precem pro omnium salute faciamus, ut quomodo in caelo id
est in nobis per fidem nostram voluntas Dei facta est ut essemus e caelo,
ita et in terra hoc est in illis credere nolentibus fiat voluntas Dei,
ut qui adhuc sunt prima nativitate terreni incipiant esse caelestes ex
aqua et spiritu nati" (DO 17). By his referring here to I Cor 15, 47-49
Cyprian exhorts his people to pray for their persecutors. If they do so,
he argues, they are patterning their lives on Christ. Living no longer
as pagans do, with the life of Adam (de terrae limo), they share the
life (caelestes) of him who is from heaven (de caelo). In fact, they are
identified fully with that life, they are heaven (in caelo, id est, in
nobis). Their imitation is not mere mimickry of Christ, but a participation in his inner holiness, that is, in his (a) doing the will of God
(b) by his sacrificial prayer for the salvation of all humanity.
    To Cyprian, Christ's prayer partook in the power of his sacrifice.
Just as the notion of "passio" includes the Last Supper offering, so too
does the Calvary sacrifice include the high priestly prayer for the unity
of all in God: "Deus pacis et concordiae magister qui docuit unitatem,
sic orare unum pro omnibus voluit, quomodo in uno omnes ipse portavit"
(DO 8). Also: "et utique quod orabqt orabat pro nobis, cum peccator
ipse non esst, sed nostra peccata portaret" (Ep 11, 5, 2): "rogantis
autem desiderium videte quo fuerit, ut quomodo unum sunt pater et filius,
sic et nos in ipsa unitate maneamus" (DO 30). It is also clear from
these texts that the integral place Christ's Last Supper prayer for our
unity has in his overall passio-sacrifice is the basis for Cyprian's
understanding of the salvific effectiveness of our sacrificial prayer
at the Eucharist.

lived before his earthly existence.[224] As we have already seen, holiness (veritas) enters all human history only through the historical activities of Christ's passio: his life, death, resurrection and sending of the Spirit. Abraham, Isaac, Joseph, Moses and David, therefore, are said to 'bear the figure of Christ' (Pat 10), not primarily because their external behavior resembled the historical Christ's. More correctly and fundamentally, their outward actions resembled Christ's only because, and to the extent to which, Christ in his holy passio is already present and active within them.[225]

It is clear from this analysis that "portare typum" and "portare figuram" have the same basic meaning as the Pauline phrase "portare imaginem." Furthermore, all three phrases point to the same kind of ontological relationship between two realities as that expressed by that absolute use of portare found in phrases such as "in uno omnes ipse

---

[224]For example, "Abel pacificus et iustus ... martyrium primus ostendens initiaret sanguinis sui gloria dominicam passionem qui et iustitiam Domini habuerat et pacem" (DO 24).
Witness the joint use of initiare and primus both in this text and in Ep 73, 5, 2, where Christ is the subject: "[Christus] resurrection carnis per semetipsum primus initiaverit:" Just as Christ's personal resurrection is meaningless for human beings apart from his own membership in the human race, so does any individual life have value only by virtue of its participation in the historical life and holiness of Christ. To be human is to be found in Christ.

[225]That outer imitation is worthless without inner participation in the holiness of Christ is evident in Cyprian's argument against heretical baptism: "Quae est haec aqua mendax et perfida? Utique ea quae baptismi imaginem mentitur et gratiam fidei adumbrata simulatione frustratur" (Ep 73, 6, 1). Also: "Vanum prorsus et stultum est, ut quia Novatianus extra ecclesiam vindicat sibi veritatis imaginem, relinquat ecclesia veritatem" (Ep 73, 2, 3). For the most recent treatment of Cyprian's notion of salvation outside the Church, see M. Bevenot, "Salus Extra Ecclesiam Non Est," in Fides Sacramenti - Sacramentum Fidei: Studies in honour of Pieter Smulders, edd. H.J. Auf der Maur et al. (Assen, Netherlands: van Gorcum, 1981), pp. 97-105.

portavit" (DO 8) and "nos omnes portabat Christus qui et peccata nostra portabat" (Ep 63, 13, 1). It should also be noted that in this absolute use of portare, where Christ is the grammatical subject, the stress is on the participation of all other human beings in the reality of Christ: He carries us; we do not carry him.[226] It is his reality that is paramount. Cyprian continues this stress in his writings on the role of Christ even where typological individuals (e.g. Abraham, Moses, David) or members of the Church are the grammatical subjects of portare. The verb in these instances is almost always qualified by imaginem, typum or figuram. Christ is thereby seen to be that one full reality which supports all others in being, for to the degree to which others truly exist (in veritate) do they also bear his image.

Cyprian's "portare," according to this interpretation, coincides fully with the vision of salvation history found in his "sacramentum." Just as does "sacramentum," "portare" in the great majority of its uses declares that a human being "carries," that is   existentially realizes, Christ in his saving deeds to the degree that that person possesses Christ's inner dispositions of obedience to God and self-sacrifice for others. This is true whether the person is thematically conscious of Christ in doing so or not. Furthermore, the relative intensity of these

---

[226]Although Cyprian's Christians are the grammatical subject of the absolute use of portare in the imperative, "portate Deum in corpore vestro" (Test III, 11 & 63; Vir 2; DO 11; Fort 6), that sentence is a direct quote from I Cor 6, 20 and not something original to the bishop of Carthage. In light of his other uses of portare, Cyprian might easily see in "in corpore vestro" the equivalent of "imaginem" as it occurs in the other Pauline text, "portemus imaginem eius qui de caelo est" (I Cor 15, 49).

dispositions (veritas) can be seen in the similarity of that person's outward behavior (imago) to the deeds of Christ's life. Particularly intense examples of this identity with Christ are expressly named "sacramenta," and through meditation and reflection it is continually possible to find further examples.[227] On the other hand, participation in Christ is only possible because he carried us "first" (primus). In the events of his life on earth, his death, resurrection and sending of the Spirit, all human nature in principle is taken up in his humanity into the fulness of life in the Trinity. In Christ is found that true humanity, the veritas, which all other human beings share in to the degree that Christ in his saving deeds acts through them and allows them to be truly themselves as human beings (in veritate). According to Cyprian's use of "portare" and "sacramentum," then, all history finds its true foundation, its fulness and its explanation in the ever-present history of Christ.

Adunare

Adunare and its substantive adunatio[228] can be shown to reflect the same theology in Cyprian's writings as that discovered in his use of

----

[227]The four confessors, Nemesianus, Dativus, Felix and Victor write to Cyprian expressing their gratitude for his having pointed out other instances in salvation history besides those already recognized of "sacramenta:" "... non desinis tractatibus tuis sacramenta occulta nudare, sic nos in fidem facis crescere et de saeculo homines ad credulitatem accedere" (Ep 77, 1, 1). On the theological legitimacy of finding additional types and sacramenta in salvation history, see the opening arguments of Chapter Two, Section I, above, pp. 35-39.

[228]Adunare-adunatio is not classical Latin, but it does occur in Latin translations of the Bible before the time of Cyprian and in the works of Tertullian: E.W. Watson, "The Style and Language of St. Cyprian,"

portare. According to J. Daniélou, Cyprian's <u>adunatio</u> "stresses the realism of a unity which is physical and not simply moral."[229] As evidence of this, Daniélou cites Ep 62, 1, 2 where Cyprian appeals to a "bond" uniting Christians to one another which is more fundamental than are the moral demands of love:

> ... nobis captivitas fratrum nostra captivitas
> computanda est ..., cum sit scilicet <u>adunationis</u>
> et corpus unum, et non tantum dilectio sed et
> religio instigare nos debeat et confortare ad fra-
> trum membra redimenda (Ep 62, 1, 2).
> (We must consider the captivity of our brothers
> our own captivity ... since precisely out of our
> union there is but one body, and it is not love
> alone but the bond which ought to incite us to
> strengthen us to redeem those members which are
> our brothers.)

The "bond" (<u>religio</u>) spoken of here, which unites Christians to one another in a way deeper even than do the bonds of charity, is in fact the very same bond which Christ forged when, in his <u>passio</u>, he bore in himself all other human beings:

228(cont)in <u>Studia Biblica et Ecclesiastica</u> IV (Oxford: Clarendon, 1896), p. 301. See also L. Bayard, <u>Le Latin de Saint Cyprien</u> (Paris: Hachette, 1902), p. 178; H. Pétré, <u>Caritas: Etude sur le vocabulaire latin de la charité chrétienne</u>, Spicilegium Sacrum Lovaniense XXII (Louvain: Université Catholique, 1948), pp. 330-332: B. Renaud, "L'Eglise comme assemblée liturgique selon saint Cyprien," <u>Recherches de Théologie ancienne et médievale</u> XXXVIII (1971), 8-9, n. 9: Scholars disagree on whether Cyprian's <u>adunare</u> is a translation of the Greek, <u>SUNAGO</u>.

[229]J. Daniélou, S.J., The Origins of Latin Christianity (Phila-delphia: Westminster, 1977), p. 462. Others refer to this bond as "mystical:" L. Bayard, <u>Le Latin</u>, p. 178; H. Pétré, <u>Caritas</u>, p. 329; M. Reveillaud, <u>Saint Cyprian: Oraison dominicale</u>, pp. 149, 150.

> ... nos omnes _portabat_ Christus ... quando
> autem in calice vino aqua miscetur, _Christo populus_
> _adunatur_ ... quo et ipso sacramento populus noster
> ostenditur _adunatus_, ut quemadmodum grana multa in
> unum collecta et conmolita panem unum faciunt, sic
> in Christo qui est panis caelestis unum sciamus esse
> corpus, cui coniunctus sit noster numerus et _adunatus_
> (Ep 63, 13).
> (Christ carried us all ... when water is mixed
> with wine in the chalice, the people are united to
> Christ ... and by the same _sacramentum_ our people
> are shown to be united [to one another], so that,
> just as many grains gathered together and ground
> together and mixed together into one make one bread,
> so are we to know that there is in Christ who is the
> heavenly bread one body, to which our membership is
> joined and united.)

The source of the unity of Christians with one another is their unity
with Christ. As argued above, Christ by his _passio_ "carried us all" in
his humanity and he realized our union with himself already in the outward ritual which expressed that inner _passio_-intention: the Last
Supper offering of wine mixed with water. As the _sacramentum_ of that
total _passio_-event (Last Supper, Calvary), the Eucharist also realizes
that same unity with Christ (_adunatur_) in the lives of those who offer
it. Furthermore, the unity of all in Christ necessarily includes in it
the unity of all with one another. As a result, one and the same _sacra-_
mentum (_quo et ipso sacramento_) points to (_ostenditur_) this two-fold
unity: The water (the people) is united to the wine (Christ), illus-
trating our union with Christ; the many grains of wheat forming one
bread show that the many individuals united to Christ constitute with
each other one body (_unum ... corpus_) in Christ.[230]

---

[230]As Daniélou notes, it is clear that Cyprian here is borrowing
the image of many grains of wheat making up one bread from _Didache_ 9 .
His borrowing is made complete in Ep 69, 4, 2, where the cup of wine is
seen as formed by the pressing together of many grapes. Danielou, _Origins._
p. 463.

The ultimate source of the unity by which Christ "carries us" in himself, and which in turn binds Christians to one another, is the unity by which the three persons in God are one: "unitatem ille portabat ... de caelo et a patre venientem" (Un 7), "de unitate patris et filii et spiritus sancti plebs adunata" (DO 23).[231] The unity, therefore, by which Christ bears us in himself in his passio is the identical unity by which he shares in the Trinity, a unity which furthermore serves to bind the Christian people toegether. Cyprian uses "adunare-adunatio" precisely to point to this unity.

Daniélou names the unity signified by Cyprian's adunatio "physical" because he sees in it "the ultimate point of realism in the question of the unity of the Church."[232] In order to demonstrate this realism, he quotes the following passage:

> Denique unanimitatem christianam firma sibi adque inseparabili caritate conexam etiam ipsa dominica sacrificia declarant. Nam quando Dominus corpus suum panem vocat de multorum granorum adunatione congestum, populum nostrum quem portabat indicat adunatum; et quando sanguinem suum vinum appellat de botruis adque acinis plurimis expressum adque in unum coactum, gregem item nostrum significat commixtione adunatae multitudinis copulatum. Si Novatianus huic pani dominico adunatus est, si Christi poculo et

---

[231]See also Ep 66, 8: "plebs adunata;" Epp 61, 3; 66, 8; 69, 5: "populus adunatus." A. Demoustier remarks that Christian participation in the Trinity according to Cyprian is accomplished only in a sacramental context: "Cyprien ne semble pas parler de l'unité trinitaire à propos de l'Eglise en dehors d'un contexte baptismal," ("L'Ontologie de l'Eglise selon Saint Cyprien," Recherches de Science Religieuse LII (1964), 563, n. 36). For example, Zel 18: Cogita quod filii Dei hi soli possint vocari qui sint pacifici, qui nativitate et lege divina ad similitudinem Dei patris et Christi respondeant adunati."

[232]Daniélou, Origins, p. 463.

> ipse commixtus est, poterit videri et unici
> ecclesiastici baptismi habere gratiam posse,
> si eum constiterit ecclesiae unitatem tenere.
>   Denique quam sit inseparabile unitatis
> sacramentum et quam sine spe sint ... qui
> schisma faciunt et relicto episcopo alium sibi
> foris pseudoepiscopum constituunt ... (Ep 69,
> 5 & 6).
>   (In a word, then, the Lord's sacrifices them-
> selves also proclaim that Christian unanimity is
> forged by a firm and inseparable charity. For
> when the Lord names bread his body, bread fash-
> ioned from the union of many grains, he is
> indicating that our people whom he bore are
> united; and when he calls wine pressed from many
> bunches of grapes and gathered together his blood,
> he again signifies our flock joined together by
> the mutual mixing of the union of a multitude.
> If Novatian is united to this dominical bread,
> if he is also mixed in with the cup of Christ,
> he would also be seen as able to possess the
> grace of the one baptism of the Church, if it
> were established that he upholds the unity of
> the Church.
>   Finally, how unbreakable is the sacramentum
> unitatis and how hopeless they are who create a
> schism and who, abandoning the bishop, set up for
> themselves a false bishop outside [the Church]...)

As noted above, Daniélou states that Cyprian's adunatio signifies a union more profound than that arising from the demands of love. How-ever, in this passage from Ep 69 Cyprian states that Christian solidarity does in fact rest on love: "inseparabili caritate." Therefore the question arises: To what charity is Cyprian referring? The phrase, "inseparabili caritate" bears a striking resemblance to Ep 63, 13, 2: "unde ecclesiam ... nulla res separare poterit a Christo," which in turn recalls Paul's exclamation: "Quis ergo nos separabit a caritate

122

Christi?" (Rom 8, 35).[233] The love referred to by "inseparabili
caritate" is none other than the love Christ has for us, a love which
on his part will never fail. However, by serious sin the Christian can
cut himself off from that love. Furthermore, for Cyprian, separation
from Christ's love uniting us to himself is separation from his "body:"
"contra timendum est orandum, ne dum quis abstentus separatur a Christi
corpore remaneat a salute ..." (DO 18). (We ought to pray to ward off
the fearful possibility that someone cut off and separated from the body
of Christ might so remain as to be cut off from salvation ...) There is
therefore an intimate connection, even an identity, made between allowing oneself to be loved by the all-victorious love of Christ and belonging to his "body." In fact, in the passage from Ep 69, 5 & 6 quoted
above, Cyprian argues that when Christ named bread at the Last Supper
"his body" (corpus suum), he actually meant to signify that his "carrying" (portabat) us was an act of his love (inseparabili caritate)[234]
uniting us together (adunatum). Likewise, when Christ called his blood
"wine," he showed that we Christians, like many grapes crushed together
into one cup, are by that same loving act (portabat) united to one
another (adunatae multitudinis). That is to say, belonging to Christ's
"body" (corpus) means sharing in the irreversible love by which Christ
"carried us all" (Ep 63, 13, 1), so that the unity of the Church is the

[233]Rom 8, 35 is quoted in Test III, 18; Ep 11, 5, 3; and Fort 6.
The importance that Cyprian gives to this passage and to the thought it
contains is seen in the repeated use of separare and inseparabilis
throughout his writings.
[234]See also Zel 17: "adunata dilectione."

unbreakable bond of his charity uniting Christians to one another.[235]

The statement in Ep 69, 5 quoted above that Novatian must be joined
(adunatus) to the bread of the Lord and be "mixed with" (commixtus) the
cup of Christ in order to be in union with the Church is obviously the
basis for Daniélou's conclusion that Cyprian has reached "the ultimate
point of realism" in his understanding of Church unity. According to
this view, the consecrated bread and wine are the "physical" objectifi-
cations of the two-fold unity of Christ with his people and of the
people among themselves. A. Demoustier finds this "realism" expressed in
Ep 63, 13:

> Nam quia nos omnes portabat Christus qui et
> peccata nostra portabat, videmus in aqua populum
> intellegi, in vino vero ostendit sanguinem Christi.
> Quando autem in calice vino aqua miscetur, Christo
> populus adunatur et credentium plebs ei in quem
> credidit copulatur et iungitur. Quae copulatio et
> coniunctio aquae et vini miscetur in calice Domini
> ut conmixtio illa non possit ab invicem separari.
> Unde ecclesiam id est plebem in ecclesia constitutam
> fideliter et firmiter in eo quod credidit persever-
> antem nulla res separare poterit a Christo quo minus
> haereat semper et maneat individua dilectio. Sic
> autem in sanctificando calice Domini offeri aqua
> sola non potest quomodo nec vinum solum potest.
> Nam si vinum tantum quis offerat, sanguis Christi
> incipit esse sine nobis. Si vero aqua sit sola,
> plebs incipit esse sine Christo. Quando autem
> utrumque miscetur et adunatione confusa sibi invicem
> copulatur, tunc sacramentum spiritale et caeleste

---

[235]Ep 60, 1: "inseparabilem fratrum caritatem." That Christ's
unconquerable love realized in his historical, saving deeds (passio)
is the source of the unity of the Church is witnessed in Cyprian's
writings by the frequency and variety of words connected with love:
"caritas," "dilectio," "amare," "concordia," "unanimitas," "humanitas,"
"pax," "frater," etc: H. Pétré, Caritas: Etude sur le vocabulaire
latin de la charité chrétienne, Spicilegium Sacrum Lovaniense XXII
(Louvain: Université Catholique, 1948), passim. See also B. Renaud,
"L'Eglise comme assemblée," p. 24, n. 72.

perficitur. Sic vero calix Domini non est aqua sola
aut vinum solum, nisi utrumque sibi misceatur, quomodo nec corpus Domini potest esse farina sola aut
aqua sola, nisi utrumque adunatum fuerit et copulatum
et panis unius conpage solidatum. Quo et ipso
sacramento populus noster ostenditur adunatus, ut
quemadmodum grana multa in unum collecta et conmolita
et conmixta panem unum faciunt, sic in Christo qui
est panis caelestis unum sciamus esse corpus, cui
coniunctus sit noster numerus et adunatus.
    (For because Christ carries us all who also
carries our sins, we see the people to be understood
in the water, but in the wine he shows the blood of
Christ. But when the water is mixed in the chalice
with the wine, the people are united to Christ and
the corps of believers are linked and joined to him
in whom they believed. This linking and joining of
water and wine is mixed in the chalice of the Lord
so that that mixture is unable to be separated from
each other. Thus, no reality will ever be able to
separate the Church from Christ, that is, the people
faithfully rooted in the Church and firmly persevering
in what they believe, so that the love might hold
firm forever and remain undivided. Accordingly, then,
in sanctifying the chalice of the Lord water cannot
be offered alone just as neither can wine alone. For
if someone offers only wine, the blood of Christ
begins to be without us. But if water would be alone,
the people begins to be without Christ. But when both
are mixed and, confused in a union, are joined to each
other, then the spiritual and heavenly sacramentum is
completed. Therefore, the chalice of the Lord is not
water alone or wine alone without the mixing of both
together, just as the body of the Lord cannot be flour
alone or water alone without both being united and
joined and forged by the union of one bread. By this
very same sacramentum our people are shown to be united,
so that just as many grains collected into one and
ground together and mixed together make up one bread,
so in Christ, who is the heavenly bread, we can understand that there is one body, to which our membership
is conjoined and united.)

For Demoustier, the figural dimension of the Eucharist according
to Cyprian, e.g., that water signifies the people, does not cause what
it signifies. Rather, he interprets the phrase, "in sanctificando
calice Domini," as pointing to a "consecration" of the bread and wine

which "makes this mixture exist as the blood of Christ, [and] of Christ who is united to his people."[236]   In other words, in Demoustier's interpretation, within the Eucharist itself there is no imitation-presence economy of salvation history at work, one which would make Christ in his historical _passio_ present through the typological repetition of his saving actions. Demoustier states to the contrary that according to Cyprian, "... the eucharist is _sacramentum_ ... only in regard to the sacrifice, and not as signifying the body."[237]   That is to say, the eucharistic rite _signifies_ and points to Christ's historical death, but in contrast, the consecrated bread and cup _are_ his body and blood. This supposed complete identity in Cyrpian's mind between the consecrated bread and cup and Christ, and a Christ who furthermore is seen as united to his people, the Church, is what Daniélou names "the ultimate point of realism in the question of the unity of the Church." In other words, the unity of the Church with Christ and among its members is so objectified in the eucharistic bread and cup that this two-fold unity forms a _tertium quid_, an independently existing reality which in fact is neither Christ nor his Church.

The fact is that Daniélou and Demoustier are not alone in discerning this kind of excessive "realism" in Cyprian's eucharistic theology. J. Betz states simply, "Cyprian believes in the identity of the conse-

---

[236]A. Demoustier, S.J., "L'Ontologie de L'Eglise selon saint Cyprien," _Recherches_ _de_ _Science_ _Religieuse_ LII (1964), 566.

[237]_Ibid_., p. 567, n. 48: "... si l'eucharistie est _sacramentum_ c'est en tant qu'elle renvoie au sacrifice, non pas comme signifiant le corps."

crated contents of the chalice with the once-poured-out blood of Christ.[238]

A. Gerken observes, "Eucharist and unity of the community are for Cyprian almost an identity."[239] Although Demoustier eschews approaching Cyprian's eucharistic thought in terms of "real presence,"[240] commentators from F. Probst[241] and H.B. Swete[242] to H. Grass[243] have kept the question open. H. Feld tells us that there is still no consensus on the issue.[244] The contention of the present author is that the questions of "real presence" and of identifying Christ (united to his Church) with the consecrated bread and wine cannot be asked of Cyprian, since they are conceived of in such objectivistic categories of thought. A closer analysis of Ep 63, 13 quoted above will reveal a much more "symbolic" view of reality in Cyprian's writings than has heretofore been recognized.

---

[238] Johannes Betz. Eucharistie in der Schrift und Patristik, Handbuch der Dogmengeschichte, edd. M. Schmaus, A. Grillmeier, L. Scheffczyx and M. Seybold, IV, 4a (Freiburg: Herder, 1979), p. 145: "Cyprian glaubt also die Identität des konsekrierten Kelchinhaltes mit Jesu einst vergossenem Blut."

[239] Alexander Gerken, O.F.M., Theologie der Eucharistie (München: Kösel-Verlag, 1973), p. 85: "Eucharistie und Einheit der Gemeinde ist für Cyprian fast eine Identitat."

[240] Demoustier, "L'Ontologie," p. 567.

[241] Ferdinand Probst, Liturgie der drei ersten christlichen Jahrhunderten (Tübingen, 1870), p. 227: "Cyprian die Gegenwart Christi in der Eucharistie lehrt."

[242] H.B. Swete, "Eucharistic Belief in the Second and Third Centuries," The Journal of Theological Studies III (1902), 174.

[243] H. Graß, "Abendmahl II. Dogmengeschichtlich," Die Religion in Geschichte und Gegenwart (Dritte Auflage), (Tübingen: J.C.B. Mohr, 1957), I, 24.

[244] Helmut Feld, Das Verständnis des Abendmahls (Darmstadt: Wissenschaftliche Buchgesellschaft, 1976), p. 89: "Umstritten ist ebenso wie bei Tertullian auch bei Cyprian, ob er an die Realpräsenz Christi im Abendmahl gedacht hat."

Just as Daniélou finds an excessive "realism" in Cyprian's Ep 69,5 statement that Novatian must be "joined to the bread of the Lord" and "mixed in with the cup of Christ" if he is to belong to the Church, so does Demoustier find in Ep 63, 13 similar realistic language. For the martyr-bishop clearly says, "If someone offers only wine, the blood of Christ begins to be (incipit esse) without us," and "if water would be alone, the people begins to be (incipit esse) without Christ." Obviously, because of the simple declarative nature of these two statements and the repetition of the unconditioned phrase, "incipit esse," Demoustier finds no other option but to take these statements as direct predications of reality as Cyprian sees it. However, all the commentators on this text seem to overlook the larger context of typological discourse in which these statements are made:

(1) As already noted, M. Fahey indentifies "ostendere" as a sign of Cyprian's speaking in categories of typology.[245] The bishop of Carthage uses this code-word both at the beginning and at the end of Ep 63, 13, as if to signal the symbolic nature of his analysis: "ostendit ... ostenditur." These uses of ostendere are furthermore re-inforced by clues throughout the passage that the bread and wine are to be understood metaphorically: "videmus ... intelligi;" "Unde;" "Sic;" "quemadmodum ... sic;" "sciamus."

(2) Next, Cyprian in this passage explicitly interprets the Eucharist as a symbolic continuation of particular biblical images. Thus,

---

[245]Michael Fahey, S.J., Cyprian and the Bible: a Study in Third-Century Exegesis (Tübingen: J.C.B. Mohr, 1971), pp. 615, 621.

128

(a) the unseparable union of water and wine ritualizes St. Paul's
assertion that nothing can separate us from the love of Christ (Rom 8,
35), and (b), the eucharistic bread expresses tangibly Christ's metaphor
of himself as the "Bread from heaven" (Jn 6): "sic in Christo qui est
panis caelestis unum sciamus esse corpus." In a parallel passage interpreting the Eucharist, DO 18, Cyprian recalls the same metaphor: "panis
vitae Christus est" (Jn 6, 35). By recalling these metaphors, he in
effect argues that at the Last Supper Jesus was using the bread and wine
of the meal as a visible metaphor of himself, and that He intends that
Christians do the same in their Eucharists.[246]

(3) All of this is not to say that Cyprian envisions the Eucharist
as an empty symbol of an absent Christ. On the contrary, because he
understands the eucharistic bread and cup as sacramenta, the African
bishop precisely affirms that Christ in his passio is present and active
in the eucharistic celebration. It is because Demoustier sees "sacramentum" in this passage as something less than salvific that he translates
the phrase, "tunc sacramentum spiritale et caeleste perficitur," "Then,
that which is revealed on the noetic level of figures (sacramentum) is
accomplished (perficitur)."[247] For Demoustier, Christ's presence is
accomplished by the words of consecration, not by the symbolism of the

---

[246] See Ep 69, 5 quoted above: "... Dominus corpus suum panem
vocat..., ... populum nostrum indicat adunatum; ... sanguinem suum vinum
appellat..." These acts of naming which Cyprian repeatedly predicates of
Christ indicate that he sees Christ speaking in symbolic language, and
not in terms of complete physical identity.

[247] Demoustier, "L'Ontologie," p. 567: "alors, ce qui est révélé au
plan encore noétique des figures s'accomplit."

sacramentum. Furthermore, the sacramentum as symbol points to the fulness of Christ's presence in the eucharistic bread and cup, and not, as was argued earlier in this chapter, to the saving deeds of Christ in his historical life: his passio.[248]

If "sacramentum" in this passage were understood as making Christ's passio present through a typological repetition, then the phrase in question would more properly be translated: "Then (when water and wine are thoroughly mixed) the spiritual and heavenly sacramentum is made complete." That is to say, only when water and wine are mixed together in the cup can they truly symbolize and therefore allow us to be united consciously with the passio of Christ where "He carried us all" (nos omnes portabat) in himself. In other words, the mixing of water and wine does not point primarily to the objective, "realistic" union of Christ and the Church in the consecrated bread and cup; but rather, the eucharistic bread and mixed cup point to the union of Christ and the Church in the passio, and as a sacramentum of the passio[249] they allow the Church in the present moment to ratify and more fully realize its union with Christ. Hence the "real presence" of Christ united to his Church.

---

[248]Ibid., p. 566: "L'acte de mêler le vin et l'eau ... signifie l'union du Christ et de son Eglise. Puis il passe à sa réalisation. La Consécration fait exister ce mélange ..." [emph. mine].

[249]Ep 63, 9, 3: "oblatio et sacrificium nostrum responderit passioni;" Ep 63, 14, 3: "dominicae passionis et nostrae redemptionis sacramentum;" Zel 17: "de sacramento crucis et cibum sumis et potum."

The question remains: If Cyprian does not envision the eucharistic bread and mixed cup as an objective, "physical" realization of the unity of Christ and the Church, why does he employ such "realism" language in regard to the Eucharist? Why does he speak of the need for Novatian to be "mixed in with" the cup? Or why does he claim that by offering water alone in the cup the people "begin to be" without Christ?

First of all, Cyprian speaks in such "realistic" fashion precisely because he wants to affirm in the strongest terms that the sacramentum of the Eucharist does cause the presence of Christ, but of a Christ in union with his Church. Secondly, that Cyprian's use of "corpus" (body) in regard to the Eucharist is a symbolic one is consistent with what Demoustier himself observes:

> For the Stoics and again for Tertullian distinct
> elements that are in continuity form one unique
> entity: This is the representational basis for
> the concept of Body as a unique totality made up of
> distinct elements. One finds this kind of image
> again in the De Unitate, and one can assert that
> the whole of Cyprian's christology is expressed by
> means of such metaphors: induere, e.g. De Unitate
> 7; portare, e.g. Ep 63, 13.250

In other words, the union of the Church with Christ is not so radically "physical" as Daniélou contends. Rather, the words, "corpus,"251

250Demoustier, "L'Ontologie," p. 569, n. 55: "Pour les stoïciens et encore pour Tertullien des éléments distincts qui sont en continuité, forment un être unique: c'est la base représentative du concept de Corps comme totalité unique composée d'éléments distincts. On retrouvera ce type d'image dans De Unitate et l'on peut constater que l'ensemble de la christologie de Cyprien s'exprime à l'aide de telles représentations: induere par ex. de Unitate 7; portare par ex. Ep 63, 13."

251H. Pétré notes that Cyprian adopts St. Paul's metaphor for the Church as the "corpus Christi" (Caritas: Etude sur le Vocabulaire Latin de la Charité Chrétienne [Louvain: Spicilegium Sacrum Lovaniense, 1948], p. 284). For Cyprian the Church obviously is the "corpus Christi" because

"induere," and "portare" are metaphors[252] using analogues from the

physical world to point to a real, although spiritual ("sacramentum

---

251(cont)when Christ _called_ bread his "body" at the Last Supper, he
was referring to the union his passio forges between himself and the
Church: "Nam quando Dominus corpus suum panem vocat..., populum nostrum
quem portabat indicat adunatum" (Ep 69, 5, 2). Thus, "corpus" is a metaphor Christ used for the Church's union in him. Coming from its divine
origin, it also effects the union it signifies. See also Ep 62, 1, 2:
"adunationis nostrae et corpus unum." Further indication that "corpus"
is a metaphor for union in Christ is Cyprian's use of "corpus" to refer
to the union of bishops. Since the "corpus" of the Church is held together by the union of bishops with each other (Ep 68, 3, 1: "...
copiosum corpus est sacerdotum concordiae mutuae glutino atque unitatis
vinculo copulatum"), that union itself is called "corpus:" Epp 55, 24;
68, 1; 68, 3. Consequently, when Cyprian notes that Christ calls bread
his "body," the martyr-bishop sees in that bread a type or sacramentum
of the union forged in the passio between Christ and the Church, with
which he forms one "corpus."
    B. Renaud fails to recognize the typological nature of the eucharis-
tic bread and mixed cup. For him, one "body" is as independently "real"
as the other: "Cyprien ne confond pas le corps eucharistique et le
corps de l'Eglise ... [The use of "corpus" for both] prouve le réalisme
de sa croyance en l'Eglise comme en l'eucharistie; et même alors, le mot
garde chaque fois une nuance particulière qui lui fait signifier
davantage l'Eglise ou davantage l'eucharistie" ("L'Eglise comme assemblée,"
pp. 33, 34). In contrast, W. Simonis asserts that for Cyprian the only
raison d'etre of a Church sacramentum is in its being a symbolic self-
expression of the Church itself: [Cyprian] überhaupt im Sakrament nicht
in erster Linie eine eigenständige, von der jeweiligen Kirche loslösbare
und in sich eindeutige Größe sah, sondern dass es für ihn nur eine
konkrete Weise der verwirklichung der kirchlichen disciplina war ..."
"Ecclesia Visibilis et Invisibilis [Frankfurt: Josef Knecht, 1970], p.
12).
    252The scandal that results from reading Cyprian with a strict
literalism is reflected in the words of one scholar: "It is one thing
to say, as did earlier writers, that the eucharist is a sacrifice of
thanksgiving to God and also to say that it is the body and blood of
Christ on which we feed. It is altogether another thing to put them
together, as Cyprian does, and to say that in the eucharist we offer
the body and blood of Christ as our sacrifice. This is the step which
Cyprian took, and it was fraught with enormous consequences for the whole
subsequent history of the development of eucharistic doctrine" (M.F.
Wiles, "The Theological Legacy of St. Cyprian," Journal of Ecclesiastical
History XIV [1963], 148).

spiritale et caeleste") bond (adunatio). And the bond to which they
point is the love of Christ (inseparabili caritate)[253] which is recalled
by and expressed through the eucharistic bread and mixed cup as sacramentum of his passio (Ep 63, 14, 3: "dominicae passionis ... sacramentum").

sacramentum unitatis

An important corrollary needs to be added to the foregoing study of
"adunare-adunatio" in Cyprian: An investigation into his meaning of
"sacramentum unitatis." In Ep 69, 6, after demanding that Novatian be
"united to the Lord's bread" (adunatus), the bishop of Carthage remarks:

> Denique quam sit inseparabile unitatis
> sacramentum et quam sine spe sint ... qui schisma
> faciunt et relicto episcopo alium sibi foris
> pseudoepiscopum constituunt...
> (Finally, how unbreakable is the sacramentum
> unitatis and how hopeless they are who create a
> schism and who, abandoning the bishop, set up for
> themselves a false bishop outside [the Church]...)[254]

Let us examine "sacramentum unitatis" in this and related texts according
to the basic characteristics arrived at earlier in this chapter of any
use of "sacramentum" by Cyprian:

(1) Christological: U. Wickert argues that for Cyprian the unity
of the Church is one of charity: (a) "unitas" and "vinculum caritatis"
in Ep 41, 1 are roughly equivalent in meaning; (b) "unitatis sacramentum"

---

[253]Notice Cyprian's conviction, "qui caritatem non habet, deum non
habet" (Un 14).

[254]Other examples and variations of "unitatis sacramentum" include:
Epp 45, 1; 54, 1; 55, 21; 59, 2; 73, 11; 74, 11 (2x); Un 4; Un 7.

is equated with "vinculum concordiae inseparabiliter cohaerentis" in

Un 7: and (c) in Ep 69, 6 (quoted above) the identity between unity and

charity is "even clearer:" "inseparabile unitatis sacramentum."[255]

Evidently this identity is clear to Wickert because "inseparabile unitatis

sacramentum" obviously recalls the phrase in Ep 69, 5: "unianimitatem

christianam ... inseparabili caritate conexam." Furthermore, as we have

already argued, the charity that unites the Church is the love of Christ

realized in his passio. Thus, in line with our previous analysis of

sacramentum according to Cyprian, "sacramentum unitatis" is christological:

It refers to and makes present the veritas of Christ in his historical,

saving events.

(2) Perceptible Reality: Nowhere within his study of "sacramentum

unitatis" does Wickert define Cyprian's understanding of "sacramentum."

He comes closest to such a definition where he remarks: "The ecclesio-

logical difference between the mystery (emph. mine) of unity and the un-

mysterious singleness of the first Apostle (Peter) must be clearly

seen."[256] This present study, on the other hand, has attempted to show

that nowhere does Cyprian understand "sacramentum" as "abstract mystery."

On the contrary, a basic characteristic of this word is that it always

denotes a "perceptible reality," one found within a direct experience of

the here and now. Thus, for example, the very uniqueness or "singleness,"

---

[255]Ulrich Wickert, Sacramentum Unitatis: Ein Beitrag zum Verständnis
der Kirche bei Cyprian (Berlin: Walter de Gruyter, 1971), p. 29, n. 81.
Similar evidence can be found in Ep 55, 21, where "catholicae ecclesiae
individuo sacramento" echoes the parallel found in Ep 54, 1 between
"individuae caritatis" and "sacramenti unitas."

[256]Op. cit., p. 59: "Die ekklesiologische Differenz zwischen dem
Geheimnis der Einheit und der geheimnislosen Singularität des Erstapostels
muss klar gesehen werden."

134

as Wickert puts it, of the first Apostle would in fact help qualify, rather than disqualify, him to be in Cyprian's eyes a "sacramentum."

But to what "perceptible reality" does Cyprian refer in his formula, "sacramentum unitatis?" The answer comes in the demands he puts upon Novatian if the Roman presbyter is to belong to the Church: Novatian must be "mixed in with" the cup of the Lord and "be united" (adunatus) to His bread. In other words, Novatian must share concretely in the life of the church: gather with it in its assemblies, partake in the one cup and bread of the community, and submit himself to community life together under the one bishop (episcopo). Only if there is this perceptible, outward unity OF Christians with one another can there be a true inward community of Christians with Christ.

(3) A-Temporal: As a sacramentum, the sacramentum unitatis is not confined to any single, unique occurrence but refers to the concrete, lived unity of the Church at any given time and place in history where it is experienced as the saving continuation of Christ in his life, death and resurrection.

(4) Divine Action: Finally, as a sacramentum, the concretely shared life of the Church (sacramentum unitatis) effects what it signifies. It does so because, as in every sacramentum, it is God who acts: Christ in his passio uniting the Church to himself and ultimately to the Trinity. "The sacramentum unitatis is the unity of the Trinity reproducing itself in the unity of the Church and, in doing so, making itself known as the origin of this unity."[257] Demoustier bases this

---

[257]A. Demoustier, "L'Ontologie de L'Eglise selon saint Cyprien," Recherches de Science Religieuse LII (1964), p. 583: "Sacramentum unitatis, c'est l'unite de la Trinité se reproduisant dans l'unité de l'Eglise et se faisant ainsi reconnaître comme l'origine de cetta unité."

conclusion on Cyprian's discussion of Christ's seemless robe in Un 7.[258]

For the martyr-bishop, the robe of Christ is a type (sacramento vestis)

which, in the life of Christ, points to his bearing divine unity into the

human condition: unitatem ille portabat de superiore parte venientem, id

est de caelo et a Patre. As part of the historical phenomenon of Christ,

the robe witnesses that all that Jesus was and did served to unite human-

kind inseparably to God.

On the other hand, Cyprian uses the indivisible, physical robe as a

metaphorical analogue of the Church's concrete life together, which in

turn is the sacramentum of its unity achieved in Christ. The visible,

physical robe of Christ during his passio could not be possessed by anyone

if it were severed. As unseverable, the robe is a type of the Church's

---

[258]Un 7: "Hoc unitatis sacramentum, hoc vinculum concordiae
inseparabiliter cohaerentis ostenditur quando in evangelio tunica Domini
Iesu Christi non dividitur omnino nec scinditur sed, sortientibus de
veste Christi, quis Christum potius indueret, integra vestis accipitur
et incorrupta adque indivisa tunica possidetur. Loquitur ac dicit
scriptura divina: 'De tunica autem, quia de superiore parte non consu-
tilis sed per totum texilis fuerat, dixerunt ad invicem, Non scindamus
illam sed sortiamur de ea cuius sit.' Unitatem ille portabat de
superiore parte venientem, id est de caelo et a Patre venientem, quae
ab accipiente ac possidente scindi omnino non poterat, sed totam semel
et solidam firmitatem inseparabiliter obtinebat: possidere non potest
indumentum Christi qui scindit et dividit ecclesiam Christi. Contra
denique cum, Solomone moriente, regnum eius et populus scinderetur, Achias
propheta Hieroboam regi obvius factus in campo in duodecim scissuras
vestimentum suum discidit, dicens: "Sume tibi decem scissuras, quia haec
dicit Dominus, 'Ecce scindo regnum de manu Solomonis, et dabo tibi
decem sceptra, et duo sceptra erunt ei propter servum meum David et
propter Hierusalem civitatem, quam elegi ut ponam nomen meum illic.'"
Cum duodecim tribus Israel scinderentur, vestimentum suum propheta
Achias discidit; at vero quia Christi populus non potest scindi, tunica
eius per totum textilis et cohaerens divisa a possidentibus non est:
individua, copulata, conexa ostendit populi nostri, qui Christum
induimus, concordiam cohaerentem; sacramento vestis et signo declaravit
ecclesiae unitatem."

136

unseverable unity with God through Christ's _passio_. One must therefore
remain united in a _visible_, _concrete_ unity with the Church (= _unitatis
sacramentum_) if he or she is to remain united with God.[259] Just as there
is no union of God with humanity except in the concrete life and existence
of Jesus (represented by the physical clothes he wore), so is there no
unity with God through Christ for other human beings except in the concrete life and existence of Christ's "body," the Church.[260] Such, then,
is Cyprian's meaning behind the phrase, _sacramentum unitatis_.

repræsentare

An investigation into Cyprian's understanding of salvation history,
and specifically of the imitation-to-presence relationship behind the
eucharistic leader's acting in the place of Christ, logically includes a

---

[259]Cyprian's unnuanced identification of participation in the
external life of the Church with interior union with Christ needed the
theological refinements of Augustine: "Anders als jene afrikanischen
Theologen, bei denen die Kirche wesentlich die heilige Gemeinde ist,
welche die Sakramente als ihr eigenes, untrennbar mit der Kirche ver-
bundenes, heiliges Tun vollzieht, unterscheidet Augustinus scharf das
äußere, sichbare Sein und Tun der Kirche von der existentiellen,
letzlich nie ganz nach aussen sichtbar werdenden Situation des einselnen
Gliedes der Kirche" (W. Simonis, _Ecclesia Visibilis et Invisibilis_
[Frankfurt: Josef Knecht, 1970], pp. xi, xii.).

[260]Cyprian gives this same conviction in his celebrated expression,
"_salus extra ecclesiam non est_ (Ep 73, 21). M. Bevenot has plausibly
argued that the bishop of Carthage speaks so absolutely only in regard to
those who are under pressure to break from the Church, and that "_salus_"
in this phrase is better interpreted as "the helps to salvation" than
merely as "salvation" itself. As in other difficult questions, Cyprian
would have allowed that God would somehow deal mercifully with those
inadvertantly cut off (by deception or circumstance) from concrete
ecclesial life. "Salus Extra Ecclesiam Non Est," in _Fides Sacramenti -
Sacramentum Fidei_, H.J. Auf der Maur, L. Bakker, A. van de Bunt, J.
Waldram, edd. (Assen, The Netherlands: van Gorcum, 1981), pp. 97-105.

study of his use of "repraesentare." In contrast to "adunare,"
"repraesentare" is used widely by classical Latin authors. P.G.W. Glare
in the Oxford Latin Dictionary[261] lists seven meanings for the word. As
in our study of "sacramentum," we propose first to seek the common meaning to "repraesentare" in classical times at work in the seven analogous
variations. Next, Tertullian's use of this word will be investigated.
Finally, the texts from Cyprian involving "repraesentare" will be
considered.

Glare's first meaning for "repraesentare" in classical Latin is (1)
"To give immediate effect (to something that would normally take place
later), bring forward to the present." The phrase, "to bring (something)
forward to the present time," demands that the item in question also
exist at some other point in history. In fact, the next four definitions
set forth by Glare also presuppose this existence of a reality in two
separate places in history: (2) "To pay (a sum) in ready money" implies
the outward actualization of a payment existing previously, albeit only,
in the barterers' minds. The third meaning, (3) "To present to view,
exhibit," fairly demands that the reality exhibited exist previously in
order for it then to be demonstrable. The same holds true for (4) "To
show or present in person," and also for (5) "To make present to the
mind." Consequently, the first five definitions of "repraesentare"
presuppose the existence of a reality in more than one place and time in
history, even if that existence be only in one's previous (2) or subse-

---

[261]P.G.W. Glare, ed., Oxford Latin Dictionary, Fascicle VII:
Qualiterqualiter--Sopitus (Oxford: Clarendon, 1980), 1621.

quent (5) imagination. Furthermore, this same presupposition also holds true for Glare's sixth definition: (6) "To bring back into the present (what is dead, lost, etc.), revive," or "to serve as the equivalent of." The combination of the sixth (6) with the first (1) definition, "To bring forward to the present," suggests furthermore that behind "repraesentare" is the awareness that one and the same reality is truly present and active in two separate points in history.

Finally, Glare's seventh and last definition: (7) "To represent in art, poetry" or "to resemble, imitate," connects the notion of repeated real inner presence to outward resemblance or imitation. Given Glare's definitions, then, there is solid basis in the classical Latin "repraesentare" for an intrinsic connection between the resemblance or imitation of a past, future or distant reality and its effective presence in the here and now.

Turning to Christian Latin, we find in J. van der Geest's study that Tertullian also used "repraesentare" in order to denote that presence which is achieved through an intended imitation of the original reality.[262] In the bread of the Last Supper, asserts Tertullian, "[Christus] corpus suum repraesentat" (Christ "represents" [i.e. makes present] his body) (Adv Marc I, 14, 3). Christ also made himself present in Old Testament types: "se illum repraesentare gestavit, quem demonstraverat per Esaiam" (Adv Marc IV, 14, 13). Here van der Geest remarks, "prophecy made [Christ] already present, but not in his full reality."[263] In other

---

[262] J.E.L. van der Geest, Le Christ et L'Ancien Testament chez Tertullien, Latinitas Christianorum Primaeva XXII (Nijmegen: Dekker & van de Vegt, 1972), p. 114.
[263] Ibid.

words, the type, like a platonic image, because it points to the historical Christ as its full reality, makes Christ partially present by participating in him.

Although Cyprian's "repraesentare" does not differ substantially from the meanings of that word in classical Latin and in Tertullian's writings, a survey of his uses confirms that this word also reflects his imitation-to-presence understanding of salvation history:

(1) In Ep 27, 3, 1 the bishop of Carthage remarks that throughout Africa those who lapsed from the faith during persecution have pressured their bishops to grant that the reconciliation promised by the martyrs "be realized immediately:"[264] "pacem ... repraesentari coegerunt." Thus, "repraesentare" has the force of "to make present in a palpable and thoroughly effective way."

(2) In Ep 43, 7, 2 Cyprian assures his people that the persecution is almost over, so that he with his colleagues will soon be out of exile and with them: "ut repraesenter [sic] ... cum collegis meis." In this use of "repraesentare" its identity with "praesens" is foremost: "to be present again."

Its basic "praesens" meaning is made explicit in Ep 12, 1. Here Cyprian expresses the wish that he could be present ("praesens") to his people. However, since circumstances forbid that, he next wishes that the "diligence (of his presbyters and deacons) might make his [episcopal] office present" for them: "... officium meum vestra diligentia repraesentet ..." In this example, according to Cyprian's "repraesentare,"

---

[264] L. Bayard, Le Latin de Saint Cyprien (Paris: Hachette, 1902), p. 107.

someone else can serve to make a person present.

(3) In Ep 62, 4, 2 Cyprian states that he has included the names
of imprisoned brothers and sisters in his letter to Januarius and other
bishops. He did so in order that these bishops might remember ("in
mente habeatis")[265] those unable to offer the Eucharist for themselves.
By their remembrance, Januarius and the other bishops "make [themselves]
present on behalf of [the incarcerated], supplying for the alms[266] in the
sacrifices, and in prayers:" "eis vicem boni operis in sacrificiis et
precibus repraesentatis." Thus, Cyprian's "repraesentare" signifies that
one makes one's own presence the vehicle of another's real and effective
presence, and does so in mental (in mente), verbal (precibus), or ritual

---

[265]B. Renaud questions whether "in mente habere" might have been a
Carthaginian liturgical formula for introducing prayer: e.g. Epp 78, 2,
1; 79, 1, 2. He concedes that in any case this phrase also has the mean-
ing of "to remember" ("Eucharistie et culte eucharistique selon Saint
Cyprien," [Unpublished doctoral dissertation, Université Catholique de
Louvain, 1967], pp. 186-188).

[266]H. Pétré argues that "bona opera" signifies "almsgiving" for
Cyprian: Op 11; 16; 18. Also, "opus bonum": Ep 31, 1 (Caritas: Etude
sur le vocabulaire latin de la charité chrétienne, Spicilegium Sacrum
Lovaniense XXII [Louvain: Université Catholique, 1948], p. 243). The
social dimension of the physical offering which participants in the
Eucharist were expected to bring forward is emphasized by Cyprian's naming
it "alms." In this present text, Ep 62, 4, 2, "boni operis" witnesses
that for Cyprian the bringing forward or "offering" of bread and wine on
behalf of the physically absent one is a ritual way of "remembering" that
person and thereby making him or her present. Another such way is
(naming them?) in prayers: "in precibus." On the relationship of the
offering to the Eucharist as "sacrifice," see Victor Saxer, Vie liturgique
et quotidienne à Carthage vers le milieu du IIIe Siècle, Studi di Antichità
Cristiana XXIX (Citta del Vaticano: Pontificio Istituto di Archeologia
Cristiana, 1969), 245; and Rupert Berger, Die Wendung "Offerre Pro" in
der Römischen Liturgie, Liturgiewissenschaftliche Quellen und Forschungen
XLI (Münster: Aschendorff, 1965), 60-64.

(boni operis in sacrificiis) remembrance.[267]

(4) In Ep 6, 3 Cyprian argues that the martyrs, a group made up of both sexes and all ages, even boys, make the Lord present in the same way that mere youths, Hananiah, Asariah and Mishael, did in the fiery furnace. That is, they show that the strength in them is the Lord's and not theirs. "repraesentans nobis tale aliquid quale Ananias, Azarias, Misael ... facerunt, ... praesente cum illis Domino." In Ep 61, 2, 2 Cyprian states that he "sees present again" in Lucius, the bishop-confessor, what the three youths embodied in their witness: reliance on God and evidence of his saving power: "repraesentatum videmus in vobis quod ... pueri praedicaverunt ..." Consequently, "repraesentare" in Epp 6, 3 and 61, 2,2 signifies that the Lord makes himself present in the person of the Christian according to the same causality of imitation-to-presence by which He did so through Old Testament types.

If the basic significance of "repraesentare" for Cyprian is "to make present," one can ask: What does "to be present" mean in his writings? In Ep 66, 9, 1 Cyprian states that Christ 'directs the bishops themselves and the Church with the bishops by his presence:' "praesentia ... gubernat." In Ep 43, 1, 1 he writes that the deacons serve the people by 'affording them the full diligence of their presence:' "plenam vobis praesentiae suae diligentiam praebeant." Cyprian parallels "presence" in this context to their work of exhorting the people ("exhortantionibus"), reassuring them ("corroborare") and reforming them

---

[267]For Cyprian's understanding of the salvific value of verbal remembrance, see the "mentio" subsection below, pp. 142-144.

("reformare"). In a word, "to be present" means "to witness one's faith."
Christians, especially Church leaders, make Christ present to one another in
their own persons to the degree that they embody and effectively communicate their personal (appropriation of the Church's) faith in the Lord.[268]

We conclude from this investigation of Cyprian's "repraesentare"
(1) that it always involves some kind of making oneself or another present
again; (2) that, accordingly, a person can truly be present in more than
one place or time in history; (3) that presence is effected through
personal identification, expressed in remembering words or actions, with
a physically absent other; (4) finally, that Cyprian's "repraesentare"
thus reflects his understanding of how the imitation of Christ by Old
Testament types and by faithful Christians results in his effective
presence.

"mentio"

Cyprian's conviction that Christ is made present in the eucharistic
celebration by means of a remembering imitation is confirmed by his use
of the word, "mentio." B. Renaud observes that "mentio" derives from the
same root as "memini" and "memoria," suggesting the explicit expression

---

[268]For the best modern theological presentation of the relationship
of Christ's presence in the Church to the faith of the Church, see E.J.
Kilmartin, S.J., "Apostolic Office: Sacrament of Christ," Theological
Studies XXXVI (1975), 243-264: "The life of faith, as Paul calls it,
includes the presence of Christ in the Christian and the personal laying
hold of Christ in such a way that he becomes the principle of life. It
is a presence analogous to intentional presence experienced by [a
person] through memory, but comes about only through the Spirit and
results in the believer and Christ being two in one Spirit. The believer
is thus able to live out of the mystery of Christ 'in us'" (p. 254).

of the remembrance of someone or some thing.[269] He then cites Ep 63, 17,
1:

> Et quia passionis eius mentionem in sacri-
> ficiis omnibus facimus, passio est enim Domini
> sacrificium quod offerimus...
> (And because we make mention of his passio
> in all of the sacrifices, it is therefore the
> passio of the Lord that we offer ...)

Commenting on this text, Renaud asserts that the "mentio passionis" is
the explicit remembrance of the Last Supper in the institution narrative.
Because that narrative prescribes the repetition of the actions it
describes, the phrase, "to make mention of the passio," therefore
includes the outward performance of the Last Supper actions of Jesus:
"c'est rappeler la cène en en faisant le récit."[270]

For our present purposes, what is most important to recognize in
this text is the identity made by Cyprian between the "mentio" and the
presence in the Eucharist of the passio: "quia passionis eius mentionem
..., passio est." For the saintly bishop, simply because the eucharistic
celebration is a "mentio," an explicit remembering imitation, of the
passio, it is the passio. Once again, the easy, unquestioned identity
made here between the imitation of Christ and the presence of Christ

---

[269]Renaud, "Eucharistie," p. 259.

[270]Ibid., p. 260. Renaud rightly implies that "doctor" in the
phrase, "Iesus Christus ... sacrificii huius auctor et doctor" (Ep 63,
1, 1) means that according to Cyprian the institution narrative itself
demands that the actions described be imitated and, furthermore, that it
tells how they are to be imitated (p. 257). He also clearly shows that
"mentio" in the present context is the equivalent of "commemoratio" of
Paul's institution narrative in I Cor: e.g. Ep 63, 10, 2; 63, 17, 1
(p. 260).

144

argues that Cyprian presupposed in regard to Church <u>sacramenta</u> the same imitation-to-presence economy as is affirmed by Church Tradition for the relationship of New Testament to Old, that is, for Christ's presence in Old Testament types.

Conclusions

The task set for this chapter was to discover whether there be any evidence at all that Cyprian sees an imitation-presence relationship between Christ and historical figures living before as well as historical figures living after the time of Christ. Studies of the key words to his theology of salvation history, "sacramentum," "imago," "veritas," "portare," "adunare," and "repraesentare," repeatedly support a single conclusion: Cyprian does in fact envision such an imitation-presence relationship between Christ and all persons, objects and events regardless of when they occur in history.

In order to convey this vision of inner consistency in all of salvation history, Cyprian uses the term "sacramentum" just as surely of a Melchisedech offering bread and wine as he does of the Church's eucharistic cup. Both for him are "sacramenta" of Christ in his saving life, death and resurrection.

In our study of Cyprian's use of "portare" are uncovered the basic elements in his understanding of salvation history: Christ, through the power of his divine love, irrevocably united himself in his humanity to "us all" and thereby transformed us through communion in the life of the Trinity. Consequently, to the extent that anyone anywhere in history lives and acts according to true human existence, the existence of Christ (veritas), to that extent is Christ present and acting through that person. Furthermore, wherever the dispositions of Christ are present in someone (obedience to God and self-sacrifice for others), that person's actions will also resemble the external actions of the historical Christ. For Cyprian there is only one history: the history of Christ. Everything in this world exists only as an indication and reminder of, and in solidarity with, the historical Christ. Thus, even the objects and events of the "natural" world are explainable only in terms of our relationship to God forged through the passio of Christ. If the sun shines equally on us all, for example, it does so only in order to indicate that Christ, our sun, pours out eternal life for all in and through the Church (Ep 69, 14, 1). And if men naturally are joyful to have sons who resemble them, it is only because God intends by that to show us how much He wishes us to be like Him (Zel 15).

While all things potentially point to Christ and to our relationship to God foundationally accomplished in his passio, for Cyprian this is especially true of the Church. To the degree that the Church lives in a fellowship of concord and mutual love, it is truly united to Christ and imitates his historical life. By making its own the Last-Supper sign of Christ's ultimate self-gift, the Church in the Eucharist lives out in history its identity as the "body" of Christ. It is Christ himself who, as priest, offers himself in its Eucharist.

If, then, physical objects, such as bread and the mixed cup, can be such intense forms of Christ's presence as even to be named his "body" and "blood," would not human persons for Cyprian potentially be even more capable of being "sacramenta," of bearing and conveying Christ's presence? In our next and final chapter, then, we will investigate in what way

Cyprian sees one human person, the leader of the Eucharist, as an imitator and consequent bearer of Christ's presence.

CHAPTER IV

"SACERDOS VICE CHRISTI"

Introduction

The search for the theological foundations which ultimately support Cyprian's theology of eucharistic leadership has up to this point led us through three preliminary stages. First, we looked into sacred Scripture for the roots of the presupposition that the imitation of Christ by the leader results in the presence of Christ. Next, the Christian writings of the second and early third centuries were studied in order to determine to what degree their authors see the presence of Christ in the imitation of him by those living after his historical life on earth. Thirdly, we investigated in the writings of Cyprian himself the place this kind of imitation-presence ontology might have in his overall theology of salvation history.

The task of this fourth chapter finally is to study the role which, according to Cyprian, the eucharistic leader has in the course of salvation history. If, as we have found in the Carthaginian's writings, all persons, objects and events in the created world participate in Christ to the extent that they exist, is there a special participation exhibited by the eucharistic leader which prompts Cyprian to state, "That priest truly functions in the place of Christ who imitates what Christ did" (Ep 63, 14)?

In order to answer this question adequately, we must first discover in Cyprian's theology that imitation-presence relationship which any Christian, cleric or lay, would have to Christ. As we have seen already, for Cyprian the intensity of Christ's presence depends on the personal holiness of the one who imitates his saving deeds. We will therefore study next the relationship which the outstanding Christian, the martyr, has to Christ and to the rest of the Church. Determining the role of the martyr will allow us a point of comparison for another role in the Church, that of the eucharistic leader as ordained minister. This will be the final topic of our investigation. The chapter will therefore be comprised of three major sections: I. The Christian; II. The Martyr; III. The Leader of the Eucharist.

I. The Christian[271]

The Dying World

In the "Conclusions" section to Chapter Three it was noted that for Cyprian the created world only exists to the degree that it images Christ in his death-resurrection, the ultimate reality. Along with the other Fathers of the Church, Cyprian sees creation therefore as essentially sacramental[272] and as fundamentally good.[273] To the bishop of Carthage no one has a right to glory in anything as being his or her own since everything that is is a gift from God.[274]

On the other hand, Cyprian also sees the natural world as a world

---

[271]For a fuller treatment of Christian life according to Cyprian, see Josepho Capmany, "Miles Christi" en la Espiritualidad de San Cipriano, Colectanea San Paciano, serie teologica I (Barcelone, 1956); Pierre Gaudette, "Baptême et vie chrétienne chez Saint Cyprien de Carthage," Laval Theologique et Philosophique XXVII (1971), 163-190, 251-279; Simone Deléani, Christum Sequi: Etude d'un thème dans l'oeuvre de saint Cyprien (Paris: Études Augustiniennes, 1979). Deléani's work brings Cyprian to light as a giant in Christian spirituality.

[272]Yves Congar, O.P., Tradition and Traditions (New York: MacMillan, 1966), p. 65: "There is for [Patristic and Medieval writers] one understanding of God's three books -- each through each --: the book of creation, the book of the soul, and the book which resumes and explains them both, Scripture."

[273]Ep 64, 2, 2: "... quaecumque a Deo fiunt Dei factoris maiestate et opere perfecta sunt."

[274]Test III, 4: "In nullo gloriandum, quando nostrum nihil est." This chapter quotes and explains I Cor 4, 7bc: "What have you that you did not receive? If then you received it, why do you boast as if it were not a gift?"

in decay.[275] It is like a house falling into ruins (Mort 25). This is
true because, although God made everything good, human beings in their
free will[276] have misused creation and have chosen death instead of life.
Natural humanity, the humanity that comes from Adam, has lost all fear of
God. In its pride it no longer worships him.[277] That is the reason God
allows the ancient enemy of the human race, the devil, to punish and tempt
to further sin.[278] It is also the reason the natural world itself is
dying, why there are persecutions and plagues throughout the Roman
world.[279]

~The natural world is now ruled by the devil and all who are under

---

[275] Apparently Cyprian is influenced by Stoic cosmology. Patterned
after the life-span of a natural man, the natural world is growing old.
Now in its sixth age, according to Cyprian, it is close to death. Dem 3:
"Haec sententia mundo data est, haec Dei lex est ut omnia orta occidant
et aucta senescant et infirmentur fortia et magna minuantur et cum
infirmata et deminuta fuerint finiantur." Also, Un 16 ("occasus mundi");
Ep 67, 7; Mort 25; Mort 27. For a development of this topic, see Jean
Daniélou, S.J., The Origins of Latin Christianity (Philadelphia: Westminster, 1977), Ch. IX: "Cyprian and the Age of the World," pp. 251-258.

[276] Ep 59, 7: "...homo libertati suae relictus et in arbitrio
proprio constitus sibimet ipse vel mortem adpetit vel salutem." See
Gaudette, "Baptême et vie chrétienne," p. 172.

[277] Dem 9: "Indignari se Deus dicit quod agnitio Dei non sit in
terris, et Deus non agnoscitur nec timetur."

[278] Cyprian records a "vision" of a father with a youth (Christ) at
his right hand. The youth is saddened because the father's laws are not
obeyed. At the father's left is one (the Devil) who is gleeful at being
allowed to strike the evil-doers (Ep 11, 4). Section III below will
discuss whether, as A. von Harnack argues, Cyprian governed his church
as a visionary. See A. Harnack, "Cyprian als Enthusiast," Zeitschrift
fur die neutestamentliche Wissenschaft III (1902), 177-191, esp. 179-
191. See below, pp. 215-217.

[279] Gaudette, "Baptême et vie chrétienne," p. 169: "La cause
véritable de tous ces fléaux, ce n'est rien d'autre que l'abondance du
péché qui a déchaîne la colère de Dieu."

his power are devoured with envy, the root of all other vices.[280] Like Adam, they have lost their created resemblance to God.[281] Having rejected the Truth, they are no longer able to receive its light.[282] In this condition, the cry of St. Paul could be put in their mouths: "Who will deliver [us] from the body of this death?" (Rom 7, 24).

Baptism: "sacramento utroque"

Just as in regard to the Eucharist Cyprian separately names the mixed cup one "sacramentum" of the Lord's passio ("sacramento calicis:" Ep 63, 12, 2), and the bread another ("panis unius ... sacramento:" Ep 63, 13, 3-4), so also in baptism does he see two sacramental aspects: the water-bath and the after-bath laying on of the hand (Ep 72, 1, 2):

---

[280] Zel 6: "Radix est malorum omnium, fons cladium, seminarium delictorum, materia culparum. Inde odium surgit, animositas inde procedit." That envy for Cyprian is the fundamental evil follows naturally from his understanding of God as the source of unity in the Church, which in turn is the "sacramentum unitatis." Envy is precisely that disposition by which one looks upon others, along with their possessions, as ultimately alien and separated from oneself. It is the exact opposite to seeing everything existing in and belonging to all in Christ.

Cyprian's description of the bodily effects of envy highlights the radical unity he sees between one's internal disposition and one's outward expression: "Hinc vultus minax, torvus aspectus, pallor in facie, in labiis tremor, stridor in dentibus, verba rabida ..., odio tamen furiatae mentis armata" (Zel 8).

[281] Pat 5: "... similitudo divina quam peccato Adam perdiderat ..."

[282] Op 12: "Quales nunc in ecclesia quosdam videmus, quorum praeclusae aures et corda caecata nullum de spiritalibus ac salutaribus monitis lumen admittunt ..."

"utroque sacramento").[283]

Water is the sacramentum by which one is washed clean of sin in
Christ's loving self-sacrifice (passio) for the Church.[284] The water-
bath is the place where Mother Church, the bride of Christ, gives birth
to her children.[285] By means of the saving water one is given a share

---

[283]J. Ysebaert points out that where Stephen, bishop of Rome,
insisted that those baptized by heretics were truly baptized and needed
only the reconciliation laying on of the hand for full admission to the
Church (Ep 74, 1, 2), Cyprian thought he meant the baptismal laying on
of the hand (Ep 74, 5, 1; Ep 69, 11, 3), including the consignatio (Ep
73, 6, 2). The confusion stems from the fact that in Rome, following
the immersion, the laying on of the hand was part of the anointing.
In North Africa, however, the laying on of the hand took place at the
end of the rite, after the immersion, the anointing, and the vesting,
almost as a post-baptismal event. It is for this reason that Cyprian
could conceive of the laying on of the hand as a separable rite. J.
Ysebaert, "L'Imposition des Mains, Rite de Reconciliation," La Maison-
Dieu 90 (1967), 101-102.
    Although some scholars see in Cyprian's use of "manus" in the
singular a collective plural, signifying the use of two hands, P. van
Beneden opts for the use of one hand. Aux Origines d'une terminologie
sacramentelle: ORDO, ORDINARE, ORDINATIO dans la litterature chretienne
avant 313, Spicilegium Sacrum Lovaniense XXXVIII (Louvain, 1974), p. 111,
n. 116.
[284]Ep 69, 2, 3: "'Christus dilexit ecclesiam et se ipsum
tradidit pro ea, ut eam sanctificaret purgans eam lavacro aquae' (Eph 5,
26-27). ...una est ecclesia quae a Christo diligitur et lavacro eius
sola purgatur..."
[285]Cyprian combines the Song of Songs (4, 12) metaphors for the
beloved as a garden, a sister, a fountain and a well and then applies
them to the Church as the bride of Christ: "Si autem hortus conclusus
est sponsa Christi quae est ecclesia ... Et si fons signatus est ...
Puteus quoque aquae vivae si unus est ..." (Ep 69, 2, 1).
    Un 5: "unum ... caput est et origo una et una Mater fecundi-
tatis successibus copiosa: illius fetu nascimur, illius lacte nutrimur,
spiritu eius animamur." Un 6: "Sponsa Christi ... nos Deo servat, haec
filios regno quos generavit, adsignat. ... Habere non potest Deum patrem
qui Ecclesiam non habet matrem."

in the "grace of Christ,"[286] that is, the Holy Spirit.[287] Through the work of the Spirit conforming the baptized to Christ in his saving events, Christ becomes present again in salvation history.[288] The baptized person, who once lived in the darkness and imprisonment of sin, now lives by the Spirit in the light of Christ.[289] Furthermore, since there is but one baptism in the Church,[290] the Holy Spirit is given initially in baptism to all in equal measure regardless of age, sex, or position in the world,[291] as a sharing in the life of the Trinity.[292]

---

[286]Ep 69, 13, 1: "... salutari aqua et fide legitima Christi gratiam consecutos..." Ep 69, 6, 2: "...aquam baptismi salutarem et gratiam caelestem..."

As noted in Chapter Three, Christ in his saving events is for Cyprian "veritas," the fundamental reality. "gratia Christi," on the other hand, is the participation by the Christian in that reality. Therefore, "gratia" and "veritas" are one and the same: "gratia et veritas una est" (Ep 71, 1, 3).

[287]By apposition Cyprian equates "gratia" with "Spiritus Sanctus:" "...consecuti sunt quidem gratiam dominicam.......imo Spiritus Sanctus non de mensura datur..." (Ep 69, 13, 3; 69, 14, 1). In this text he goes on to compare the sun pouring out equal light on everyone to Christ giving his grace, the Holy Spirit, equally to all. Just as the sun and its light are one, so is Christ one with the Spirit. Yet within that unity is a distinction between the source of the light (sun Christ) and the light that is sent forth (light, Spirit).

[288]Just as the sun puts people by its rays into its own light, so too by the Spirit are the baptized immersed into Christ in his saving deeds (veritas): "dies verus" (Ep 69, 14, 1).

[289]Ep 69, 14, 1: "...quanto magis Christus sol et dies verus in ecclesia sua lumen vitae aeternae pari aequalitate largitur?"

[290]Ep 70, 3, 1: "...baptisma unum sit et Spiritus Sanctus unus et una ecclesia a Christo Domino nostro ... fundata."

[291]Ep 69, 14, 2. Also, Ep 64, 5: "...omnem omnino admittendum esse ad gratiam Christi ..."

[292]Another "sacramentum" to be found in baptism is the triple immersion coupled with the triple profession of faith: "[Matt 28, 18-19] insinuat trinitatem, cuius sacramento gentes tinguerentur" (Ep 73, 5, 2).

In addition to water and the laying on of the hand, Cyprian also
sees the anointing as an essential part of the rite:[293]

> Ungi quoque necesse est eum qui baptizatus
> est, ut accepto chrismate id est unctione esse
> unctus Dei et habere in se gratiam Christi possit
> (Ep 70, 2, 2).
> (It is necessary that he who is baptized also
> be anointed, so that, receiving the chrism, that
> is, the anointing, he is able to be the Anointed
> of God and have the grace of Christ in himself.)

The Christian, therefore, is anointed with the anointing of Christ
("the Anointed of God"). He is given the same mission that was given to
Christ himself in his earthly life, a mission which led to his suffering,
death and resurrection. In other words, the rite of anointing clarifies
that the Christian in baptism is empowered to become a living type of
Christ.

"Induere Christum"

In his study of the liturgical life at Carthage in the time of
Cyprian, V. Saxer sets out the probable ordering of events in the baptismal rite:[294]

---

[293]That Cyprian sees anointing also as a sacramentum is revealed in
his finding it so already in the Old Testament. Jacob's anointing the
stone on which he slept signifies that the stone was Christ: "quem
lapidem consecravit et uncxit sacramento unctionis Christum significans"
(Test II, 16).

[294]Victor Saxer, Vie liturgique et quotidienne à carthage vers le
milieu du IIIe siècle: Le Témoignage de Saint Cyprien et de ses Contemporains d'Afrique, Studi di Antichita Cristiana XXIX (Citta del Vaticano:
Pontificio Istituto di Archeologia Cristians, 1969), pp. 106-144.

1. Blessing of the Water
2. Renunciation of the Devil
3. Triple Immersion with the Triple
     Profession of Faith
4. Anointing
5. Imposition of the Hand with a Prayer
6. Consignation
7. Handing over the Pater Noster
8. Kiss of Peace
9. Eucharist

Cyprian, like Tertullian before him, makes no reference to a possible
rite of vesting the newly baptized. Nevertheless, his writings are
peppered with the verb, "induere," often in the pharse, "induere Christum."
His inspiration for using this word is once again Pauline: "As many of
you who were baptized into Christ have put on (induistis) Christ" (Gal
3, 27).[295] He quotes this passage five times in the course of his writings
(Epp 62, 2, 2: 74, 5, 2; Lap 30; Op 14; Pat 9). The fact that Cyprian
finds Paul's words particularly appropriate in explaining the deeper
meaning of baptism[296] suggests that at Carthage the vesting of the newly
baptized was indeed an explicit part of the ritual. It is already
evident from his letter on the Eucharist (#63) that he is very conscious
of the typological nature of Christian rites. If, therefore, he insists
that in baptism the Christian "puts on Christ," the probability is strong
that he once again is interpreting the typology of a liturgical rite, the
rite of vesting the newly baptized. In fact, in one passage he even uses

---

[295]See also Rom 13, 14: "But put on the Lord Jesus Christ and make
no provision for the flesh, to gratify its desires."

[296]See also Ep 74, 5, 4: "Qui potest apud haereticos baptizatus
Christum induere, multo magis potest Spiritum Sanctum quem Christus
misit accipere."

the phrase, "indumento Christi candido" (the white garment of Christ).[297]

For the ancients, clothing shared in the being of the person who wore it.[298] Thus, the image, "induere Christum," denotes a participation in the person of Christ. Furthermore, for Cyprian the kind of clothes a person wears colors his or her relationship to Christ. To the virgins in the Church he states categorically, "[Those who are] dressed in silk and purple cannot put on Christ.[299] Elsewhere he tells his people that they should not mourn the martyrs "nor wear dark clothing here [on earth], since there [in heaven] they have already taken up white garments."[300] Those who denied the faith during the persecutions he advises to wear only sackcloth, telling them "to desire no other apparel after the vesture of Christ has been lost."[301]

---

[297]Op 14. Sharing possessions, almsgiving, is a participation in the Christ who offered himself for us: "Eme tibi albam vestem, ut qui secundum Adam nudus fueras et horrebas ante deformis, indumento Christi candido vestiaris."

[298]J.J. von Allmen, "Vêtement," in Vocabulaire Biblique (Neuchâtel-Paris: Delachaux et Niestlé, 1956), pp. 303-304, cited in Pierre Gaudette, "Baptême et Vie Chrétienne chez Saint Cyprien de Carthage," Laval Théologique et Philosophique XXVII (1971), 187.

[299]Vir 13: "Sericum et purpuram indutae Christum induere non possunt."

[300]Mort 20: "quotiens revelatum est ... ut publice praedicarem fratres nostros debere non plangi nec accipiendas esse hic atras vestes, quando illi ibi indumenta alba iam sumpserint ..." The use of the Apocalypse 7, 9 imagery of the white-robed Elect strongly suggests that the same rite was in vogue in Cyprian's church. Elsewhere there is evidence that Cyprian was aware of vesting as a rite: his reference to Numbers 20, 25-26 where Aaron puts his stole on Eleazar: "exue Aaron stolam eius et indue Eleazar filium eius" (Ep 67, 4, 1).

[301]Lap 35: "post indumentum Christi perditum, nullum iam velle vestitum."

Cyprian's use of "induere" is more than a delightful borrowing of scriptural imagery. This word is in fact a correlative to "portare" and, as such, fundamental to his theology of salvation history.[302] Alluding to I Corinthians 15, 27-49,[303] Cyprian speaks, not of our putting on Christ, but of his first putting on our humanity. Christ's "putting on human flesh" is thus paralleled to his "carrying our sins:"

> ...quod primum de illa sublimitate caelesti
> ad terrena descendens non aspernatur Dei filius
> carnem hominis induere et cum peccator ipse non
> esset aliena peccata portare (Pat 6).
> (...from the first moment of his descent from
> the sublimity of heaven to earthly things he did
> not disdain, though the Son of God, to put on
> human flesh, and although He himself was not a
> sinner, to bear the sins of others.)

To the holy bishop of Carthage Christ's "putting on human flesh" is no theological abstraction. In his commentary on Acts 9, 40 where Peter raises to life the widow, Tabitha, Cyprian states how fitting it was that the clothes which the widow fashioned be displayed as evidence of her good works, since Christ "himself had been clothed in widows" ("quando esset in viduis ipse vestitus:" Op 6). In his assuming fully our human

---

[302] For the place of "portare" in Cyprian's theology of salvation history, see Chapter III, Section II, above.

[303] "Primus homo e terrae limo, secundus e caelo: qualis ille e limo, tales et qui de limo, qualis caelestis, tales et caelestes. Quomodo portavimus imaginem eius qui de limo est portemus et imaginem eius qui de caelo est" (Quoted in: Test II, 10; Test III, 11; Vir 23; Zel 14). Cyprian's frequent use of the word, "caelestis," can almost certainly be linked to his understanding out of this passage of Christ's redeemed humanity, in which we all participate by baptism. E.g., DO 17: "..in caelo, id est, in nobis... ...ut qui adhuc sunt prima nativitate terreni incipiant esse caelestes ex aqua et spiritu nati." And the bread of the Eucharist which nurture's Christ's humanity in us Cyprian calls "panis caelestis" (Ep 63, 13, 4).

condition, the Lord has "put on" and personally realized in his _passio_ all human suffering, including that of being bereft of the beloved (a husband).[304] Cyprian's reflection that Christ "put on human flesh" is therefore not a statement on the Incarnation as a physical event. It is rather a meditation on the living mystery of Christ in his _passio_, where he "carried us and our sins."

Just as in the case of "_portare_," where Christ's "carrying us" implies in return that we "carry his image," so too Christ's "putting on human flesh" (_induere_) demands that the Christian also "put on Christ." In _De Ecclesiae Catholicae Unitate_, 7, Cyprian argues: Christ wore an undivided tunic, that is, in his _passio_ he inseparably united us to himself. When the soldiers cast lots for his tunic, they did so to determine which of them would "put on Christ" ("_quis Christum potius indueret_"). The seamless robe _is_ Christ, and we, who by our baptism "put on Christ" ("_Christum induimus_"), are actually then "putting on" the unity of the Church ("_unitatis sacramentum_"). Stated simply, to "put on Christ" is to foster and preserve the unity of the Church, the unity of Christians with one another:

---

[304] One could possibly see in the phrase, "_in viduis_," an understanding that Christ during his earthly ministry was ministered to by women who were widows. Part of their ministry would have been to provide him with clothing. Thus "_in viduis_" would mean "by those who were in fact widows also." In that case, Tabitha's preparing clothing for the poor would align her with those who clothed Christ during his lifetime, since indeed the poor are Christ. On the other hand, although "_in viduis vestitus_" may seem a jarring metaphor, "clothed in widows" is in fact the _lectio facilior_. Furthermore, one person's being clothed in another has solid precedent in Cyprian's frequent use of the phrase, "_Christum induere_." Thus, by the metaphor "_in viduis_," Cyprian states that by her good works Tabitha is clothed in Christ, who by his _passio_ was "clothed in widows."

> Nam cum dicat Paulus apostolus: "Quotquot
> in Christo baptizati estis, Christum induistis"
> (Gal 3, 27), in captivis fratribus nostris con-
> templandus est Christus ... (Ep 62, 2, 2).
> (For when Paul the Apostle says: "As many
> as were baptized in Christ have put on Christ,"
> Christ ought to be seen in our brothers in
> prison ...)

Our "putting on Christ" in baptism means that we somehow ontologically

participate in the being of Christ. Cyprian argues further on in this

same passage that those with faith ought to see in anyone baptized the

person of Christ himself -- him to whom they have been united. They

should therefore deliver their brothers from prison: They should free

from prison the Christ "who delivered [them] from the jaws of the devil"

(Ep 62, 2, 2).

"Putting on Christ" in baptism is, however, meaningless if one does

not then follow the example of Christ:

> Christi nomen induere et non per Christi viam
> pergere quid aiud quam praevaricatio est divini
> nominis, quam desertio itineris salutaris? (Zel
> 12).
> (To put on the name of Christ and not continue
> along the way of Christ -- what else is that but a
> prevarication of the divine name, a desertion of
> the saving journey?)

Thus, one's ontological participation in Christ begun in baptism demands

imitation of the deeds of Christ if that identity is not to be a lie and

to cease altogether:

> Quodsi et nos, ... si ipsum induimus, ... qui
> Christum vestigiis salutaribus sequimur, per Christi
> exempla gradiamur ... (Pat 9).
> (But if we too ... have put him on, ... we who
> follow Christ in saving footprints, ought to go for-
> ward according to the examples of Christ.

Our study of "induere" has shown once again the radical identity in Cyprian's theology between the imitation of Christ and the presence of Christ in Christian salvation history: 'As many as are baptized into Christ have "put on Christ" in order to become living types of Christ.'

The Consignation

The last step in the baptismal ceremony is that of the consignation:[305]

> Quod nunc quoque apud nos geritur, ut qui in ecclesia baptizantur praepositis ecclesiae offerantur et per nostram orationem ac manus impositionem Spiritum Sanctum consequentur et signaculo dominico consummentur (Ep 73, 9, 2).
> (What is now also our custom is that those baptized in the Church are brought to the presiders, and by our prayer and imposition of hand they receive the Holy Spirit and with the Lord's sign they are fully christened.)

"The Lord's sign," or as Cyrpian names it elsewhere, "the sign of Christ" (signum Christi),[306] is the rite whereby the presiding minister traces a cross on the candidate's forehead. The Israelites of old were once preserved from death by marking their doorposts with the blood of a lamb, a marking that united them typologically to the death of Christ.

---

[305] Ep 73, 6, 2: "manum imponi ut Spiritum Sanctum consequatur et signetur." Test II, 22: "in hoc signo crucis ... in frontibus notentur." Ep 58, 9, 2: "muniatur frons, ut signum ... servetur."

[306] Dem 22: "renati et signo Christi Signati ... hoc signum qua in parte corporis positum ... super frontes." Dem 26: "Hanc gratiam (immortalitatem) Christum inpertit ... subigendo mortem trophaeo crucis, ... vivificando mortalem regeneratione caelesti. ... huius sacramento et signo censeamur." Once again "sacramentum" is applied to a single element in the overall baptismal rite.

In the same way, explains Cyprian, Christians by their baptismal marking
are preserved from eternal death and are radically oriented to the passio
of Christ.[307]

"Miles Christi" - "Christum Sequi"

That Cyprian, along with Tertullian and most early Christian authors,
was fond of expressing Christian existence in military imagery is well
documented.[308] We have already seen how Tertullian compares the committment of the Christian in baptism to the military oath, the "sacramentum,"
which the recruit made to his commanding general. Cyprian does the
same.[309] Furthermore, his constant interpretation of Christian life is
that it is a battle fought by the Christian to persevere in and be
faithful to what he or she has 'begun to be' by baptism.[310] In this

---

[307]Dem 22: "Quod ante occiso agno praecedit in imagine impletur in
Christo secuta postmodum veritate. Ut illic percussa Aegypto Iudaicus
populus evadere non nisi sanguine et signo agni potuit, ita et cum
vastari coeperit mundus et percuti quisque in sanguine et signo Christi
inventus fuerit solus evadit."

[308]Adolf Harnack, Militia Christi: Die christliche Religion und
der Soldatenstand in den ersten drei Jahrhunderten (Tübingen: J.C.B.
Mohr, 1905), ET: tr. David Mcl. Gracie (Philadelphia: Fortress, 1981);
Josepho Capmany, "Miles Christi" en la Espiritualidad de San Cipriano,
Colectanea San Paciano, serie teológica, I (Barcelone, 1956); Christine
Mohrmann, "Statio," in Etudes sur le latin des Chrétiens, III (Roma:
Edizioni di Storia e Letteratura, 1965), 307-330 = Vigiliae Christianae
VII (1953), 221-245.

[309]Ep 74, 8, 3: "Divinae militiae sacramenta." Also, Ep 10, 2, 3:
"sacramento ac devotione militis eius;" Lap 7; 13.

[310]Don 5: "sis tantum quod esse coepisti." Don 14: "id esse
incipit, quod esse se credit." Vir 22: "ut coepit fortiter, jugiter
perseveret." See Gaudette,"Baptême et Vie Chrétienne," pp. 251-253.

164

battle, Christ is the general (imperator) and the Christian, by
receiving the signum Christi in baptism, is the soldier (miles) who has
been entrusted with the "sign," the standard of Christ. The camp
(castra) is the Church which needs defense against its schismatics
(rebelles) and enemies (hostes), those controlled by the devil:

> Boni militis est adversus rebelles et hostes
> imperatoris sui castra defendere. Gloriosi ducis
> est commissa sibi signa servare (Ep 73, 10, 1).
> (It is the part of the good soldier to defend
> the camp against rebels and enemies of his commander.
> He is entrusted with safeguarding the standards of
> his glorious leader.)

The signs to be defended (signa) include the victorious "trophy of the cross "
by which Christ overcomes death and brings Christians to life in baptism:

> Inmortalitatem ... Christus inpertit ...
> subigendo mortem trophaeo crucis, redimendo
> credentem pretio sui sanguinis, reconciliando
> hominem Deo patri, vivificando mortalem
> regeneratione caelesti. Hunc si fieri potest
> sequamur omnes, huius sacramento et signo cen-
> seamur (Dem 26).
> (Christ bestows immortality by overcoming
> death with the trophy of his cross, by redeeming
> the believer with the price of his blood, by
> reconciling humanity to God the Father, by bring-
> ing the dead to life in the heavenly rebirth. If
> possible, may we all follow him, may we be
> identified with his sacramentum and his sign.)

The sign of the cross received at baptism is therefore meant to characterize the continued existence of the Christian (censeamur),[311] to make him

---

[311]Moses, who expressed bodily the sign of the cross, is presented
as an example of perseverence in Christian life: "Quod exemplum perse-
verandi et permanendi designatur in Exodo, ubi Moyses ad superandum
Amalech qui figuram portabat diaboli in signo et sacramento crucis adlevabat supinas manus, nec vincere adversarium potuit, nisi postquam
stabilis in signo adlevatis jugiter manibus perseveravit" (Fort 8).

a follower of Christ (sequamur).

The following of Christ, as a theme, has been admirably studied

by S. Deléani. In the Introduction to his work he states:

> The importance of the theme of the sequela Christi
> in the history of Christian spirituality suffices
> to justify its study in any given author. Never-
> theless, if we have chosen Cyprian of Carthage, it
> is because in our opinion his work marks a decisive
> turning-point in the interpretation and exploitation
> of the formula Christum (or Dominum) sequi, or of
> synonymous formulas, such as vestigia Christi sequi,
> per vestigia Christi gradi, etc.[312]

Deléani goes on to remark that "Christum sequi," as a metaphor taken

from life,[313] is actually scriptural. Based on a johannine image, that

of following Christ into the kingdom, it is developed in Cyprian to the

point where the following of the Lord is intimately associated with the

notion of resemblance to God or to Christ.[314]

> To follow Christ is notably to imitate his Passion
> by ... the renunciation of possessions or by
> patience. Imitation allows the baptized to
> resemble his model and to identify with him.

---

[312]Simone Deléani, Christum Sequi: Étude d'un thème dans l'oeuvre de Saint Cyprien (Paris: Etudes Augustiniennes, 1979), p. 13.

[313]Ibid., p. 22: "...les Anciens percevaient le langage symbolique comme un moyen d'approcher la divinité, de passer du visible a l'invisible."

[314]Ibid., p. 66. Once again, as in the case of all of Cyprian's great metaphors -- portare, corpus, induere --, it emerges how radically scriptural is Cyprian's language and theological thought. His platonism is merely the glue that holds together a personal appropriation of the Word of God.

> The context of <u>sequi Christum</u> often permits the
> separating out of other values as well, such as
> that of obedience to the commandments and to the
> teachings of the Lord, that of personal attach-
> ment in an exclusive and indefectible way to his
> person, an attachment which is that of a slave
> to his master (<u>dominus</u>), a disciple to his
> teacher (<u>magister</u>), a traveler to his guide, a
> soldier to his general, a friend to a friend,
> that of the renouncing of riches and, more gen-
> erally, of the world and everything earthly.[315]

In a word, "<u>Christum sequi</u>" presupposes <u>imitation</u>, "that one conform one's

conduct to the words and the acts of the Lord,"[316] which ultimately means,

to the <u>passio</u> of Christ.[317]

Deléani records the understanding of imitation which Cyprian's bio-

grapher, Pontius, ascribes to his subject:

> Imitation in the eyes of Cyprian consists, less
> in taking as a rule of life the principle by which
> the person chosen for a model has governed his con-
> duct, than in reproducing as if by blueprint the
> acts of the model. ....
> Being a fervent admirer of Job, "[Cyprian] taught
> that we should do everything that Job once did,
> so as to generate in our regard by identical
> actions a similar approval from God."[318]

---

[315]<u>Ibid.</u>, p. 16.

[316]<u>Ibid.</u>, p. 15.

[317]<u>Ibid.</u>, p. 74: "Pour Cyprian ... suivre le Christ -- et il
n'est jamais question, chez lui, de suivre Dieu le Père --, c'est se
conformer, par chacun de ses gestes ou de ses paroles, à ce qu'a fait
et dit concrètement le Jesus de l'histoire, et notamment à l'acte
essentiel de sa vie terrestre, la Passion." Cyprian's <u>Christum sequi</u>
thus patterns his <u>sacramentum</u>: all reference is to Christ in his historical, saving events. The <u>passio</u> is the prototype (<u>veritas</u>) in
which, by their imitation, all other realities participate.

[318]<u>Ibid.</u>, pp. 99, 100.

In this presentation Deléani seems to accuse Cyprian of the "crude typology" described by de Lubac, where similar exterior circumstances by themselves effect a common interior salvation.[319] However, Deléani himself states elsewhere:

> [Cyprian] recalls with force that, without the intention and without charity, without the continual practice of Christian virtues, martyrdom has no value (Un 14); whereas conversely, the practice of the virtues and it alone confers the crown of the victor (Epp 14, 2, 2; 10, 5, 2; etc.).[320]

It is true that Cyprian has a platonic world-view. The prototype of all reality is found in the saving events of Christ's historical life, so that items found outside the life of Christ exist by imaging that prototype.[321] Nevertheless, Christ's life itself is the realization of a

---

[319]Henri de Lubac, S.J., The Sources of Revelation, tr. Luke O'Neill (New York: Herder and Herder, 1968), pp. 47-48. On this point, see Chapter Two, "Matthaean Exegesis," above, pp. 43-47.

[320]Deléani, Christum Sequi, p. 91.

[321]Alexander Gerken's views on platonic thought in the Greek Fathers applies as well to Cyprian's theology of salvation history: "Das platonische Denken in der Zeit der griechischen Patristik kannte zwei grundlegende Strukturprinzipien: Es war Denken angesichts der Idee, und es was Stufendenken im Sinne einer Heils- und Erlösungslehre ... (p. 65).
"Fast alle griechischen Väter sind ... von diesem Denken affiziert ... Man könnte von ihrem Denken sagen, daß es sich im Verstehenshorizont des Realsymbols bewegte. Mensch und Welt werden gedeutet in einer Weise, daß eine Wirklichkeit Symbol einer anderen, höheren Wirklichkeit ist, aber nicht Symbol bloss in dem Sinne, daß wir eine Ähnlichkeit sehen und eine Beziehung herstellen, sondern Symbol in dem Sinne, daß die höhere Wirklichkeit sich selbst in der niederen ausdrückt, in ihr gegenwärtig ist und durch sie wirkt, wenn auch in einer defizienten, abgeschwächten Weise ... (p. 67).
"Nicht nur Christus selbst, nicht nur der erhöhte Herr, sondern das Erlösungs-geschehen ist für uns erreichbar, so daß wir an ihm teilhaben können. An dieser Stelle erkennen wir, wie das platonische Bilddenken durch seine Anwendung im christlichen Bereich eine Umwandlung erfahren hat. Während Platon die Beziehung Urbild - Abbild zwischen

168

spiritual reality: the inner communitarian life of the Trinity. Therefore, no imago in this world has any value for the bishop of Carthage
outside of its manifesting the interior presence of the veritas.[322] The
imitation of Christ by the Christian consequently must first of all and
throughout it all be an imitation of the interior dispositions which
Christ realized outwardly during his passio. For Cyprian, these are the
dispositions of (1) patience, (2) humility, and (3) obedience.

Patience

A succinct, yet profound, resume of Cyprian's teaching on Christian
patience in De bono patientiae is given by D. Lang-Hinrichsen:

> We who are born to be servants and children of
> God are to imitate the patience of the Father.
> The goal of patience is similarity to God. Sim-
> ilarity to God shines forth in our actions (Ch.
> 5). Because the life of Christ was a life of
> suffering in patience, if Christ is the way of
> our salvation and we have "put on" Christ -- in
> a word, if we are Christians--, then we are so
> only to the degree that we undergo his sufferings
> in the same disposition (Ch. 9). Only by partici-
> pating in his sufferings in patience do we partici-
> pate in Christ. Being patient and heroically
> persevering is the only Way of the following of
> Christ.[323]

321(cont)statischen Wirklichkeiten dachte und für ihn ein eigentlich
geschichtliches Denken nicht vollziehbar war, wird die Beziehung Urbild -
Abbild von den greichischen Vätern auf Ereignisee, auf Vorgänge angewandt"
(p. 70). Theologie der Eucharistie (Munchen: Kosel-Verlag, 1973).
    322Ep 73, 2, 3: "Vanum prorsus et stultum est, ut quia Novatianus
extra ecclesiam vindicat sibi veritatis imaginem, relinquat ecclesiā
veritatem."
    323Dietrich Lang-Hinrichsen, "Die Lehre von der Geduld in der
Patristik und bei Thomas von Aquin," Geist und Leben XXIV (1951), 221.

Lang-Hinrichsen states further that for Cyprian the virtue of Christian patience is an "ontological reality:" it is existence in Christ (das Sein in Christus). It is so vital for the Christian precisely because, as seen in the life of Christ, his sufferings are the only path to life with the Father (Pat 20). Patience does not tell us what we are to do or not do. Rather, it is that inner attitude of Christ toward suffering characterizing all the Old Testament types: Abel, Abraham, Isaac, Jacob, Joseph, Moses, David (Pat 10), and especially Job (Pat 18), and which allows us to bear sufferings without being broken by them and to praise God even in the midst of them (Pat 18).[324]

By characterizing it as patience, patientia, Cyprian actually points out that the roots of Christian life are in the passio (pati) of Christ.[325] Chapter One of this study argued that Christ is the fulfillment and savior of human history only because he wills it so, only because it is his intention. In Chapter Three we found that Cyprian includes within the saving passio the event in which Christ expressed his inner intention of self-sacrifice: the Last Supper. In his treatise on patience Cyprian again stresses the inner dispositions of Christ and reasons that the Christian partakes in the same sufferings which Christ went through

---

[324]Ibid., pp. 221, 222.

[325]Fort 5: "... post omnes iniurias et contumelias [Christus] passus quoque et crucifixus [est], ut nos pati et mori exemplo suo doceret, ut nulla sit homini excusatio pro se non patienti, cum passus sit ille pro nobis, et cum ille passus sit pro alienis peccatis, multo magis pro peccatis suis pati unumquemque debere." Deléani concludes: "il semble bien que Cyprien conçoive la vie chrétienne, le comportement de celui qui a donné son adhésion au Christ, comme un cheminement douloureux à la suite du Maître souffrant." Christum Sequi, p. 87.

(passio) only if he or she possesses interiorly the same mind "that was in Christ Jesus" (Phil 2, 5). Consequently, the true imitation of Christ is found only in the living out of the same inner dispositions that led him to sacrifice himself for the Church. Nevertheless, Cyprian as a platonist is also convinced that, on the one hand, identical dispositions will express themselves in similar outward actions; on the other, actions imitating the actions of Christ will deepen those dispositions within and will realize outwardly Christ's presence again in salvation history. The Christian will become a living type of Christ.

Obedience and Humility

Cyprian looks upon Christ as the teacher of all the virtues of Christian life:

> Voluntas autem Dei est quam Christus et fecit
> et docuit. Humilitas in conversatione, stabilitas
> in fide, verecundia in verbis, in factis iustitia,
> in operibus misericordia, in moribus disciplina,
> iniuriam facere non nosse et factam posse tolerare,
> cum fratribus pacem tenere, Dominum toto corde
> diligere, amare in illo quod pater est, timere quod
> Deus est, Christo nihil omnino praeponere, quia nec
> nobis quicquam ille praeposuit, caritati eius inse-
> parabiliter adhaerere, cruci eius fortiter ac fidenter
> adsistere, quando de eius nomine et honore certamen
> est, exhibere in sermone constantiam quo confitemur,
> in questione fiduciam qua congredimur, in morte
> patientiam qua coronamur: hoc est coheredem Christi
> velle esse, hoc est praeceptum Dei facere, hoc est
> voluntatem patris inplere (DO 15).
> (The will of God is in fact what Christ did and
> taught. To have humility in conversation, stability
> in faith, reverence in words, justice in deeds, mercy
> in one's actions, discipline in behavior, to be inno-
> cent of wrongdoing and to suffer it in oneself, to
> live in peace with the brethren, to love the Lord with
> one's whole heart, to love what is the Father in him,
> to fear what is God, to exalt nothing above Christ

since he preferred nothing over us, to cling
inseparably to his love, to stand by his cross
bravely and faithfully when there is a struggle
involving his name and his honor, to profess in
our speech the constancy of our faith, in doubt
the source of our trust, and in death the patience
that wins us the crown. Herein lies the will to
be an heir with Christ, the doing of God's law,
and the fulfilling the Father's will.)

Here we find that the life of Christ can be summed up in one sentence:

"Voluntas autem Dei est quam Christus fecit et docuit." Since Christ's

fundamental relationship, the relationship to his Father, is essentially

one of obedience, all other virtues in his life are expressions of his

obedience, but especially so his humility:[326]

in ipsa militia primus ambulaverit Dominus,
humilitatis et tolerantiae et passionis magister
(Ep 58, 3, 1).
(The Lord is the first to march in that army,
the teacher of humility and of forebearance and of
the passio.)

As the teacher of humility,[327] Christ is the total adversary of the

devil and those who, by causing disunity, are his minions. Novation,

therefore, is seen as the "teacher of pride" (doctor superbiae: Ep 60,

3).

Although Cyprian does not directly quote the passage in order to

highlight Christ's humility,[328] he nevertheless seems to have Matthew

---

[326]See Josepho Capmany, "Miles Christi" en la Espiritualidad de San
Cipriano (Barcelone, 1956), pp. 167-185; 221-235.

[327]Ep 59, 3, 2: "humilitatem docet."

[328]Cyprian quotes Mt 11, 29 in Test I, 13 and Test III, 119. As
Fahey notes, Cyprian's interest in these citings is the yoke of Christ,
rather than the humility of Christ. Michael Fahey, S.J., Cyprian and the
Bible: A Study in Third-Century Exegesis (Tübingen: J.C.B. Mohr, 1971),
p. 302.

11, 29 in mind in his reflections on Christ's humility: "Learn from me, for I am meek and humble of heart." Cyprian accordingly exhorts the virgins to be "mites" and "humiles," since in their virginity they image Christ himself, "hanc imaginem virginitas portat."[329] Abel, as an Old Testament type of Christ, prefigured the passio of Christ in his meekness and humility:

> Sic Abel originem martyrii et passionem iusti initians primus et dedicans adversus fratrem parricidam non resistit nec reluctatur, sed humilis et mitis patienter occiditur (Pat 10).
>
> (Thus Abel, as the first to inaugurate the origin of martyrdom and to offer up the passio of the Just One, did not resist his fratricidal brother or struggle against him, but in humility and meekness patiently allowed himself to be killed.)

Consequently, the ultimate motive for Christian humility is found in its being an imitation of Christ in his passio: "Imitentur Dominum qui sub ipso tempore passionis non superbior sed humilior fuit" (Let them imitate the Lord who, at the time of his passio, did not become more proud, but rather more humble).[330]

Humility, together with its basis in obedience, therefore, make up the essence of the imitation of Christ.[331] By living in humble obedience

---

328(cont)Cyprian also alludes to Phil 2, 8: "Humiliavit se ut populum qui prius iacebat erigeret" (Op 1). Here the salvific nature of Christ's humility and its roots in the passio are stressed.

[329]Vir 23.

[330]Ep 14, 2, 3. Deléani concludes that, in general, imitation for Cyprian always refers to the passio of Christ. Christum Sequi, p. 86, n. 394.

[331]Deléani, Christum Sequi, p. 86: "'Le Christ a souffert pour vous, vous laissant un example, pour que vous suiviez ses traces' (Zel 11), et en terminant son développement par cette citation, il établit implicitement une relation entre la Passion du Christ et l'obéissance aux préceptes divins" [emph. mine].

to the will of God as Christ did, the Christian lives as a veritable
type _of_ _Christ_.

Disciplina

Humility and Obedience are not conceived of by Cyprian as private
virtues, marking off individual Christians from one another. Rather, they
appear in individual lives as expressions of the very nature of the Church.
For there to be unity in the Church -- its very nature, there must be
order. However, order is impossible without obedience:

> Paenitentiam autem ille agit qui divini
> praecepti memor mitis et patiens et sacerdotibus
> Dei obtemperans obsequiis suis et operibus iustis
> Dominum promeretur (Ep 19, 1, 1).
> (Indeed that person does penance [becoming
> reconciled to the Church] who, conscious of the
> divine precept, with meekness and patience obeys
> the priests of God, and thereby becomes deserving
> before the Lord by obedient and holy deeds.)

The name that Cyprian attaches to this overall order in the Church,
a name that he inherits from Tertullian[332] and from Roman culture, is
"disciplina." This word includes in its meaning much more than our

---

[332]On "Disciplina" according to Tertullian, see H.-I. Marrou, "'Doctrina' et 'disciplina' dans la langue des Pères de l'Eglise," Archivum Latinitatis Medii Aevi (Bulletin Du Cange) IX (1934), 5-25; Valentin Morel, "Le développement de la 'discipline' sous l'action du Saint-Esprit chez Tertullien," Revue d'Histoire Ecclésiastique XXXV (1939), 243-265; Rene Braun, Deus Christianorum: Récherches sur le vocabulaire doctrinal de Tertullien, Publications de la Faculté des Lettres et Sciences Humaines d'Alger XLI (Paris: Presses Universitaires de France, 1962), 423-425; Dimitri Michaélidès, Sacramentum chez Tertullien (Paris: Etudes Augustiniennes, 1970), p. 338; Jean Daniélou, S.J., The Origins of Latin Christianity (Philadelphia: Westminster, 1977), p. 430.

174

contemporary notion of "Church discipline." S. Hübner, in his
excellent analysis, points out that the bishop of Carthage grounds his
understanding of "disciplina" on its use in Scripture.[333] Hübner outlines
Cyprian's concept of "disciplina" as follows:

(1) Cyprian's "disciplina" in the wide sense signifies Christian
teaching as a whole, that is, everything that Christ taught. Accordingly,
he parallels "disciplina" to "doctrina" and "traditio" (Test III, 66, 67,
68).

(2) "Disciplina" is its narrower, more proper meaning denotes
Christian life lived according to Christian teaching. Consequently it
includes (a) the order found in Church structure (Epp 17, 3; 59, 6),
(b) the orders of baptism (Ep 74, 4), Eucharist (Ep 63, 15), and reconciliation (Epp 16, 2; 19, 1; 20, 2).

(3) "Disciplina" has God as its origin (Test III, 66).[334] It is
therefore the "disciplina Dei" (Vir 23), "caelestis" (DO 28; Pat 1),
"deifica" (Zel 15; Pat 1), "religiosa" (Ep 75, 10). Christ is its teacher,
"disciplinae magister" (Ep 11, 5, 1).

(4) This "disciplina ecclesiastica" (Ep 43, 3) comes to the Church
from God substantially as passed on through the Apostles ("disciplina
antiqua:" Ep 30, 2) and as expressed in the Scriptures (Lap 5; Ep 14,

---

[333]Siegfried Hübner, "Kirchenbuße und Exkommunikation bei Cyprian,"
Zeitschrift für katholische Theologie LXXXIV (1962), 58-60. Test III, 66:
Jer 3, 15; Prov 3, 11f.; Ps 2, 12; etc.
[334]"disciplina Dei in eccelsiasticis praeceptis observanda."

2).[335] Because they embody the Church's disciplina, the Scriptures are
normative and are variously named: "lex evangelica," "Christi praecepta"
(Ep 59),"Domini mandata" (Ep 43, 2), etc.

(5) "Disciplina" defined in the foregoing fashion is necessary for
salvation (Ep 13, 2),[336] so that those without disciplina (indisciplinati)
are also without the grace of Christ and consequently headed for destruc-
tion (Id 10; Ep 4, 4).

Disciplina: The Church as Liturgical Assembly

Hübner's analysis of "disciplina" in Cyprian's writings demonstrates
its centrality within his theology. Our previous study gives us the
reasons for this: The goal of Christ in his passio, according to Cyprian,
is the unity of the Church in himself. Therefore, those dispositions by
which a Christian "follows" and "imitates" Christ (patience, humility,
obedience) must at the same time be the virtues which most give unity to
the Church. Furthermore, Christ's saving deeds bring salvation to humankind only because they are the expressions of his inner patience,
humility and obedience to God and of his "inseparable love" for his Church.
In the same way, then, the unity of the Church must consist in more than
external order and efficient management. "Disciplina" is essential to the

---

[335]Lap 5: "disciplina nobis divinitus tradita." Ep 14, 2: "secundum
scripturarum magisterium ecclesiastica disciplina."

[336]Ep 13, 2: "recedente ab his disciplina dominica recessit et
gratia."

For a list of the occurrences of "disciplina" in Cyprian's
writings, see Gaudette, "Baptême et Vie Chrétienne," p. 260, n. 74.

Church only insofar as it engenders and deepens within the community the saving dispositions of Christ. As such, "disciplina" signifies the Church itself in its outward configuration to the life of Christ: that by which the Church lives as a type, a "sacramentum" (unitatis) of Christ. By forming it as a sacramentum, disciplina reveals within the Church the presence of Christ as the true source of its unanimity, its common love, its concord and peace:

> Pacificos enim et concordes adque unanimes
> esse in domo sua Deus praecepit et quales nos fecit
> secunda nativitate tales vult renatos perseverare,
> ut qui filii Dei sumus in Dei pace maneamus, ut
> quibus spiritus unus est unus sit et animus et
> sensus. Sic nec sacrificium Deus recipit dissidentis
> et ab altari revertentem prius fratri reconciliari
> iubet, ut pacificis precibus et Deus possit esse
> pacatus. Sacrificium Deo maius est pax nostra et
> fraterna concordia et de unitate Patris et Filii et
> Spiritus sancti plebs adunata (DO 23).
>
> (God indeed ordained that people of peace and
> of one heart and mind should reside in His house, and
> this is how He made us by the "second birth," and
> this is how He wishes those reborn to continue to
> be, in order that we who are the offspring of God
> might remain in the peace of God, and we whose spirit
> is one might also have one mind and one common feel-
> ing. For that matter, neither does God accept the
> sacrifice of a dissenter, but rather demands that he
> turn away from the altar first to be reconciled to his
> fellow, so that with prayers prayed in peace, peace
> might also be made with God. A greater sacrifice to
> God is our mutual peace and fraternal concord and our
> being a people united by the unity of the Father and
> the Son and the Holy Spirit.)

This passage, by alluding to Mt. 5, 23-24, also hints at the relation-ship in the Church of liturgy to Christian living. It has already been noted that, according to Cyprian, in the Eucharist the Church imitates the actions of Christ at the Last Supper. In the liturgy of offering and com-municating in his bread and mixed cup, the Church proclaims the identity

of its lived existence in Christ as that of being his "Body." In the
passage quoted from De dominica oratione 23 above, Cyprian alludes to the
command of the Lord that the liturgy which Christians perform ritually
coincide with their actions and attitudes during the rest of their lives.
The Lord himself in Mt 5, 23-24 allows that coming to the altar is what
makes the Church realize the true inner meaning of the rest of its
existence, and which sends it forth in urgency to live more fully that
meaning in the world at large.

All human existence is symbolic for Cyprian and capable of manifesting Christ in his saving events. However, for the believing Church,
in the Eucharist Christ reaches across history to act in its midst. That
is to say, Christ, who in his passio commanded that the Eucharist be done
in memory of him, expressly continues the action of his passio through the
gathering[337] and action of the Church. Thus, in the actions of its
liturgy the Church already exists in the full realization to which the
rest of its life points. By its being involved in the very action in
which Christ irrevocably united himself in his humanity to the Church,
the Church is in fact already involved in the goal of all creation; the
eschatological union of all in Christ.[338]

Since the actions of the liturgy are structured by Christ precisely
in order to express and deepen the unity of the Church, the liturgy is the

---

[337]Ep 63, 16, 1: "sacramenti veritatem fraternitate omni praesenti."
See also, Bruno Renaud, "L'Eglise comme assemblée liturgique selon saint
Cyprien," Recherches de Theologie ancienne et médiévale XXXVIII (1971),
5-68.

[338]Dem 25; "Hic vita aut amittitur aut tenetur: hic saluti
aeternae cultu Dei et fructu fidei providetur."

most intense form of its "disciplina." The liturgy is that which orders
the Church most profoundly by establishing it in its deepest mystery:
that of being the "Body" of Christ.[339]

Summary

According to Cyprian the world is sacramental and oriented to Christ.
However, as tainted by human sin, it also shares in the mortality of
Adam and is under the devil's control. By renunciation of the devil and
incorporation into Christ, the heavenly one ("caelestis"), the Christian
is reborn in the baptismal water of "Mother Church." Besides the sacramentum of water, there are other sacramenta or types at work in the
initiation rite which illustrate and inaugurate Christian life.

The triple immersion and confession of faith reveal that the Church
is a sharing in the unity of Trinitarian life. The anointing teaches and
commits the baptismal candidate to a sharing in the mission of Christ
himself. The rite of investing (?) asserts that baptism inaugurates a
personal participation in Christ in his passio. The laying on of the
hand recognizes and helps confer this life in Christ as a sharing in his
Spirit. The signing with the cross emphasizes and marks the Christian
as one who begins an inner imitation of Christ in patience, obedience and
humility, and an outer participation in the very same sufferings which

---

[339]Walter Simonis, Ecclesia Visibilis et Invisibilis (Frankfurt:
Josef Knecht, 1970), p. 12: "Sakrament für [Cyprian] nur eine konkrete
Weise der Verwirklichung der Kirchlichen disciplina war." Also, Adrien
Demoustier, S.J., "L'Ontologie de l'Église selon Saint Cyprien,"
Recherches de Science Religieuse III (1964), 587: "[L'Église] est
l'unique assemblée eucharistique qui réalise, en l'assemblée sociologique,
l'unité trinitaire."

Christ accepted for human salvation.

In a word, the rite of baptism proclaims that the new Christian, by his or her initiation into the Church, begins the life of a type of Christ. By living in a unity of love and self-sacrifice with other Christians in the Church, the baptized "carries" the other members of the Church, thereby expressing and making present in his or her human existence the Christ who in his passio carried us all and our sins in himself.

II. The Martyr

The Martyr as "Sacramentum" of Christ

That martyrdom plays a fundamental role in the thought of Cyprian of Carthage is well known.[340] Indeed, little else could be expected of a bishop entrusted with a church in constant threat to its existence. In such conditions, all of Christian life is naturally measured against the ultimate vocation of martyrdom.[341]

As we have seen, Christian life in general is a life in imitation of the passio of Christ. This holds true in a preeminent way for martyrdom. As a martyr, a Christian follows Christ through the culmination of his

---

[340]See especially E.L. Hummel, The Concept of Martyrdom According to St. Cyprian of Carthage (Washington: The Catholic University of America Press, 1946); Marc Lods, Confesseurs et martyrs, Cahiers Théologiques XLI (Neuchâtel-Paris: Delachaux et Niestlé, 1958); Michele Pellegrino, "Eucaristia e Martirio in San Cipriano," pp. 135-150, in Convivium Domini-cum (Catania: Centro di Studi Sull'Antico Cristianesimo, 1959); _____ _____, "Le Sens Ecclesial du Martyre," Revue des Sciences Religieuses XXXV (1961), 151-175; H.A.M. Hoppenbrouwers, Recherches sur la terminologie du martyre de Tertullien à Lactance, Latinitas Christian-orum Primaeva XV (Nijmegen: Dekker & van de Vegt, 1961).

[341]Simone Deléani states in Christum Sequi (Paris: Études Augustiniennes, 1979), "pour Cyprien, c'est la vie chrétienne dans son ensemble qui est martyre" (p. 89). Pierre Gaudette in "Baptême et Vie Chrétienne chez Saint Cyprien de Carthage," Laval Théologique et Philoso-phique XXVII (1971) adds: "Or il est facile de voir que toute la théologie du martyre exprimée dans les écrits de saint Cyprien est enracinée dans sa théologie du baptême" (p. 263). For Cyprian, martyrdom is a vocation. It is God's power acting through the martyr, not something one can presume to have on one's own. Therefore, no one should rashly offer him- or herself for martyrdom (Ep 81, 1, 4).

passio, his death: "_nos_ _pati_ _et_ _mori_ _exemplo_ _suo_ _doceret_" (He taught us by his example to suffer and die).[342] Similarly, just as living the virtues of Christ daily (patience, humility, obedience, etc.) is participation in Christ suffering,[343] by his death the martyr identifies fully with Christ: "_Qui_ _pro_ _nobis_ _mortem_ _semel_ _vicit_ _semper_ _vincit_ _in_ _nobis_" (He who once conquered death for us is always conquering it in us).[344]

Martyrdom, then, is Christian living to its fullest. With this understanding, Cyprian can argue that just as ordinary Christian life is life according to the _disciplina_ of the Church, those imprisoned and empowered by Christ to undergo a martyr's death ought by that very fact to be outstanding in exhibiting Christ's virtues in the _disciplina_ of ordinary Christian living:

---

[342]Fort 5.

[343]DO 20: "Eum dicit posse se sequi et _gloriam_ _dominicae_ _passionis_ _imitari_ qui expeditus et succinctus nullis laqueis rei familiaris involvitur, sed solutus ac liber facultates suas ad Dominum ante praemissas ipse quoque comitatur."

[344]Ep 10, 3. Also Ep 10, 4: "ipse luctatur _in_ _nobis_ ... et coronat pariter et coronatur." That Christ is present in the martyr is a long-standing Christian tradition. Tertullian: "Christus in martyre est, ut moechos et fornicatores martyr absolvat ..." (_De_ _Pudicitia_ 22): _Passio_ _Sanctorum_ _Perpetuae_ _et_ _Felicitatis_ 15, 6: "Modo ego patior; illic (in martyrdom) autem alius (Christ) _erit_ _in_ _me_ qui patietur pro me, quia ego pro illo passura sum." See M. Lods, _Confesseurs_ _et_ _martyrs_, pp. 24-27.

The exact meanings of "_martyr_" and "_confessor_" in Cyprian's writings are disputed. In general, "_martyr_" is applied to one who has died or is imprisoned to die for the faith. "Confessor" is one who professed the faith before pagan authorities and/or suffered punishment for the faith. See E.L. Hummel, _The_ _Concept_ _of_ _Martyrdom_, pp. 5-20; H.A.M. Hoppenbrouwers, _Recherches_, pp. 91-105.

> Hoc est esse confessorem Domini, hoc est esse
> martyrem Christi: servare vocis suae inviolatam
> circa omnia et solidam firmitatem, nec per Dominum
> martyrem fieri et praecepta Domini destruere conari.
> Uti adversus illum dignatione quam tibi dederit,
> armis ab illo acceptis rebellem quodammodo fieri,
> hoc est Christum confiteri velle et evangelium
> Christi negare (Ep 28, 2, 3).
> (This is what being a confessor of the Lord is,
> what being a martyr of Christ is: protecting the
> solidity of his voice unblemished and unbroken in
> all circumstances. It means not becoming a martyr
> by the Lord's power only then to try to destroy the
> precepts of the Lord. To use against him the dig-
> nity which he has given you, to somehow become a
> rebel with the very weapons received from him: this
> is wanting to confess Christ at the same time as
> denying the Gospel of Christ.)

Extending the comparison between martyrdom and ordinary Christian
life further: Just as Christian life is entered into by baptism, Cyprian
cites Christ's naming his _passio_ a "baptism" to show that in martyrdom
one is truly baptised. Martyrdom is true baptism into Christ because, by
their suffering the _passio_ of Christ, the martyrs' blood is actually the
blood of Christ:

> ... illos ... nec privari baptismi sacramento,
> utpote qui baptizentur gloriosissimo et maximo
> sanguinis baptismo, de quo et Dominus dicebat
> "habere se aliud baptisma baptizari" (Lk 12, 50).
> Sanguine autem suo baptizatos et passione sancti-
> ficatos consummari ... declarat in evangelio idem
> Dominus ... (Ep 73, 22).
> (Neither are those deprived of the sacramentum
> of baptism who in fact are baptized in the most
> glorious and greatest baptism of blood, about which
> the Lord said that "he has another baptism to under-
> go." The same Lord declares in the Gospel that those
> are made complete who are baptized in his blood and
> sanctified by his _passio_.)

The baptism of martyrdom is initiation into the fulness of life (_consummari_)

toward which ordinary water-baptism is directed: the glory of heaven.[345]
Most importantly, we can also conclude from this passage that, by becoming
so identified with Christ in his _passio_ through the shedding of blood, the
martyr has become for Cyprian a personal "_sacramentum_" of Christ.

The Martyr as Ecclesial Person

The figure of the martyr for Cyprian is not the one of the modern
hero, facing overwhelming odds alone and coming out victorious by calling
upon the ultimate energies of his own personality. The martyr is not a
witness to his own heroism. He is rather a witness to the glory of
Christ:

> cuius est spes et fides et virtus et gloria
> omnis in Christo est (Lap 20).
> (All of his or her hope and faith and strength
> and glory is in Christ.)

Martyrdom expresses the inner nature of the Church as that community which
is bound together by the victorious love of Christ (_inseparabili_ _caritate_).
a love victorious even over death. Therefore, the martyr is one who
chooses death rather than deny Christ's love within the Church binding
members to one another: "_in persecutione fratres a fratribus non_
separari" (brothers not being separated from brothers even in persecution:

345
 Ep 31, 2: "Vidimus gloriosos illos martyrum triumphos ... et inter
angelos ac potestates dominationesque caelestes constitutos ..." Dem 26:
"Erimus christiani cum Christo simul gloriosi, de Deo patre beati, de
perpetua voluptate laetantes semper in conspectu Dei et agentes Deo gratias
semper."

Ep 60, 2, 1).[346] This complete act of love by the martyr for the Church
witnesses both to the truth of the Church's faith and to the inner
victorious love of Christ at work within its fellowship. Above all,
then, the martyr is an ecclesial reality, so much so that his or her
glory is actually the glory of the Church: "in quibus mater ecclesia
gloriatur" (Ep 10, 1, 1). Cyprian therefore sees his own martyrdom as
an honor to an already glorious church: "honor ecclesiae nostrae tam
gloriosae" (Ep 81, 1, 2).

The Martyr and the Eucharist

Because the martyr expresses the nature and holiness of the
Church, it is the Church itself which must empower its members to face
martyrdom. It does this primarily by means of the Eucharist:

> Gravior nunc et ferocior pugna imminet, ad quam
> fide incorrupta et virtute robusta parare se debeant
> milites Christi, considerantes idcirco se cotidie
> calicem sanguinis Christi bibere ut possint et ipsi
> propter Christum sanguinem fundere (Ep 58, 1, 2).
> (Now a more serious and ferocious battle
> threatens, for which the soldiers of Christ ought
> to prepare themselves with uncorrupted faith and
> sturdy virtue, understanding to that end that they
> ought to drink the chalice of the blood of Christ so
> as to be able themselves to shed blood for the sake
> of Christ.)[347]

---

[346]See also Ep 76, 6, 2: "connexa vobis vinculo fortissime caritatis ... nec carcere nec metallis separata." Ep 37, 1: "Honori nos
vestro caritas vestra individua connectit, separari dilectionem spiritus
non sinit." Un 14: "esse martyr non potest qui in ecclesia non est."

[347]See also Ep 57, 2, 2: "Aut quomodo ad martyrii poculum idoneos
facimus, si non eos prius ad bibendum in ecclesia poculum Domini iure com-
municationis admittimus?"
  Cyprian's emphasis on the sign-value of the Eucharist is so strong
that he claims Christians will become ashamed of Christ's blood and not be
willing then to shed their own if at their Eucharists they offer water

Just as Abel was found worthy[348] to "bear the image of Christ" in his death because of his pious offering at the altar,[349] so also are the martyrs made into types of Christ by their liturgical union with him. Those who lead the Eucharist in the Church are thus preparing Christians by ritual to be sacrificial victims with Christ in the fullest degree: "<u>sacerdotes</u> <u>qui</u> <u>sacrificia</u> <u>Dei</u> <u>cotidie</u> <u>celebramus</u> <u>hostias</u> <u>Deo</u> <u>et</u> <u>victimas</u> <u>preparemus</u>" (We priests who celebrate the sacrifices of God daily are preparing offerings and victims for God: Ep 57, 3). That martyrs are seen as types of Christ in his sacrifice emerges from Cyprian's explication of one <u>sacramentum</u> found in their ordeal: When they are beaten by wooden clubs by their captors, they are to see in that wood the wood of the cross of Christ.

> Neque enim ad fustes christianum corpus
> expavit, cuius spes omnis in ligno. Sacramentum
> salutis suae Christi servus agnovit, redemptus
> ligno ad vitam aeternam ligno provectus est ad
> coronam (Ep 76, 2, 1).
> (For neither is the Christian body terrified in
> the face of clubs, since all of its hope is found
> in wood. The servant of Christ recognizes the
> <u>sacramentum</u> of his salvation: redeemed by wood for
> life everlasting, he is propelled by wood to the
> crown.)

347(cont)instead of wine, since wine alone signifies the blood of Christ (Ep 63, 15).

Simone Deléani in <u>Christum</u> <u>Sequi</u> (Paris: Études Augustiniennes, 1979) states, "le martyre est conçu par Cyprien comme un acte de vie ecclésiale. Il est participation au sacrifice eucharistique" (p. 92).

348DO 23: "Merito ille dum in sacrificio Dei talis est, ipse postmodum sacrificium Deo factus est, ut martyrium primus ostendens initiaret sanguinis sui gloria dominicam passionem ..."

349Pat 10: "qui figuram Christi imagine praeeunte portabant ... Sic Abel ..."

In other words, for Cyprian, in the suffering and death of the martyr the actual suffering and death of Christ is taking place. By virtue of the typological nature of history there can be no question for the bishop of Carthage or, indeed, for the martyrs themselves, that the wood of the clubs is in fact the wood of the cross. This and this alone is sufficient to assure the martyr that that same wood will 'ferry him forth' (provectus) to the victory of Christ.

That the martyrs, like Abel, image in their sufferings and death the ritual sacrifice of the liturgy is also a teaching of Cyprian. When certain incarcerated bishops and presbyters express their concern to Cyprian that they are not able now to offer the Eucharist, Cyprian reassures them that in their sufferings they are living their sacrifice to God, an offering just as pleasing and effective as the Eucharist itself:

> Celebratis immo atque offertis sacrificium Deo
> et pretiosum pariter et gloriosum et plurimum vobis
> ad retributionem praemiorum caelestium profuturum,
> cum scriptura divina loquatur et dicat: 'sacrificium
> Deo spiritus contribulatus, cor contritum et humilia-
> tum Deus non despicit' Ps 50, 10. Hoc vos sacrificium
> Deo offertis, hoc sacrificium sine intermissione die
> ac nocte celebratis, hostiae facti Deo et vosmet ipsos
> sanctas atque immaculatas victimas exhibentes (Ep 76,
> 3).
> (You indeed celebrate and offer a sacrifice to
> God equally precious and glorious and filled for you
> with the returns of future heavenly rewards since divine
> Scripture speaks and says, "A burdened spirit is a
> sacrifice to God, a contrite and humbled heart God does
> not spurn." You offer this sacrifice to God, you cele-
> brate this sacrifice ceaselessly day and night. Made
> into sacrificial offerings to God, you show yourselves
> to be holy and immaculate victims.)[350]

---

[350]Michele Pellegrino in "Eucaristia e Martirio in San Cipriano," in Convivium Dominicum (Catania: Centro di Studi Sull'Antico Cristianesimo, 1959) finds the basis for Cyprian's equating the offering of one's life

188

For Cyprian, then, martyrdom is the full living out of the Eucharistic sacrifice.

Because the blood shed by the martyr is none other than the blood of Christ, and because the wood used to beat the martyr is the wood of the cross, the sacrifice of the martyr is in fact the sacrifice of Christ. It is therefore the same sacrifice as that of the Eucharist: "hostias Deo et victimas preparemus" (Ep 57, 3). At the Eucharist the Church in each of its members offers itself in an intense typological fashion, as part of its overall typological presentation of Christ's passio in the daily sufferings of its life in the world, and especially in the ultimate sacrifice of martyrdom: "passio est enim Domini sacrificium quod offerimus" (Ep 63, 17, 1).

The Martyr's "Gloria" as "Veritas"

Throughout his interpretation of martyrdom Cyprian continually characterizes it as something "glorious." His inspiration for doing so comes from St. Paul:

> Rom 5, 2: "Gloriamur in pressuris" (Test III, 6; Fort 9).
> (We glory in our sufferings.)

> Gal 6, 14: "mihi autem absit gloriari nisi in cruce Domini nostri Iesu Christi, per quem mihi mundus crucifixus est et ego mundo" (Test III, 11; Vir 6).
> (But far be it from me to glory except in the cross of our Lord Jesus Christ, through whom the world is crucified to me and I to the world.)

350(cont)with the ritual offering in the martyr-bishop's reference to II Tim 4, 6: "Item suum certamen ostendens et hostiam se Domino cito futurum esse promittens ait, 'ego iam libor, et tempus instant assumptionis'" (Ep 10, 4). p. 147.

Cyprian's use of "gloriari," based on these texts, is a revolutionary one.
Whereas those under the influence of the devil "boast about" and "take
pride in" their worldly achievements or adornments (Vir 5),[351] Christians
are to "glory" rather in their weakness and sufferings because those very
sufferings are their participation in the passio of Christ:

> Quid enim gloriosius ... quam collegam passionis
> cum Christo in Christi nomine factum fuisse (Ep 31, 3)?
> (For what is more glorious than to be made a
> companion of the passio with Christ in the name of
> Christ?)
> Maior est qui est in nobis quam qui est in hoc
> mundo (Ep 10, 1).
> (He is greater who dwells in us than he who dwells
> in this world.)

The motive for "glorying" in the sufferings of Christ is based on something more for Cyprian than the sheer overturning of the world's expectations.
There exists in the passio an objective glory. In Christ's saving deeds God
himself shines through -- the Ultimate Reality, Truth itself:

> 'Multi, inquit venient in nomine meo ...' (Mk 13,
> 6). Unde apparet non ea statim suscipienda et adsumenda
> quae iactantur in Christi nomine, sed quae geruntur in
> Christi veritate (Ep 73, 16, 2).
> ('Many, he says, will come in my name ...' Hence
> it is evident that things which are boasted as being in
> Christ's name are not to be immediately taken up and
> absorbed, but rather only those things which are performed
> in the reality of Christ.)

---

[351]See Dennis E. Groh, "Tertullian's Polemic Against Social Co-optation," Church History XL (1971), 7-14: For Tertulliam, "the very essence
of gloria ... is the direct opposite of the Christian virtue of humilitas"
(p. 11). "Ambitio and gloria are passions -- categories of concupiscentia"
(p. 12).
  In the same vein, Cyprian declares: "In Deum solum fidendum, et in
ipso gloriandum" (Test III, 10), and again, "In nullo gloriandum, quando
nostrum nihil sit" (Test III, 4).

For Cyprian, therefore, only that which reveals the veritas of Christ is
glorious. Its glory, then, increases with its sharing in the fulness of
reality: "Quae gloria est similem Deo fieri" (What glory it is to
become like unto God: Pat 5). However, because Christ as veritas reveals
God most intensely in his sufferings, his passio, the same is true for
Christians who follow Christ: "gloriam dominicae passionis" (DO 20).
This, then, is the ontological basis for Cyprian's observation, "Dolor,
qui veritatis testis est" (Suffering proves the presence of true reality:
Id 14). This is also why those closest to God seem to suffer most:
"Quos diligo, inquit Dominus, redarguo et castigo" (Apoc 3, 19) (Those
I love, says the Lord, I upbraid and chastise: Lap 14).[352]

In her study of the word, "passio," C. Mohrmann observes that during
the age of persecutions this word "forceably suggests the idea of the
victory and of the heavenly glory which follow upon the passion." She notes
this as particularly true for Cyprian.[353] In other words, the reason the
passio of Christ is glorious lies in the fact that, as a manifestation of
Ultimate Reality (veritas), it is already victorious and suffused in
heavenly light. To the bishop of Carthage, the death of a martyr is therefore glorious, not simply in his heavenly reward, but even in the here and
now. His death is a manifestation of the veritas: true reality. As
such it shares in the glory of God. This is why Cyprian is careful to be

---

[352]For Cyprian, the greater the suffering, the greater the glory:
"Confessio tamen praesens quantum in passione fortior, tantum clarior et
maior in honore est: crevit pugna, crevit et pugnantium gloria" (Ep 10,
1).
[353]Christine Mohrmann, "Pascha, Passio, Transitus," Ephemerides
Liturgicae LXVI (1952), 41.

martyred within the confines of his own episcopal see, so that the glory
of his death might reflect in this world on the Church from which he
comes (Ep 81, 1, 2). His suffering and death witness to the depth of
reality present within the Church (Dolor ... veritatis testis est).

The Authority of the Martyr

Inasmuch as "gloria" for Cyprian refers to the presence of Christ's
veritas in a person, it likewise signifies the presence of holiness.
Therefore, in the Christian community it is holiness that is honored
("honor ecclesiae nostrae tam gloriosae" Ep 81, 1, 2).[354] What is more,
recognized holiness endows a person with a certain authority in the Church.
Cyprian speaks of the dignity (dignitas) given by the Lord to the martyr
as a kind of weapon (arma), a source of power (Ep 28, 2, 3). He also
argues that Numidicus deserves to become a presbyter because of the
"honor" of his confession, his virtue and his faith: "luce clarissima
confessionis inlustris et virtutis ac fidei honore sublimis" (Ep 40, 1).
The holiness of his life is therefore seen as having endowed him with a
personal recognition in the Church, a recognition which in turn befits
him to be a holder of office. By the same reasoning, Cyprian appointed
certain others to be lectors:

---

[354] People who live holy lives gain honor in the Church: "Qui zelare
non novit quique unanimus et mitis fratres suos diligit dilectionis et
pacis praemio honoratur" (Zel 16). Virginity causes "gloria," so that
a virgin who is martyred has a double glory: "gloria gemina" (Ep 76,
6). Lap 2: "militiae suae gloria virginis."

> Hos ... lectores ... constitutos sciatis,
> quia oportebat ... gloriosos vultus in loco
> altiore constituti (Ep 39, 5).
> (Be informed that these lectors were in-
> stalled, because glorious visages should be
> set up on a higher position.)

The power which the martyr, confessor or otherwise holy person
possesses is clearly that of Christ himself acting through his Spirit:
"Vox plena spiritu sancto de martyris ore prorupit" (A voice full of
the holy Spirit bursts forth from the mouth of the martyr: Ep 10, 4,
1).[355] In all that he says and does, if it be in humility[356] and according to Church disciplina,[357] the martyr especially, but any holy person,
shares in the holiness and therefore the authority of the Church itself:
"ecclesiae catholicae auctoritatem ... et veritatem" (Ep 73, 2).[358]

Finally, because the martyr or confessor is a follower of Christ,
he or she in turn becomes someone whose deeds are authoritative to the
point of deserving imitation themselves:

---

[355]See also Ep 76, 5.

[356]Ep 14, 2: "Imitentur Dominum qui sub ipso tempore passionis non
superbior sed humilior fuit ..." Also, Ep 28, 2, 3.

[357]DO 24: "Ceterum discordans et dissidens et pacem cum fratre non
habens ... Quale delictum est quod nec baptismo sanguinis potest ablui,
quale crimen quod martyrio non potest expiari!" Un 14: "esse martyr non
potest qui in ecclesia non est."

[358]See Thomas G. Ring, O.S.A., Auctoritas bei Tertullian, Cyprian
und Ambrosius, Cassiciacum XXIX (Würzburg: Augustinus-Verlag, 1975),
esp. p. 95.

Peter Brown in The Cult of the Saints (Chicago: The University
of Chicago Press, 1981) states that even after death, by means of the
relic, a holy person possessed a "praesentia" for the Church: "a token
of the unalloyed mercy of God" (p. 101).

> Nec non et cetera stantium multitudo vestram
> gloriam sequitur, proximis et paene coniunctis
> laudis insignibus vestigia vestra comitatur (Lap
> 2).
> (Indeed, even the remaining multitude of the
> faithful follow your glory, tracing your footsteps
> with laurels of praise rivaling and fairly joined
> with your own.)

For Cyprian, the vocation of the Christian is the following of Christ:
sequi Christum. Therefore, if he also exhorts Christians to follow
(sequitur ... comitatur) or imitate the martyrs and confessors, it is
only because of his imitation-presence understanding of salvation history:
The martyrs and confessors are living types of Christ, personal sacramenta
making the veritas ("gloria") of Christ present in the time of the
Church.

Summary

By their following of Christ in his passio even unto death,[359]
the martyrs, like Abel, become types of Christ to the fullest. In fact,
the martyr's body is a sacramentum for Cyprian: The blood of the martyr
is, by participation, the blood of Christ.

Although martyrdom is a special grace from God, the martyrs do not
form any hierarchical order in the Church. Rather, martyrdom expresses
to the fullest the common vocation of all Christians to live typologically

---

[359]Karl Rahner in On the Theology of Death (New York: Herder and
Herder, 1961) says, "In order to understand martyrdom, death must be
understood" (p. 83). "Martyrdom is ... Christian death as such. It is
not only what Christian death in general should be, but it appears as
such as well ... death in freedom and faith" (p. 101). Cyprian would say,
'Martyrdom is the death of Christ. As such, it is also Christian death.'

the _passio_ of Christ. Therefore, a martyr is above all an expression of
that inner life of the Church brought about by Christ: the unity of
mutual love. The martyr dies rather than deny that fellowship; he or
she preserves to the utmost and to the end the _sacramentum unitatis_.

Embodying Church unity, the martyr also expresses the holiness of
the Church. Consequently, individuals need the grace-filled support of
the Church, especially in the celebration of the Eucharist, in order to
live out the martyr's vocation. The martyr's ordeal and the Eucharist
both express typologically the same reality: the _passio_ of Christ, and
so each is imaged in the other.

The "_gloria_" of the martyr is the manifestation of his or her sharing
in the _veritas_ of Christ. Therefore, even in the midst of suffering are
the martyrs "glorious." They are manifestations of the depth of reality
for all to see, but for the faithful to understand. Their _gloria_ is
actually that of the Church whose holiness they express to an eminent
degree.

The _gloria_ or holiness of the martyr, as a participation in Christ,
gives the martyr great influence in the Church: a kind of authority, and
it makes his actions deserving of imitation. Imitation of the martyr is
ultimately imitation of Christ.[360] In other words, the martyr is a true
sacramentum or type of Christ.

_____

[360] I Cor 11, 1: "Become imitators of me, just as I am an imitator
of Christ." For St. Paul's understanding of this mutual imitation, see
D.M. Stanley, S.J., "'Become Imitators of Me': The Pauline Conception
of Apostolic Tradition," _Biblica_ XL (1959), 859-877.

III. The Leader of the Eucharist

"Sacerdos"

The terms, "sacerdos" (priest), "sacerdotium" (priesthood), and
their Greek equivalents were never used at all within the first two
centuries C.E. to signify Christian ministry.[361] Although Tertullian
applies "sacerdos" in different passages to Christ, to the bishop, and
to ordinary Christians,[362] he does not directly link its meaning to
eucharistic ministry. Used of Christ, it expresses his self-sacrifice
to the Father ("summus sacerdos Patris:" de Pudicitia 20, 10) in terms
of the Letter to the Hebrews. Christians in general are called
"sacerdotes" (De monogamia 7, 8) as those who offer up prayer, in line
with Jn 4, 23-24. Finally, the bishop himself is named "summus
sacerdos" only once in Tertullian's writings, but then only as if by
metaphor, through a comparison of his position in the Church to the Old
Testament priest at the top of the Israelite hierarchy. Tertullian's
inspiration for doing so appears to be I Clement 40, 5, which also
emphasized the divine origin of good order in the Church (De baptismo

---

[361]Maurice Bevénot, "Tertillian's thoughts about the christian
priesthood'," in Corona Gratiarum, I (Brugge: Sint Pietersabdij, 1975),
p. 125. The material found in this background paragraph is derived
completely from this article.
[362]Ibid., pp. 125-137, passim.

17, 1-2).[363]

Cyprian, on the other hand, continually names the bishop "_sacerdos_."
Christ alone, in line with the Letter to the Hebrews, is called "_summus
sacerdos_" (Ep 63, 14). He is "High Priest" because, by the offering of
his life, he has replaced Old Testament priesthood completely. He did so
by doing the will of God (Heb 10: 7):

> QUOD SACERDOTIUM VETUS CESSARET ET NOVUS
> SACERDOS VENIRET, QUI IN AETERNUM FUTURUS ESSET.
> In psalmo CVIIII: Ante luciferum genui te.
> Iuravit Dominus, hec paenitebit eum, tu es
> sacerdos in aeternum secundum ordinem Melchisedech.
> Item in Regnorum primo ad Heli sacerdotem: Et
> suscitabo mihi sacerdotem fidelem, qui omni quae
> sunt in corde meo faciet (I Sam 2, 35ff) (Test I,
> 17).
> (THAT THE OLD PRIESTHOOD CEASED AND THE NEW
> PRIEST CAME, WHO WILL REMAIN SO FOREVER. In Psalm
> 109: "Before the day star I begot you. The Lord
> has sworn and he will not repent: You are a priest
> forever according to the order of Melchisedech.
> Again, in the first book of Kings, to Eli the priest:
> "I will raise up for me a faithful priest, who will
> do all that is in my heart.")

The bishop, by acting in the place of Christ at the Eucharist, is also
given the title, "_sacerdos_:"

> Nam si Christus Iesus Dominus et Deus noster
> ipse est summus sacerdos Dei patris et sacrificium
> patri se ipsum primus optulit et hoc fieri in sui
> commemoratione praecepit, utique ille sacerdos vice
> Christi vere fungitur qui id quod Christus fecit
> imitatur et sacrificium verum et plenum tunc offert
> in ecclesia Deo patri, si sic incipiat offerre
> secundum quod ipsum Christum videat optulisse. (Ep
> 63, 14, 4).

---

[363]Ibid., p. 130. Bévenot attributes "nonne et laici sacerdotes
sumus?" (De exhortatione castitatis 7, 3) to his Montanist period. See
also P. van Beneden, Aux origines d'une terminologie sacramentelle, Spicilegium sacrum Lovaniense XXXVIII (Louvain, 1974), p. 31, n. 69, p. 34, n.
74.

(For if Christ Jesus our Lord and God himself
is the <u>High</u> <u>Priest</u> of God the Father and first
offered himself as sacrifice to the Father, and commanded that this take place in his memory, that priest
indeed truly functions <u>in the place of Christ</u> who
imitates that which Christ did, and consequently
offers a true and complete sacrifice in the Church to
God the Father, if he so begins to offer in accordance
with what he sees that Christ offered.)

When Test I, 17 and Ep 63, 14, 4 are thus set side by side, it becomes

evident that Cyprian understands Christ as "High Priest," not as an

expression of Aaronic priesthood, but as its fulfillment. Christ is

therefore "High Priest" in the sense of being priest <u>par</u> <u>excellence</u>:

        Nam <u>qui</u> <u>magis</u> <u>sacredos</u> Dei summi quam Dominus
noster Iesus Christus <u>qui</u> sacrificium Deo patri
optulit et optulit hoc idem quod Melchisedech op-
tulerat, id est panem et vinum, suum scilicet corpus
et sanguinem (Ep 63, 4, 1).
        (For <u>who</u> <u>is</u> <u>more</u> <u>a</u> <u>priest</u> of the High God than
our Lord Jesus Christ who offered a sacrifice to God
the Father and offered this same thing that Melchisedech
had offered, that is, bread and wine, indeed, his own
body and blood.)

By the sacrifice of himself, Christ is the prototype "priest." Conse-

quently, the priesthoods of Aaron and Melchisedech are mere prefigurements

of his own.[364] Furthermore, the leader of the Eucharist is named

---

[364]R.L. Zell in "Priesthood of Christ in Tertullian and Cyprian,"
<u>Texte und Untersuchungen</u> CVIII, Studia Patristica XI, 2 (Berlin:
Akademie-Verlag, 1972) states, "Cyprian considered the Risen Jesus as
glorified High Priest in an Aaronic sense ... it follows quite logically
that he would understand Christian ministry and Eucharist under Levitical
aspects. This is, in fact, what we find him doing" (p. 286). As our own
argument here shows, Zell's premise is unfounded. Therefore, the reason
he gives for Cyprian's comparing the bishop to Old Testament priests has
no basis. In his position, Zell agrees with S.L. Greenslade, "Scripture
and Other Doctrinal Norms in Early Theories of the Ministry, <u>Journal of</u>
<u>Theological Studies</u> XLIV (1944), 173.

"sacerdos" (Ep 63, 14, 4), not primarily in order to assert a similarity to Old Testament priests, but rather, to ascribe participation in the priesthood of Christ to the degree of the leader's imitation of Christ in his Last Supper offering ("summus sacredos"). "Sacerdos," then, is a typological word for Cyprian. To the degree that one is a "priest," he is also a type of Christ.

Were presbyters "sacerdotes?"

Whereas Cyrpian constantly names the bishop "sacerdos," it is disputed whether in his writings he gives that title to the presbyter.[365]

[365]Among those in the affirmative are: Adolf von Harnack, History of Dogma, II, tr. Neil Buchanan, orig. ca. 1900 (New York: Dover, 1961), p. 129: Gustav Bardy, "Le Sacerdoce chrétien d'après saint Cyprien," La Vie Spirituelle LX, Supplement (1939), 117; S.L. Greenslade, "The Apostolic Ministry--II," Theology L (1947), 135; Yves Congar, O.P., "Un Essai de Theologie sur le Sacerdoce Catholique," Revue des Sciences Religieuses XXV (1951), 197; Pierre-Marie Gy, O.P., "Remarques sur le Vocabulaire Antique de Sacerdoce Chrétien," in Études sur le Sacrement de L'Ordre, Lex Orandi XXII (Paris: Cerf, 1957), p. 141; Albano Vilela, La Condition Collegiale des Pretres au IIIᵉ Siècle, Théologie Historique XIV (Paris: Beauchesne, 1971), 282; Bruno Renaud, "L'Eglise comme assemblée liturgique selon saint Cyprien," Recherches de Théologie ancienne et mediévale XXXVIII (1971), 35-38; Hervé-Marie Legrand, O.P., "The Presidency of the Eucharist according to the Ancient Tradition," Worship LIII (1979),424 (Original french: Spiritus XVIII [1977], 419).
    Among those seemingly undecided are E.W. Watson, "The Style and Language of St. Cyprian," Studia Biblica et Ecclesiastica IV (Oxford: Clarendon, 1896), 258; L. Bayard, Le Latin de Saint Cyprien (Paris: Hachette, 1902), p. 179 and _____, Saint Cyprien: Correspondance, I (Paris, 1925), p. LI.
    Among those in the negative are Victor Saxer, Vie Liturgique et Quotidienne à Carthage vers le Milieu du IIIᵉ Siècle (Città del Vaticano: Pontificio Istituto di Archeologia Cristiana, 1969), pp. 85-86, n. 59; Maurice Bévenot, "'Sacerdos' as Understood by Cyprian," Journal of Theological Studies XXX (1979), 414, 421-423.

He does, however, seem to ascribe to the presbyters an association with

the bishop in "priestly" ministry:

> Ep 1, 1, 1: conpresbyteri nostri ... divino
> sacerdotio honorati
> (Our co-presbyters ... honored with the divine
> priesthood)

> Ep 61, 3, 1: Cum episcopo presbyteri sacerdotali
> honore coniuncti
> (Presbyters joined together with the bishop in
> priestly honor)

Furthermore, if we choose to take seriously the words of Ep 63, 14, 4:

"That sacerdos truly‑functions in the place of Christ who imitates what

Christ did," then, because presbyters sometimes offer Eucharist in

Cyprian's church (Epp 5, 2; 16, 4), they participate with the bishop in

the priesthood of Jesus Christ.[366]

In the following passage Cyprian's use of "sacerdotibus" clearly

seems to apply only to the presbyters:

> Ep 40, 1, 2: eum clero nostro Dominus adiungeret
> et desolatam per lapsum quorundam presbyterorum
> nostrorum copiam gloriosis sacerdotibus adornaret.
> (The Lord added him to our clergy and adorned
> the supply, desolated by the lapse of certain pres-
> byters, with glorious priests.)

In the remaining passages presbyters appear to be taken together

with bishops as forming a single body of sacerdotes in the local Church:

---

[366] See especially Bruno Renaud, "L'Eglise comme assemblée," pp.
35-38. See also Pierre Nautin, "Le rite du 'fermuntum' dans les églises
urbaines de Rome," Ephemerides Liturgicae XCVI (1982), 514-515. In
normal circumstances the bishop alone, as symbol of Church unity, leads
the Eucharist in his cathedral city.

Ep 19, 1: Paenitentiam autem ille agit qui
divini praecepti memor mitis et patiens et sacerdotibus Dei obtemperans obsequiis suis ...
(But he does penance who, recalling the divine
precept, is meek and patient and obedient to the
priests of God ...)

Un 13: Quae sacrificia celebrare se credunt
aemuli sacerdotum?
(What sacrifices do those rivals of the <u>priests</u>
believe they are celebrating?)

Ep 67, 4, 3: Nec hoc in episcoporum tantum et
sacerdotum sed et in diaconorum ordinationibus ...
(This, not only in regard to the ordinations of
bishops only and of <u>priests</u>, but also of deacons ...)

Ep 72, 2, 2: Oportet enim <u>sacerdotes</u> et ministros
qui altari et sacrificiis deserviunt integros adque
inmaculatos esse ...
(For priests and ministers who serve at the altar
and at the sacrifices ought to have integrity and be
irreproachable ...)

Taking all the foregoing evidence into account, there is a strong
case that Cyprian understands presbyters to share, along with the bishops,
in the priesthood of Christ to the degree that they too image Christ in
his priestly activity.[367]

---

[367]Since, as we have shown, "<u>sacerdos</u>" with Cyprian is a typological
word referring to the priesthood of Christ, we cannot agree with M.
Bévenot that, if Cyprian understood presbyters as <u>sacerdotes</u>, "either
... they were <u>sacerdotes</u> just as much as their bishops, <u>or</u> ... they
were honourably associated with their bishop in his sacerdotal functions,"
"'Sacerdos' as Understood by Cyprian," p. 414. On the contrary, presbyters as <u>sacerdotes</u> would be acting, not "in place of" (<u>vice</u>) the
bishop, but "in place of" Christ, doing so in conjunction with (sacerdotali
<u>honore conjuncti</u>: Ep 61, 3, 1) the bishop as primordial type of the unity
of the Church.

Priestly Prayer

In one short but powerful passage, Cyprian combines Christ's Last
Supper prayer with an allusion to his praying in the Garden of Olives,
shedding drops of blood. By doing so, Cyprian shows that Christ's outward suffering and death are really the embodiment of his inner prayerful
intention:

> Orabat autem Dominus et rogabat non pro se ...
> sed pro delictis nostris ... dicens: ... 'ut omnes
> unum sint, sicut et tu pater in me et ego in te, ut
> et ipsi in nobis sint' Jn 17, 20ff. ... ut non
> contentus quod nos sanguine suo redimeret adhuc pro
> nobis 'amplius et rogaret' Lk 22, 44 (DO 30).
> (Indeed, the Lord prayed and petitioned not for
> himself but for our failings, saying: 'may all be
> one, even as you, Father, are in me and I in you,
> that they may be so in us.' ... so not content that
> he would redeem us by his blood, 'he prayed the more
> amply' for us.)

Consequently, together with their imitating Christ's outward actions of
offering bread and wine (Ep 63, 14, 4), sacerdotes in the Church must
also imitate Christ in the offering of prayers:[368]

> quando singuli divino sacerdotio honorati et
> in clerico ministerio constituti non nisi altari
> et sacrificiis deservire et precibus adque orati-
> onibus vacare debeant (Ep 1, 1, 1).

---

[368]Rupert Berger sees the eucharistic prayer ("prex") for Cyprian
as the sacrificial essence of the eucharistic action: "Der Opferinhalt
der Eucharistie kommt für Cyprian ... aus dem sakramentalen Gehalt der
Feier, der in der "prex," dem Hochgebet, ausgesprochen wird." Die
Wendung "Offerre Pro" in der Römischen Liturgie, LQF 41 (Münster:
Aschendorff, 1965), p. 60. For Cyprian the eucharistic action, just as
the actions of the Last Supper and Calvary, is efficacious for salvation
precisely as an embodied expression of Christ's inner attitude of prayer
and self-sacrifice, of patience, humility and obedience.

(When individuals are honored with the divine
priesthood and installed in clerical ministry, they
ought to spend their time only in serving at the altar
and at sacrifices and in prayers and petitions.)

Where a false bishop has been installed against the unity of the Church, an

alien prayer is offered at the eucharistic sacrifice. As a result, it is

not Christ's sacrifice; indeed, as such, it is no sacrifice at all:

contemptis episcopis et Dei <u>sacerdotibus</u>
detelictis constituere ... aliud <u>altare</u>, <u>precem</u>
<u>alteram</u> illicitis vocibus facere, Dominicae hos-
tiae veritatem per <u>false</u> <u>sacrificia</u> profanare ...
(Un 17)
(to set up another altar, having spurned the
bishops and cast aside the priests of God, to make
a different prayer with lawless voices, to profane
the true reality of the dominical victim by false
sacrifices ...)

For this reason, only holy <u>sacerdotes</u> should be ordained in the Church.[369]

It is not enough for a <u>sacerdos</u> to imitate the outward sacrificial actions

of Christ. The prayer animating the sacrifice must imitate Christ's inner

intentions and his holiness, thereby making them present and sanctifying:

in ordinationibus sacerdotum nonnisi immaculatos et
integros antistites eligere debemus, qui sancte et digne
sacrificia Deo offerentes audiri in precibus possint quas
faciunt pro plebis dominicae incolumitate, cum scriptum
sit: 'Deus peccatorem non audit, sed qui Deum coluerit
et <u>voluntatem</u> eius fecerit, illum audit' Jn 9, 4 (Ep 67,
2, 2).
(In the ordinations of priests, we ought to choose
only unsullied leaders of integrity who, in offering

---

[369]On the connection between priestly holiness and the priest's representing Christ, see José Capmany, "El Sacerdocio Ministerial segun san
Cipriano," in <u>Teologia</u> <u>Del</u> <u>Sacerdocio</u> IV (Burgos: Ediciones Aldecoa, S.A.,
1972), pp. 158-160.
    Christ speaks in the Christian's praying the Our Father: "Agnoscat
pater filii sui verba, cum precem facimus: <u>qui</u> <u>habitat</u> <u>intus</u> in pectore
<u>ipse</u> <u>sit</u> <u>et</u> <u>in</u> <u>voce</u>" (Do 3). This applies also to the Christian's echoing
in the heart the priest's articulation of the eucharistic prayer: "et quando
in unum cum fratribus conveniums et <u>sacrificia</u> divina <u>cum</u> Dei <u>sacerdote</u>
<u>celebramus</u>, verecundiae et disciplinae memores esse debemus ... quia Deus
non vocis sed <u>cordis</u> <u>auditor</u> <u>est</u>" (DO 4).

sacrifices to God with holiness and dignity, might be
able to be heard in the prayers which they make for the
safety of the Lord's people, as it is written: 'God
does not listen to the sinner, but he who is devoted to
God and <u>does his will</u>, him God hears.')

Cyprian's <u>sacerdos</u>, therefore, fully imitates Christ and typologically

makes his priesthood present only when both the outward and the inner sacri-

fice, as presented in <u>Hebrews</u>, are imaged:

"Sacrifices and offerings thou has not desired, but
a body hast thou prepared for me; ... Then I said, 'Lo,
I have come to <u>do thy will</u>, O God'" (Heb 10, 7).
    In the days of his flesh, Jesus <u>offered prayers and
supplications</u>, with loud cries and tears, to him who was
able to save him from death, and he was heard for his
godly fear. Although he was a Son, he learned obedience
through what he suffered; and being made perfect he became the source of eternal salvation to all who obey him,
being designated by God a <u>high priest</u> after the order of
Melchizedek (Heb 5, 7-10).

Priest as Teacher and Preacher

The significance of "<u>sacerdos</u>" for Cyprian is not restricted to the

imitating of Christ's Last Supper prayerful sacrifice.[370] "<u>Sacerdotes</u>"

are also sent by Christ to teach observance of his <u>praecepta</u> (laws), that

is, to preach the Gospel (Mt 28, 18-20).[371] The presbyters, as well as the

---

[370]Christine Mohrmann, "Word-Play in the Letters of St. Cyprian," in
<u>Études sur le latin des Chrétiens</u>, I (Roma: Edizioni di Storia e Letteratura,
1958), p. 294: "Cyprian shows a particular liking for the paromasia with
'<u>sacerdos</u>,' '<u>sacrilegus</u>,' '<u>sacrificium</u>,' '<u>sacrificare</u>.'"

[371]Ep 63, 18, 3: "<u>Nam si sacerdotes</u> Dei et Christi <u>sumus</u>, ... Christum
sequi et praecepta eius observare debemus, quia et ipse ... dixit: '... Ite
ergo et <u>docete</u> omnes <u>tinguentes</u> eos in nomine Patris et Filii et Spiritus
Sancti, <u>docentes</u> eos observare omnia quaecumque praecepi vobis' Mt 28, 18-
20." Consequently, included in the identity of "<u>sacerdos</u>" is <u>baptizing</u> and
<u>preaching</u> the Gospel, in a word, passing on and continuing the <u>disciplina</u>
of the Church. Bévenot can therefore state, "'<u>sacerdos</u>' is the man chosen
by God to be <u>his instrument for the distribution of his graces</u> to those in
his charge." [emph. his] "'Sacerdos' as Understood by Cyprian," p. 417.

bishops, are called to this sacerdotal function:[372]

> Peto vos ... fungamini illic et vestris
> partibus et meis, ut nihil vel ad disciplinam
> vel ad diligentiam desit (Ep 5, 1, 1).
> (I ask that you fulfill your offices as
> well as my own where you are, so that nothing
> be lacking either in regard to disciplina or
> diligence.)

A "sacerdos" therefore imitates Christ, not only in doing what Christ did, but also in teaching what Christ taught.[373]

For Cyprian, a major symbol of the bishop's priestly function of teaching is his chair in the liturgical assembly: "cathedra sacerdotalis."[374]

---

[372]All clerical orders from deacon on down (subdeacons, acolytes, exorcists, lectors) share in the ministry of disciplina in the Church: "diaconi boni viri et ecclesiasticae administrationi per omnia obsequia devoti, cum ceteris ministeriis plenam vobis (laity) praesentiae suae diligentiam praebeant et exhortationibus adsiduis singulos corroborare sed et lapsorum mentes consiliis salubribus regere et reformare non desinant" (Ep 43, 1, 1). On the various clerical ministries in Cyprian's church, see Albano Vilela, La Condition Collegiale des Prêtres au IIIe Siècle, Théologie Historique XIV (Paris: Beauchesne, 1971), p. 267. See also, Xavier A. Thani Nayagam, The Carthaginian Clergy During the Episcopate of Saint Cyprian (Tuticorin, India: Tamil Literature Society, 1950).

[373]All Christians are to imitate what Christ did and taught: "quod Christus docuit et fecit imitatur" (Zel 11; Ep 58, 1, 3; Un 2). By their representation of Christ the priest, the sacerdotes make Christ acting and teaching present to the Church for its imitation.

[374]Epp 55, 8; 55, 9, 1; 73, 2, 3. "cathedra:" Epp 3, 1; 17, 2. Bruno Renaud concludes from Cyprian's use of "cathedra sacerdotalis" that "l'evêque résume en sa personne le sacerdoce de l'Eglise (les presbyteri n'ont pas de cathedra) ..." "L'Eglise comme assemblee," p. 41 n. 127. However, this observation must be rightly understood: Because the priesthood of Christ is directed toward the unity of humankind in the Church, priesthood in the Church is linked to the bishop who in his uniqueness images and realizes the unity of the Church. Thus, the priesthood of the presbyters is always in conjunction with the bishop, but is nevertheless parallel with the bishop's priesthood in directly imaging and acting in the place of Christ the priest.

However, because the presbyters also share in the sacerdotal function

of instructing the people ("presbyteris doctoribus:" Ep 29, 1, 2),[375]

they also share in the sacerdotal honor of sitting, along with the bishop,

at the liturgy:

> Nam admonitos nos et instructos sciatis
> dignatione divina ut Numidicus presbyter adscrib-
> atur presbyterorum Carthaginiensium numero et
> nobiscum sedeat in clero ... tam mites et humiles
> faciat in consessus nostri honore florere (Ep 40,
> 1)
> (Indeed, be informed that we were guided and
> instructed by the divine will that Numidicus the
> presbyter is to be added to the number of the
> Carthaginian presbyters and is to sit with us
> among the clergy ... May [the Lord] cause such
> meek and humble men to flourish with the honor of
> our consessus (seating together).)[376]

"auctoritas sacerdotalis"

Although E.W. Watson concludes that "Cyprian is always a careless

writer,"[377] Y. Congar finds that the martyr-bishop's "sacerdos" signifies

---

[375]Some presbyters were probably entrusted with catechizing the
catechumens. See Vilela, La Condition, p. 260.

[376]In contrast to the bishop and presbyters who sat at
the liturgy, the faithful are called "stantes:" "Ecclesia in episcopo et
clero et in omnibus stantibus sit constituta" (Ep 33, 1). See Adrien
Demoustier, S.J., "L'Ontologie de L'Eglise selon S. Cyprien," Récherches
de Science Religieuse LII (1964), 572 n. 65, and B. Renaud, "L'Eglise
comme assemblee," p. 11. Just as their sitting symbolizes the sacerdotal
teaching authority, so also with Cyprian the act of standing on the part
of the remaining faithful probably signifies for the bishop of Carthage
the faithfulness to the Gospel. Thus, those who deny the Church are the
"lapsed" or "fallen:" lapsi.

[377]E.W. Watson, "The Style and Language of St. Cyprian," Studia
Biblica et Ecclesiastica IV (1896), 258, n. 1.

the bishop and presbyter's moral authority, whereas the titles, "episcopus" and "presbyter," define their official positions within the overall constitution of the Church.[378] Is Cyprian's terminology really so precise?

(1) "Type of the Church." As "episcopus," the bishop might be called a "type of the Church:"

> Unde scire debes episcopum in ecclesia esse et ecclesiam in episcopo et si qui cum episcopo not sit in ecclesia non esse (Ep 66, 8, 3).
> (Accordingly, you ought to know that the bishop is in the Church and the Church is in the bishop, and if anyone is not with the bishop, that person is not in the Church.)

Some have mistakenly understood Cyprian to identify absolutely the Church with the bishop on the basis of this text.[379] They have done so not grasping how, for the saintly bishop, a person is able to represent typologically and thus make present another reality.[380] In describing the role of the bishop, A. Demoustier writes:

> ... if the Eucharist as sacramentum signifies that Christ brings into being this divine unity of the assembly, the bishop is the guarantee that this assembly, gathered here and now, is the same as that of the Last Supper and the same as all those which

---

[378] Yves Congar, O.P., "Un Essai de Théologie sur le Sacerdoce Catholique," Revue des Sciences Religieuses XXV (1951), 196-197.

[379] For example, Günter Klein, "Die hermeneutische Struktur des Kirchengedankens bei Cyprien," Zeitschrift für Kirchengeschichte LXVIII (1957): "Das in ecclesia esse ist identisch mit dem cum episcopo esse. ....Mit der Identität von catholicae ecclesiae unitas und collegium coepiscoporum ..." (p. 57). Klein therefore understands Cyprian to say that the holiness of the Church resides fully in the person of the bishop: "Aus seinem Handeln entspringt die Heiligkeit der Sakramente" (. 57).

[380] See above, Chapter III, Section II, "repraesentare," pp. 136-142.

derive from the Last Supper assembly by succession through time. He (the bishop) is the
<u>sign</u> that the <u>una</u> <u>Mater</u> gives life by virtue of
her divine origin to this assembly.[381]

It is not the bishop, therefore, in whom all the holiness of the Church

resides. Rather, according to Cyprian, it is the Church's holiness

which the bishop administers: "<u>Habere</u> <u>non</u> <u>potest</u> <u>Deum</u> <u>patrem</u>, <u>qui</u>

<u>ecclesiam</u> <u>non</u> <u>habet</u> <u>matrem</u>" (Whoever does not have the Church as his

mother, cannot have God as his Father: Un 6).[382] The bishop, standing

before the community as its sole bishop, and thus signifying its essential

unity in Christ,[383] is also a symbol of its link to the Lord through

the Apostles whom he first commissioned: "<u>Apostolos</u>, <u>id</u> <u>est</u>, <u>episcopos</u>

<u>et</u> <u>praepositos</u>, <u>Dominus</u> <u>elegit</u>" (The Apostles, that is bishops and

heads, whom the Lord chose ...: Ep 3, 3, 1). The bishops, therefore,

follow the Apostles in this same office as heads of churches ("<u>episcopos</u>")

by the choice and sanctification of the Lord through the lawfully con-

ducted rite of ordination: "<u>qui</u> <u>apostolis</u> <u>vicaria</u> <u>ordinatione</u> <u>succedunt</u>"

(who succeed the Apostles as vicars by ordination: Ep 66, 4).[384] By

---

[381]Demoustier, L'Ontologie," p. 587.

[382]On the theological force of "Ecclesia Mater," see Karl Delahaye,
<u>Ecclesia</u> <u>Mater</u> <u>chez</u> <u>les</u> <u>peres</u> <u>des</u> <u>trois</u> <u>premiers</u> <u>siecles</u>, Unam Sanctam
XLVI (Paris: Cerf, 1964), pp. 100-108.

[383]Ep 66, 8, 3: "ecclesia plebs sacerdoti <u>adunata</u>."

[384]For a thorough study of the meaning of "<u>ordo</u>," "<u>ordinare</u>," and
"<u>ordinatio</u>" in Cyprian, see Pierre van Beneden, <u>Aux</u> <u>Origines</u> <u>d'une</u>
<u>Terminologie</u> <u>Sacramentelle</u>, Spicilegium Sacrum Lovaniense XXXVIII (Louvain,
1974). Cyprian clearly speaks of a sacramental ordination of bishops,
presbyters and deacons.

208

ordination the Lord chooses a bishop in union with all other bishops.
Forming one body with them, the individual bishop forms part of the "glue"
which holds the Church together as one:

> copiosum corpus est sacerdotum concordiae
> mutuae glutino adque unitatis vinculo copulatum
> (Ep 68, 3, 2)
> (The body of priests is numerous, held
> together by the glue of mutual concord and the
> chain of unity.)
>
> ecclesia quae catholica una est scissa non sit
> neque divisa, sed sit utique conexa et cohaerentium
> sibi invicem sacerdotum glutino copulata (Ep 66, 8).
> (Let the Church which is universal not be split
> nor divided, but may it indeed be connected and
> joined by the glue of priests mutually cohering to
> one another.)

The body of bishops as a whole exists, therefore, as a type and a realization of the unity of the whole Church, which, in fact, is its essential
nature. "The type of spiritual unity, which is the episcopacy, is found
at the more fundamental level of the Church itself."[385]

Furthermore, the individual bishop, insofar as he is in union with
other bishops in union with the bishop of Rome,[386] shares in the office
of Peter as sign of Church unity. J. Colson sums up the role of bishop
as "type of the Church" by quoting Ep 59, 7, 3:

> The bishop incarnates, in effect, the fidelity
> of the Church to its Master. It is his profession
> of living faith, being the successor of "Peter upon

---

[385]Demoustier, "L'Ontologie," p. 574.

[386]For the best treatment of Cyprian's understanding of the place
of the bishop of Rome in the unity of the Church, see Adiren Demoustier,
"Episcopat et Union à Rome selon saint Cyprien," Récherches de Science
Religieuse LII (1964), 337-369.

whom the Church has been built by Christ, when
speaking of himself on behalf of all and
responding with the voice of the Church, Peter
said to him: 'To whom will we go? You have the
word of eternal life, and we believe and we know
that you are the Christ, son of the living God' "
(Ep 59, 7, 3).[387]

Thus, the role of the bishop in the Church as an ordained person stems

from the nature of the Church as a structured reality: "Ecclesia in

episcopo et clero et in omnibus stantibus sit constituta" (The Church is

made up of the bishop and clergy and of all the faithful: Ep 33, 1).

The purpose of Church structure is representational in the fullest sense.

By his being a "type of the Church," the bishop is in fact a "type of

Christ:" "The bishop is the guardian of the rights of the Spouse (Christ)

over his Church. His role signifies that the action of the spouse (the

Church) is in reality that of the Spouse."[388] In other words, by his

representational role, the bishop allows the Church to see itself, and

therefore to be itself, as the "body" of Christ.

(2) "Priestly Authority." Cyprian states that legitimate ordination

guarantees that only holy men are ordained in the Church:

Cum ille (Dominus) nec minima fieri sine
voluntate Dei dicat, existimat aliquis summa et
magna aut non sciente aut non permittente Deo in
ecclesia Dei fieri, et sacerdotes id est dispen-
satores eius erunt non de eius sententia
ordinari? (Ep 59, 5).

---

[387] Jean Colson, L'Évêque: Lien d'Unité et de Charité chez Saint
Cyprien de Carthage (Paris: Editions S.O.S., 1961), pp. 13, 14.

[388] Demoustier, "l'Ontologie," p. 572 n. 68.

210

> (Since the Lord says not the smallest things
> happen apart from the will of God, does anyone
> imagine that the highest matters take place in the
> Church of God without God's allowing them, and that
> priests, that is his dispensers, will be ordained
> without his willing it?)

P. van Beneden thinks that this is a "sophistic" argument, since ordination
is not only God's work, but also that of fallible human beings. He finds
that Cyprian has a "supernaturalistic theology of ecclesial function."[389]
Cyprian, however, is insistant:

> tu existimes sacerdotes Dei sine conscientia
> eius in ecclesia ordinari. Nam credere quod
> indigni et incesti sint qui ordinantur quid aliud
> est quam contendere quod non a Deo nec per Deum
> sacerdotes eius in ecclesia constituantur (Ep 66,
> 1).
> (You may think that priests of God are ordained
> in the Church without his knowledge. For to believe
> that those who are ordained are unworthy and inces-
> tuous, what else is that than to hold that priests
> are not ordained by or through God in the Church?)

For Cyprian, by the fact that God acts in Church ordinations, any
legitimately ordained bishop is guaranteed to be sufficiently "in the
Church" (episcopum in ecclesia esse et eccelsia in episcopo: Ep 66, 8,
3), that is, sufficiently holy, in order to be able to function as a
representative of the Church, as a sacramentum (Test II, 2) of its holiness. To hold open in principle the possibility that unworthy men can
legitimately be ordained is, for Cyprian, tantamount to condoning
rebellion in the Church. Such an option, inviting disunity, is patently
impossible to him since it would render ineffectual the sacrifice of

---

[389] P. van Beneden, Aux Origines, pp. 72, 80 n. 60.

Christ himself. Furthermore, the rite of ordination itself as pro-
claiming divine election would have no meaning.

On the other hand, Cyprian does not understand that the bishop's
authority depends totally on his own holiness. His office is rather to
represent the holiness of the Church. It is the Church (Mater Ecclesia)
who acts through the bishop. Thus, as we have seen, where with Tertullian
even the laity are called "sacerdotes," in Cyprian's writings only the
leaders of the Eucharist are so named. Accordingly, if the Church as a
whole offers with the "sacerdos" at the Eucharist (DO 4; Op 15; Epp 12,
2, 1; 37, 1, 2; 39, 3, 1; 51, 4, 2), it does so only through his hands
(Un 17; Ep 1, 2, 1; 65, 2, 1; 67, 2, 2; Lap 16). Furthermore, if the
sacerdos-bishop is understood to be judge over the community in the place
of Christ (iudex vice Christi: Ep 59, 5, 1), he is so only in complete
harmony with the sense and opinion of the faithful (Epp 14, 1; 16, 4, 2;
19, 2, 2; 34, 41,1).[390] In contrast, therefore, to the individual
Christian or martyr as type of the Church and of Christ, the typology at
work in the sacerdos is essential to the very nature of the Church. As
such, it is an official typology, one into which a person is ordained and
thus guaranteed by God in order that the Church continue to exist. Consequently, the bishop must incorporate at the very least that holiness
necessary to be in unity with the college of bishops. He cannot be a
"rebel" like Novatian and still be a sacerdos. Nor can he publicly deny
the faith of the Church, as did Basilides and Martialis (Ep 67, 2), and

---

[390]See Renaud, "L'Eglise comme assemblée," pp. 59, 60, on the
unanimity of sacerdos and assembly.

212

still remain a bishop. Even if such bishops later return to the Church, having once been "perfidi" (faithless) or "rebelles contra ecclesiam" (rebels against the Church: Ep 72, 2), they no longer are able to be personal symbols of the Church in its age-long faith. They can therefore no longer carry on the essential function of being "sacerdotes" and so are stripped of their official typological office.

For Cyprian there would, of course, have to be sufficient holiness in the bishop above that demanded of the ordinary Christian if he is to fulfill well the demands of his office:

> Quae ante oculos habentes et sollicite ac
> religiose considerantes in ordinationibus sac-
> erdotum nonnisi immaculatos et integros antistites
> eligere debemus, qui sancte et digne sacrificia
> offerentes audiri in precibus possint quas faciunt
> pro plebis incolumitate (Ep 67, 2).
> (Having these matters before our eyes and con-
> sidering them carefully and religiously, we ought
> to elect in the ordination of priests only blame-
> less and holy prelates, who are able as they offer
> sacrifices in a holy and worthy manner to be heard
> in the prayers which they make for the welfare of
> the people.)[391]

If, in fact, it is found that unworthy men were "ordained" in the Church, the reason in Cyprian's mind can always be traced back to an illegitimate ordination. The martyr-bishop's confidence is adamantine that if the ordination process is followed according to Church tradition, God will infallibly make his will known through the Church and worthy men will be chosen:

---

[391]For a study of the offering made by the sacerdos or others "on behalf of" the assembly or those absent, see Rupert Berger, Die Wendung "Offerre Pro" in der Römischen Liturgie, Liturgie Quellen und Forschungen XLI (Münster: Aschendorff, 1965), 60-64.

> Propter quod diligenter de traditione divina
> et apostolica observatione servandum est et tenendum
> quod apud nos quoque et fere per provincias universas
> tenetur, ut ad ordinationes rite celebrandas ad eam
> plebem cui praepositus ordinatur episcopi eiusdem
> provinciae proximi quique conveniant et episcopus
> deligatur plebe praesente, quae singulorum virorum
> vitam plenissime novit et uniuscuiusque actum de
> eius conversatione perspexit (Ep 67, 5).
> (For this reason, divine and apostolic tradition
> must be surely followed and held to, which is in
> effect among us and throughout almost all the provinces,
> namely that in regard to all rightly celebrated
> ordinations, neighboring bishops of the same province
> come together before that people for whom the prelate
> is ordained, and the bishop be chosen in the presence
> of the people that are most familiar with the lives
> of the individual men and are aware of the conduct of
> each from having lived with them.)

Thus, in order to determine between Cornelius and Novatian as to which of the two is truly bishop, he needs only to ask which underwent a lawful[392] ordination (Ep 44, 1; Ep 69, 3).

As a result of our investigation we find that the power ("potestas") or authority ("auctoritas") of a sacerdos depends on his actually operating as a representational type of the Church's holiness. "Potestas" is used by Cyprian to refer to the sacerdos in his official capacity, as one who has been entrusted with office in the Church. "Auctoritas," on the other hand, stresses the personal appropriation of the office through holiness by the sacerdos.[393] However, the two are really two aspects of

---

[392]"Legitimus" means not only "lawful," but also "legal:" something set down in law: P. van Beneden, Aux Origines, p. 131.

[393]For the best discussion of Cyprian's understanding of "auctoritas" and "potestas," see Thomas G. Ring, O.S.A., Auctoritas bei Tertullian, Cyprian und Ambrosius, Cassiciacum XXIX (Wurzburg: Augustine-Verlag, 1975), 95-110. Ring replaces the thesis of Alexander Beck in Römisches Recht bei Tertullian und Cyprian (Halle, 1930). Reprint: Aalen: Scientia Verlag, 1967) that Cyprian for the most part simply appropriated the role of the magistrate in the Roman state to his concept of bishop in the Church (pp. 130ff). For Ring, Cyprian's "episcopus" is essentially a theological reality. Auctoriats, p. 98.

one reality: representation through holiness. That is to say, whenever
he images more faithfully and fully the passio of Christ in his own life,
the sacerdos increases his "authority" in the Church. Thus, Pope Lucius
gained stature among his people by having confessed the faith in spite of
torture: "crevit sacerdotalis auctoritas" (his priestly authority in-
creased: Ep 61, 2).

Here we find that the power or authority of the sacerdos is based
upon the same foundation as the authority found in the "gloria" of the
martyr: the passio of Christ. In other words, to the degree that the
sacerdos individually (auctoritas) and as an office holder in the Church
(potestas) has power in the Church, he has that power only by virtue of
his imaging and therefore making present Christ in his saving deeds:
"glorioso episcopo" (Ep 31, 5, 2). Because of his radically representational nature, even the personal holiness of the sacerdos is also that of
his Church:

> nec fas fuerat nec decebat sine honore
> ecclesiastico esse quem sic Dominus honoraverit
> coelestis gloriae dignitate (Ep 39, 1).
> (Neither would it have been right or fit-
> ting that one whom the Lord has so honored with
> the dignity of heavenly glory be without ecclesi-
> astical honor.)

In fact, the personal identity of the bishop with the Church is so great
that the "gloria" of the Church is his own personal "gloria:" "ecclesiae
enim gloria praepositi gloria est" (Ep 13, 1, 1).

In Summary: Congar may be correct that "episcopus" and "presbyter"
refer more to the eucharistic leader's constitutional position within the
structure of the Church, and "sacerdos" more to his "moral authority."

However, there is for Cyprian no division among these titles regarding their ultimate significance. One is "episcopus," "presbyter," or "sacerdos" only by virtue of representing the holiness of the Church through representing the holiness of Christ's passio ("gloria"). This alone is the basis both for his holding office and for his authority.

"Vice Christi"

As he states more than once in his works, Cyprian sees the leader of the Eucharist acting "in the place of" (vice) Christ. The reason is that "the Lord chooses and sets up priests for himself in the Church" (sacerdotes sibi: Ep 48, 4, 2). By doing so, he is able to "govern both the leaders and the Church with the leaders by his judgment, his will, and his presence (arbitrio et nutu ac praesentia: Ep 66, 9, 1). As God is ultimate judge of his world (Ep 55, 19, 2), so has the sacerdos been set over the Church to be its "judge in the place of Christ (iudex vice Christi: Ep 59, 5, 1). Cyprian therefore sees the sacerdos in the Church as a representative of Christ in all his saving dimensions. It is Christ in the sacerdos who offers the Eucharist and guides the Church in its life in this world.

The bishop of Carthage takes the Lord's guidance of the sacerdos seriously. As noted previously, A. von Harnack sees strong evidence that Cyprian guided his church as a visionary.[394] M. Bévenot refers to his

---

[394]Adolf von Harnack, "Cyprian als Enthusiast," Zeitschrift für die neutestamentliche Wissenschaft III (1902), 177-191.

"avowed reliance on dreams" (Ep 66, 10, 2).[395] Whether or not Cyprian was favored by God with unusual communications, he clearly understood that any sacerdos-bishop needs to listen constantly to his Lord if he is in turn to teach and guide his church. The holy bishop of Carthage says that he "consults" his Lord regarding important decisions that he has to make in the Church, and in return he is "directed and guided" (Ep 66, 2, 2). He may mean by that that he follows the very advice which he gives to others, namely, to "meditate on [the Scriptures] day and night and be careful to do everything that is written in them" (Ep 74, 2, 3). In any event, he holds that bishops must be learners as well as teachers:

> Oportet enim episcopos non tantum docere sed et discere, quia et ille melius docet qui cotidie crescit et proficit discendo meliora (Ep 74, 10, 1).
> (For bishops ought not only teach but also learn, because he teaches better who daily grows and advances toward better things by learning.)

If the bishop of Carthage does receive communications from the Lord, in all important matters the Lord speaks equally to all. He does so through the Spirit within each one. In fact, Cyprian asserts that all bishops who have the Spirit are told exactly the same things by Christ:

> Neque enim poterat esse apud nos sensus diversus, in quibus unus est spiritus: et ideo manifestum est eum Spiritus Sancti veritatem cum ceteris non tenere quem videmus diversa sentire (Ep 68, 5, 2).

---

[395]Maurice Bévenot, "'Sacerdos' as Understood by Cyprian," Journal of Theological Studies XXX (1979), 413.

(Neither was there able to be differing
opinions among us in whom the Spirit is one:
And therefore it is clear that he whom we find
holding different opinions does not possess the
true reality of the Holy Spirit along with the
others.)

Thus, the picture forms here that the sacerdos of Christ is guided by his

Master through his constant meditation on the Scriptures. In his willing-

ness to learn, the Lord speaks to him through the Spirit, allowing him

thus to communicate the Lord's "judgment, will and presence" (Ep 66, 9, 1)

to his Church. In this way the sacerdos works at acting "in the place of

Christ."

Not only in his words is the sacerdos to make Christ present in the

Church, but also in his actions: "sacerdotes ... quod Christus et

docuit et fecit imitantes" (priests ... imitating what Christ both did

and taught: Ep 55, 19, 2). Consequently, he states that "priests are to

be humble because both the Lord and the Apostles were humble" (Ep 66, 3, 1).

Thus he praises Cornelius for his virginal continence and his humility

(Ep 55, 8), since both are a sharing in the passio of Christ (Vir 6).

By his following the Lord in word and action, the sacerdos becomes one of

the shepherds promised to the people by God through Jeremiah 3, 5, shep-

herds after God's own heart: "pastores secundum cor meum" (Vir 1).

Imitation-Presence

Throughout this study we have noted that for Cyprian the imitation of

Christ results in his presence. Because the sacerdos holds a position in

the Church which is itself representational, this ontology is doubly valid

218

in his regard. At the same time, Cyprian offers another instance where
someone else besides the sacerdos acts representationally. As a result,
a further insight into the Carthaginian's understanding of imitation
and presence is possible.

In Epistle 3, 1, 2, Cyprian states:

> Nam cum in lege prohibeantur viri induere
> muliebrem vestem et maledicti eiusmodi indicentur
> (Dt 22, 5), quanto maioris est criminis non tan-
> tum muliebria indumenta accipere, sed et gestu
> quoque turpes et molles et muliebres magisterio
> inpudicae artis exprimere.
> (For since in the Law men are forbidden to
> put on a woman's clothing and evildoers of this
> kind are judged, how much more of a crime is it,
> not only to take up women's clothing, but by
> action to express base, easy and effeminate
> people by the shameless artistry of acting?)

The probable reason why Cyprian and other platonist early Christians
so objected to the theatre and to acting is the very objection to it by
Plato himself:

> If [the Guardians of the State] imitate at
> all, they should imitate from youth upward only
> those characters which are suitable to their pro-
> fession -- the courageous, temperate, holy, free,
> and the like; but they should not depict or be
> skillful at imitating any kind of illiberality or
> baseness, lest from imitation they should come to
> be what they imitate ...
> Then, I said, we will not allow those ... of
> whom we say that they ought to be good men, to
> imitate a woman, whether old or young, quarreling
> with her husband, or striving and vaunting against
> the gods.[396]

---

[396] B. Jowett, tr., The Dialogues of Plato, I (New York: Macmillan,
1892; Random House, 1937), 658, 659; Orig. Greek: Platon: Oeuvres Com-
plètes, VI, ed. Emile Chambry, [Collection Budé], (Paris: Societé
d'Edition "Les Belles Lettres," 1947), 395c-395e, p. 106.

In other words, Cyprian does not object to the imitation of evil people or people of the opposite sex for fear that bad moral habits will result. He is expressing the fundamental platonic metaphysics that through imitation one reality is made present in another.

It may be that this platonic understanding is actually behind the three fantastic stories which Cyprian tells in De lapsis 25 and 26. All three deal with unworthy participants at the Eucharist. In the first story, having previously been given food at a pagan sacrifice, a baby reacts violently when brought into a eucharistic assembly and vomits back the eucharistic wine. In the second, a young girl who secretly committed a crime chokes to death on the eucharistic cup. In the third, a woman who offered sacrifice to idols causes fire to flare up when she tries to open a locket containing the eucharistic bread. It is highly probable that Cyprian recalls the warning of Paul in I Corinthians 10, 21-22:

> You cannot drink the cup of the Lord and the cup
> of demons. You cannot partake of the table of the
> Lord and the table of demons. Shall we provoke the
> Lord to jealousy? Are we stronger than he?

For Cyprian, even if he fabricated these stories, they contain an essential truth. The Eucharist, because it exactly imitates the Last Supper of Christ, is a much stronger reality than even our human bodies. Christ in his passio is the prototype of all reality. Consequently, if in our lives and in our bodies we fail to live out his passio and even by pagan rituals absolutely deny it, such physical revulsion would be altogether understandable and even expected.

Against this background, the statement "ille sacerdos vice Christi
vere fungitur qui id quod Christus fecit imitatur" (Ep 63, 14, 4),
becomes even more powerful. Cyprian sees that in his personal imitation
the sacerdos becomes medium for the presence of Christ, who is by far the
"stronger" reality.

Summary

Cyprian is the first Latin writer to use the term, "sacerdos," of
the leader of the Eucharist. In his writings, "sacerdos" is a typological word signifying participation in Christ's passio self-offering.
To the degree therefore that one is a "priest," he is also a type of
Christ.

A sacerdos is one who imitates, not only Christ's outward actions,
but also his inner attitude of obedience and sacrificial prayer. Therefore he is also one who offers prayer in the Church. In order to do so
effectively, he must appropriate the holiness of Christ.

Because presbyters also preside at the Eucharist, they share in the
role of sacerdos with the bishop. Part of that role includes teaching
and governing, and so presbyters share in the symbol of such authority,
that of being seated in the eucharistic assemblies.

The Church is essentially a structured reality. By his personally
being a type of the holiness of the Church, the bishop presents the Church
to itself in order that it be itself. It is the holiness of the Church
which acts through its type, the bishop, in dispensing the graces of God.

The authority of the sacerdos-bishop is therefore based upon his own personal appropriation of the Church's holiness, which in turn is found in his representation of the passio of Christ ("gloria"). That the sacerdos possesses such holiness is guaranteed by his legitimate ordination in the Church. In his being a type of the Church, therefore, the sacerdos is a type of Christ.

Christ himself chooses and sets up "priests" in the Church by whom he makes himself present as its actual presider and judge. The sacerdos is to be obedient to Christ, made so by meditation on his word in Scripture and by imitating his internal dispositions. He is thus enabled truly to act "in the place of Christ."

Finally, imitation-presence for Cyprian means that the more exactly the sacerdos imitates Christ's action in his passio, the more powerfully does that prototype of all reality come present in him and act through him for the good of the whole Church. Such imitation involves the whole person of the sacerdos: not only outward action, but also the inner attitudes of prayer and self-sacrifice. The sacerdos becomes the sacrifice he offers. As such, he himself becomes worthy of imitation by the Church over which he has been placed as one who leads, in life as in ritual, by example.

CONCLUSIONS

Imitation-Presence Ontology

Behind Cyprian's understanding of salvation history we have found
in our study what might be called an "imitation-presence ontology."
Throughout his writings the bishop of Carthage stresses the need to
imitate the historical Christ in what he taught and did, especially
Christ in his "passio." In fact, for him all human life has value only
insofar as it is an imitation of Christ. This is true because, in
Cyprian's eyes, the true imitation of Christ is actually also the
presence and activity of Christ.

The question then naturally arose, "Is Cyprian unique among early
Christian writers in this understanding of salvation history?" In response
to this question the first chapter attempted to show that this fundamental
theological vision is not the result of Cyprian's own personal speculation.
On the contrary, for himself as well as for his readers, Old Testament
Scriptures are a norm for Christian behavior precisely because the Church
universally believed that "types" and "figures," by imitating Christ in
their own historical lives, already participated in the sacred Reality
to which they point. In other words, there is a pre-existence of Christ
in the persons and actions of those who imaged beforehand the saving
events of his life on earth.

In examples from the New Testament we found that it is precisely

224

by a conscious appropriation of the images found in history itself
(new covenant, Moses, Jonah, etc.) that Christ fulfills and saves human
history. These "types" and "figures" of Christ, taken from throughout
history, were therefore seen as integral and essential to history's own
salvation. Consequently, it is only in the experience of these same
images of Christ that those living after Christ are able to experience
Him and be saved by the events of his life.

Similarly, Cyprian also appeals to the example of holy men and women
in the Old Testament because he is convinced that similar imitation of the
life of Christ by members of his church will result in similar participation in Christ's saving Reality. Here he echoes not only the New Testament
kerygma itself, but also the common witness of post-apostolic writers up
to his own time, including his "master," Tertullian.

Christ as Proto-Type Priest

It is with this imitation-presence understanding of salvation
history, then, that Cyprian approaches the controversy occasioning Epistle
63. As proof that wine as well as water must be offered in the chalice
at the Eucharist, the bishop of Carthage recalls the example of Melchisedech.
Just as Melchisedech, by offering wine in image of the Last Supper,
actually participated in the offering of Christ, the king of Salem is by
this very fact a witness in what way the Church must imitate the saving
actions of Christ in order for Christ to be present and active also at the
Eucharist (Ep 63, 4).

Here Christ is seen as the "proto-type" of priesthood. Any other

"priest" offering a sacrifice to God in salvation history is truly
a "priest" only to the extent that, in imitation of Christ's self-
offering, he allows Christ himself to be present and offering through
him. Just as Christ at the Last Supper in the offering of bread and wine
was actually offering the suffering and death of Good Friday, so too, any
priest who offers (in a community joined to Christ) bread and wine in
imitation of Christ actually offers Christ's body and blood.

The Sacrifice of Christ

However, contrary to the opinion of many scholars, when Cyprian
speaks of Christ's body and blood, he does not hold an extreme realism
in his eucharistic theology. Through a study of his uses of sacramentum,
portare, and adunare, we have tried to demonstrate that for Cyprian there
is no objective presence of Christ in the Church independent of the
Church's faith. Therefore, only to the degree that the eucharistic bread
and cup imitate Christ's Last Supper offering are they able to convey to
the believing Church the original intention of Christ to effect union
through them, that is, to effect his "real presence" in the life of the
Church.

Put in another way, the union which Christ effects at the Last Supper
and in his "passio" between himself and the Church is incomplete without
a continual reception and ratification on the part of the Church. That is
why Cyprian can state that, "The 'passio' of the Lord is the sacrifice
that we offer" (Ep 63, 17, 1). If in his "passio" Christ effected unity
between us and himself, to the degree that our Christian lives, especially
when celebrated in the sacramenta of the Church, bring about the unity of

226

the Church, to that degree do they also participate in Christ in his saving "passio." The "passio" of Christ is not finished. In our lives it is the sacrifice that we offer, the sacrifice of our obedience to God through the structure of the Church, our unifying love for one another, but especially as both of these are symbolized in the celebration of the Eucharist.

The Christian as Type of Christ

For Cyprian, then, the presence of Christ through imitation is not limited to ordained ministry. It is the essential vocation of every member of the Church.

Already in the rite of baptism each Christian begins to imitate and be immersed in the saving events of Christ's life. In the water-bath he or she enters into the suffering and death of Christ because Christ himself named his "passio" a "baptism" (Ep 73, 22). In being anointed, the new Christian shares in the reality and identity of Christ himself, "the Anointed of God" (Ep 70, 2, 2), thereby sharing in the mission of Christ. Taking up a theme found in St. Paul (Gal 3, 27; Rom 13, 14), Cyprian repeatedly refers to Christian life as "putting on Christ" (induere Christum). The recurrence of this image in his writings not only emphasizes a real participation in the Lord, but also raises the possibility that baptism in Cyprian's church included a rite of vesting. Finally, in the rite of consignation the Christian's body and life in this world are outwardly marked as a prolongation in history of the physically crucified Christ.

For Cyprian, even though sacramental rites are stylized and
highly symbolic, they nevertheless form part of a Christian's overall
life in the world. Accordingly, they not only instruct the Church in
the deeper meanings of Christian life, they already involve it in living
that life. As events, the rites reveal that all Christian living in the
world is a continual imitation of the historical Christ. And precisely
as imitation the rites show that the individual's Christian existence is
actually the continuation in history of the saving life, death and
resurrection of the Lord. To the extent that one is truly Christian, he
or she is also a living type of Christ.

The Leader of the Eucharist

If the ordinary Christian by his or her life in the world makes
Christ present, the bishop, the ordinary leader of the Eucharist, does
so in a special way. The leader is a type of Christ precisely to the
degree that in his person and role he images the unity of mutual love
in the gathered assembly, the unity which Christ effected in his "passio."
The office of bishop, therefore, is typological. Whereas all the members
of the Church are called to imitate and make Christ present in their
lives, on the imitation of Christ by the bishop, because of his office,
is dependent not only his own Christian identity, but that of the Church
as well. Both in his life and in the liturgy the bishop presents the true
nature of the Church to itself for its own imitation and self-appropriation,
in order that it might thereby more become itself. The singleness of
there being only one bishop in the local Church represents, not simply
the numerical unity of the Church, but also the unbreakable bond of

Christ's love among its members -- the unity of holiness. Consequently,
the potestas (power) of the bishop's office depends to some degree on
his being a concrete, representational instance of the unity and holiness
of the Church. Because this unity and holiness is actually the presence
of Christ in his saving events, only to the degree that the bishop images
the Church to itself is he also an image or type of Christ. Accordingly,
the auctoritas (authority) of the bishop in the Church increases to the
extent that the historical Christ becomes present in his person and in
his life through his faithful imitation of all that Christ did and said.

Our study of eucharistic leadership is entitled, "'Priest' as Type
of Christ," in order to underscore the fundamentally typological nature
of that liturgical role according to Cyprian. The bishop and the presbyters
who lead the Eucharist must first of all be imitators of Christ in their
lives in order to be effective leaders of the Church. But because their
actions at the Eucharist are the deepest expression of their living that
leadership, Cyprian states that at the Eucharist especially, but not
uniquely, "That 'priest' truly acts in the place of Christ who imitates
what Christ did" (Ep 63, 14, 4).

Implications for Sacramental Theology

Some years ago D. Power wrote in a survey article on symbolism in
worship:

> The most difficult [question] is to explain how
> the sign activity and the efficacious causality of
> the sacraments are to be theoretically coordinated.

> Some answers have been offered ... , but there
> is as yet no final solution.[397]

Our present study of eucharistic leadership according to Cyprian has
actually involved us in this very same question: "What is the internal
connection between the imitation of Christ by the eucharistic leader
and Christ's presence at the liturgy through him?" The answer to this
question, as this "Conclusions" section has attempted to demonstrate,
lies for Cyprian within the understanding of salvation history presented
in the New Testament and espoused by the early Church.

According to this imitation-presence ontology, the saving events of
Christ's life are those which He accomplishes precisely by _consciously_
subsuming all other events in history into his Reality. Thus, Calvary is
Christ's death in obedience to the Father; but it is also a death intended
by its divine Victim _as_ the "new covenant," that is, _as_ the fulfilling
enactment of God's one salvation in a way that makes it inchoatively
present and discoverable in all the events of history (e.g. "old covenant").
Therefore, all times and places "exist," supported by the reality of God,
only to the extent that they are actually _symbolic_, only to the degree
that they reveal and make present by their existential conformity the saving
events in which the Son of God through sacrificial love willed their
existence.

This Christocentric nature of all human history is the reason why,
as L.-M. Chauvet puts it,

> The sacramental symbolism does what it says in the
> very act of saying it. It brings about what it

---

[397]David Power, O.M.I., "Symbolism in Worship: A Survey, I," The
Way XIII (1973), 311.

> expresses in the very modalities of that expression.
> It is not an external dressing housing a hidden
> reality which might subsist by itself independently
> of its symbolic manifestation.[398]

In other words, the leader of the Eucharist becomes vehicle for the
presence of Christ in the liturgical assembly to the degree that the
Church by its faith is able to perceive in his actions, as manifestation
of his person, the leadership of Christ the priest in the sacrificial
events of his life, death and resurrection.

---

[398] Louis-Marie Chauvet, "La dimension sacrificielle de l'eucharistie," La Maison-Dieu 123 (1975), 62: "Le symbolisme sacramentel fait
ce qu'il dit, dans l'acte même où il le dit; il fait advenir ce qu'il
exprime, selon les modalités mêmes où il l'exprime. Il n'est pas un
revêtement externe enveloppant une réalité cachée qui pourrait subsister
par elle-même indépendamment de sa manifestation symbolique."

INDEX

Writings of Cyprian

Ad Demetrianum

Dem 9: 152
Dem 22: 80, 84, 93, 162-163
Dem 25: 177
Dem 26: 80, 162, 164, 184

Ad Fortunatum

Fort 5: 169, 182
Fort 6: 111, 116, 122
Fort 7: 101, 112
Fort 8: 5, 80, 103, 112, 164
Fort 9: 188
Fort 11: 87, 102, 103, 107

De bono patientiae

Pat 1: 174
Pat 5: 168, 190
Pat 6: 109, 159
Pat 9: 157, 161, 168
Pat 10: 102-103, 113, 115, 169, 172,
        186
Pat 12: 107
Pat 20: 169

Authors and Personalities

BIBLIOGRAPHY

PRIMARY SOURCES

A. Critical Editions

Bayard, Louis, ed. Saint Cyprien. Correspondance. Vols. I-II. Paris:
    Société d'Édition "Les Belles Lettres," 1925.

Cypriani, Sancti Thasci Caecilii: Opera. Edited by W. Hartel. Corpus
    Scriptorum Ecclesiasticorum Latinorum. Vol. III. 1-3. Vienna:
    C. Geroldi Sons, 1871.

Cypriani, Sancti Episcopi: Opera Pars I. Edited by R. Weber et al.
    Corpus Christianorum Series Latina. Vol. III. Turnhout: Brepols,
    1972.

Cypriani, Sancti Episcopi: Opera Pars II. Edited by M. Simonetti et al.
    Corpus Christianorum Series Latina. Vol. IIIA. Turnhout: Brepols,
    1972.

Funk, F., ed. Opera Patrum Apostolicorum. Vol. I. Tubingen: Laupp,
    1897.

Tertulliani, Quinti Septimi Florentis: Opera. Edited by J.C. Ph. Borleffs
    et al. Corpus Christianorum Series Latina. Vol. I: Opera
    Catholica. Turnhout: Brepols, 1954.

Tertulliani, Quinti Septimi Florentis: Opera. Edited by A. Gerlo et al.
    Corpus Christinaorum Series Latina. Vol. II: Opera Montanistica.
    Turnhout: Brepols, 1954.

B. Translations and Commentaries

Bévenot, Maurice. Cyprian: De Lapsis and De Ecclesiae Catholicae Unitate:
    Text and Translation. Oxford: Clarendon Press, 1971

Conway, Sister M. George Edward. Thasci Caecili Cypriani, De Bono
    Patientiae: A Translation with an Introduction and a Commentary.
    The Catholic University of America Patristic Studies, vol. XCII.
    Washington, D.C.: The Catholic University of America Press, 1957.

Deferrari, R., et al. Saint Cyprian: Treatises. Fathers of the Church,
    vol. XXXVI. New York: Fathers of the Church, Inc., 1958.

238

Donna, Sister Rose Bernard. _Saint Cyprian_. _Letters_ (1-81). Fathers of
the Church, vol. LI. Washington, D.C.: The Catholic University of
America Press, 1964.

Hannan, Mary Louise. _Thasci Caecili Cypriani De Mortalitate_: A Commentary
with an Introduction and Translation. The Catholic University of
America Patristic Studies, vol. XXXVI. Washington, D.C.: The
Catholic University of America Press, 1933.

Keenan, Sister Angela Elizabeth. _Thasci Caecili Cypriani De Habitu_
Virginum: A Commentary with an Introduction and Translation. The
Catholic University of America Patristic Studies, vol. XXXIV.
Washington, D.C.: The Catholic University of America Press, 1932.

Rebenack, E. V. _Thasci Caecili Cypriani De Opere et Eleemosynis_. A
Translation with an Introduction and a Commentary. The Catholic
University of America Patristic Studies, vol. XCIV. Washington,
D.C.: The Catholic University of America Press, 1962.

Réveillaud, Michel. _Saint Cyprien_. _L'oraison dominicale_. _Texte, traduc-_
tion, et notes. Études d'histoire et de philosophie religieuses,
vol. LVIII. Paris: Presses universitaires de France, 1964.

Staniforth, Maxwell. _Early Christian Writers_. New York: Penguin Books,
1968.

SECONDARY SOURCES

d'Alès, Adéhemar. _La Théologie de Saint Cyprien_. Paris: Gabriel
Beauchesne, 1922.

_____. _La Théologie de Tertullien_. Paris: Gabriel Beauchesne, 1905.
Brescia: Paideia, 1974.

Alexander, James, N.A. "The Interpretation of Scripture in the Ante-
Nicene Period," _Interpretation_, XII (1958), 272-280.

Alfonsi, Luigi. "Il 'De dominica oratione' di Cipriano," _Forma Futuri_:
Studi in onore del Cardinale Michele Pellegrino. Torino: Bottega
d'Efrasfo, 1975. Pp. 53-58.

Aubineau, Michel. "La tunique sans coutre du Christ: exégèse patristique
de Jean 19, 23-24," _Kyriakon, Festschrift Johannes Quasten_, I.
Edited by P. Granfield and J. A. Jungmann. Münster: Aschendorff,
1970. Pp. 100-127. Also in: _Recherches Patristiques: Enquêtes sur_
des manuscrits, Textes inédits, Études par Michel Aubineau. Edited
by A. M. Hakkert. Amsterdam: A. M. Hakkert, 1974. Pp. 351-378.

de Backer, Émile. "Tertullien," Pour l'Histoire du mot "Sacramentum," I. Les Anténicéens. Edited by J. de Ghellinck et al. Louvain: "Spicilegium Sacrum Lovaniense," 1924. Pp. 59-152.

Bakhuizen van den Brink, J. N. "Tradition and Authority in the Early Church," Texte und Untersuchungen, XVII (Studia Patristica VII) (1966). Berlin: Akademie-Verlag, 1966. Pp. 3-21.

Ball, Sister Mary Tarcisia. Nature and the Vocabulary of Nature in the Works of Saint Cyprian. The Catholic University of America Patristic Studies, vol. LXXV. Washington, D.C.: The Catholic University of America Press, 1946.

Bardy, Gustave. "Melchisédech dans la tradition patristique," Revue Biblique, XXXV (1926), 496-509; XXXVI (1927), 25-45.

_____. "La Sacerdoce chrétien d'après s. Cyprien," La Vie Spirituelle, Supplement LX (1939), 87-119.

_____. "La Sacerdoce chrétien d'après Tertullien," La Vie Spirituelle, Supplement LVIII (1939), 109-124.

_____. La théologie de l'Église de saint Irénée au Concile de Nicée. Unam Sanctam XIV. Paris: Les Editions du Cerf, 1947. Pp. 167-261.

Barr, James. Old and New in Interpretation: A Study of the Two Testaments. London: SCM Press, Ltd., 1966. Ch. IV: "Typology and Allegory," pp. 103-148.

_____. "Story and History in Biblical Theology," The Journal of Religion, LVI (1976), 1-17.

Batiffol, Pierre. "Aquariens," Dictionnaire d'Archéologie Chrétienne et de Liturgie, I, 2. Edited by Fernand Cabrol. Paris: Letouzey et Ané, 1907. Coll. 2648-2654.

_____. Cathedra Petri: Études d'Histoire ancienne de l'Église. Unam Sanctam, IV. Paris: Les Editions du Cerf, 1938.

Bayard, Louis. Le latin de Saint Cyprien. Paris: Hachette, 1902.

Beck, Alexander. Römisches Recht bei Tertullian und Cyprian. Eine Studie zur frühen Kirchenrechtsgeschichte. Halle, 1930. Aalen: Scientia-Verlag, 1967.

Benoit, Pierre. "Préexistence et Incarnation," Revue Biblique, LXXVII (1970), 5-29.

Benson, W. Cyprian, His Life, His Times, His Work. New York: D. Appleton, 1897.

Berger, Rupert. Die Wendung "Offerre Pro" in der römischen Liturgie. Liturgiewissenschaftliche Quellen und Forschungen, XLI. Münster: Aschendorff, 1965. Pp. 42-69.

Bernard, J. H. "The Cyprianic Doctrine of the Ministry," Essays on the Early History of the Church and the Ministry. Edited by H. B. Swete. London: Macmillan and Co., 1918. Pp. 217-262.

van Beneden, Pierre. Aux origines d'une terminologie sacramentelle. Ordo, ordinare, ordinatio dans la littérature chrétienne avant 313. Louvain: "Spicilegium Sacrum Lovaniense," 1973.

_____. "Ordo. Über den Ursprung einer Kirchlichen Terminologie," Vigiliae Christianae, XXIII (1969), 161-176.

Betz, Johannes. "Eucharistie als zentrales Mysterium," Das Heilsgeschehen in der Gemeinde: Gottes Gnadenhandeln. Mysterium Salutis: Grundriss heilsgeschichtlicher Dogmatik, IV, 2. Edited by Johannes Feiner and Magnus Lohrer. Einsiedeln-Zürich-Köln: Benziger Verlag, 1973. Pp. 185-313.

_____. Eucharistie in der Schrift und Patristik. Handbuch der Dogmengeschichte, IV, 4a. Edited by Michael Schmaus et al. Freiburg: Herder, 1979.

Bévenot, Maurice. "Cyprian and His Recognition of Cornelius," The Journal of Theological Studies, XXVIII (1977), 346-359.

_____. "Episcopat et Primauté chez S. Cyprien," Ephemerides Theologicae Lovanienses, XLII (1966), 176-195.

_____. "'Sacerdos' as Understood by Cyprian," The Journal of Theological Studies, XXX (1979), 413-429.

_____. "The Sacrament of Penance and St. Cyprian's De Lapsis," Theological Studies, XVI (1955), 175-213.

_____. "'Salus extra ecclesiam non est' (St. Cyprian)," Fides Sacramenti-Sacramentum Fidei: Studies in honour of Pieter Smulders. Edited by Hans Jorg Auf der Maur et al. Assen, The Netherlands: van Gorcum, 1981, 97-105.

_____. "Tertullian's thoughts about the christian 'priesthood'," Corona Gratiarum, I. Miscellanea Patristica, Historica et Liturgica, Eligio Dekkers, O. S.B. XII Lustra Complenti Oblata. Brugge: Sint Pietersubdij, 1975. Pp. 125-137.

den Boer, W. "Allegory and History," Romanitas et Christianitas. Festschrift: Iano Henrico Waszink. Edited by W. den Boer et al. Amsterdam-London: North-Holland Publishing Company, 1973. Pp. 15-27.

den Boer, W. "Hermeneutic Problems in early Christian Literature," Vigiliae Christianae, I (1947), 150-167.

Botte, Bernard. "Consummare chez Cyprien," Archivum latinitatis medii aevi (Bulletin du Cange), XII (1937), 43-44.

_____. "Secundi meriti munus," Questions liturgiques et paroissiales, XXI (1936), 84-88.

Boulet, Noëlle Maurice-Denis et Robert. Eucharistie ou La Messe dans ses Variétés, son Histoire et ses Origines. Paris: Letouzey et Ané, 1953.

Bouyer, Louis. "Mysterion," La Vie Spirituelle, Supplément, VI (1952), 397-412.

_____. "Liturgie et Exégèse Spirituelle," La Maison-Dieu, VII (1946), 27-50.

Braun, Réné. Deus Christianorum. Recherches sur le vocabulaire doctrinal de Tertullien. Publications de la Faculté des Lettres et Sciences Humaines d'Alger, XLI. Paris: Presses Universitaires de France, 1962.

Brightmann, F. E. "Terms of Communion, and the Ministration of the Sacraments, in Early Times," Essays on the Early History of the Church and the Ministry. Edited by H. B. Swete. London: Macmillan and Co., Ltd., 1918. Pp. 313-408.

Brown, Peter. The Cult of the Saints. Chicago: University of Chicago Press, 1982.

Camelot, Pierre-Thomas. Die Lehre von der Kirche Väterzeit bis ausschliesslich Augustinus. Handbuch der Dogmengeschichte, III, 3b. Edited by Michael Schmaus et al. Freiburg-Basel-Wien: Herder, 1970.

von Campenhausen, Hans. Kirchliches Amt und geistliche Vollmacht in den ersten drei Jahrhunderten. Tübingen, 1953. ET: Ecclesiastical Authority and Spiritual Power in the Church of the First Three Centuries. Translated by J. A. Baker. Stanford: Stanford University Press, 1969. Ch. IX: "Cyprian and the Episcopate," pp. 265-292.

_____. The Fathers of the Latin Church. Translated by Manfred Hoffmann. London: A. and C. Black, 1964. Ch. II: "Cyprian," pp. 36-60.

Capelle, Bernard. "L'Absolution sacerdotale chez S. Cyprien," Recherches de théologie ancienne et médiévale, VII (1935), 221-235.

Capmany, Jose. "El sacerdocio ministerial segun San Cipriano," Teologia del sacerdotio, IV: Teologia del Sacerdocio en los primeros siglos. Burgos: Ediciones Aldecoa, S.A., 1972. Pp. 145-175.

242

Capmany, José. "Miles Christi" en la espiritualidad de San Cipriano. Colectanea San Paciano, serie teologica, I. Barcelone, 1956.

Cerfaux, Lucien. "Simple Réflections à propos de l'exégèse apostolique," Ephemerides Theologicae Lovanienses, XXV (1949), 565-576.

Childs, Brevard S. Memory and Tradition in Israel. Studies in Biblical Theology, XXXVII. London: SCM Press, Ltd., 1962.

_____. "Prophecy and Fulfillment: A Study of Contemporary Hermeneutics," Interpretation, XII (1958) 259-271.

Clavier, H. "Esquisse de typologie comparée, dans le Nouveau Testament et chez quelques écrivains patristiques," Texte und Untersuchungen, LXXIX (Studia Patristica IV). Berlin: Akademie-Verlag, 1959. Pp. 28-49.

Colson, Jean. L'Evêque, lien d'unité et de Charité chez Saint Cyprien de Carthage. Unam Sanctam, XLIII. Paris: Editions S.O.S., 1961.

Congar, Yves. "L'Ancien Testament, témoin du Christ," La Vie Intellectuelle, Octobre 1949, 335-343.

_____. Tradition and Traditions. Translated by Michael Naseby and Thomas Rainborough. Orig. fr.: Paris: Librairie Arthème Fayard, 1960, 1963. ET: New York: Macmillan, 1967.

_____. "Un essai de théologie sur le sacerdoce. La thèse de l'abbé Long-Hasselmans," Revue des Sciences religieuses, XXV (1951), 187-199, 270-304.

Coppo, A. "Vita cristiana et terminologia liturgica a Carthagine verso la metà del III° secolo," Ephemerides Liturgicae LXXXV (1971), 70-86.

Daly, C. B. "Absolution and Satisfaction in St. Cyprian's Theology of Penance," Texte und Untersuchungen, LXXX (Studia Patristica II). Berlin: Akademie-Verlag, 1957. Pp. 202-207.

Daniélou, Jean. The Bible and the Liturgy. Notre Dame: The University of Notre Dame Press, 1956.

_____. "Les divers sens de l'Écriture dans la tradition chrétienne primitive," Ephemerides Theologicae Lovanienses, XXIV (1948), 119-126.

_____. Etudes d'exégèse judéo-chrétienne (Les Testimonia). Théologie Historique, V. Paris: Beauchesne, 1966.

_____. "Figure et Evénement chez Meliton de Sardes," Neotestamentica et Patristica. Supplements to Novum Testamentum, VI. Edited by W. C. van Unnik et al. Leiden: E. J. Brill, 1962. Pp. 282-292.

Danielou, Jean. "Histoire des Origines Chrétiennes," Recherches de
Science Religieuse, LVII (1969), 106-109. (Review of Coetus
Sanctorum by H. J. Vogt).

_____. The Origins of Latin Christianity. A History of Early Christian
Doctrine before the Council of Nicea, III. Translated by D. Smith
and J. A. Baker. Philadelphia: The Westminster Press, 1977.

_____. "Rahab, figure de l'Église," Irénikon, XXII (1949), 26-45.

_____. "Recherche et Tradition chez les Pères du II et IIIᵉ siècles,"
Nouvelle Revue Théologique, CIV (1972), 453-457.

_____. Sacramentum Futuri. Etudes sur les origines de la typologie
biblique. Paris: Beauchesne, 1950. ET: From Shadows to Reality.
Studies in the Biblical Typology of the Fathers. London: Burns and
Oates, 1960.

Dekkers, Eloi. "L'église ancienne a-t-elle connu la messe du soir?"
Miscellanea Liturgica in honorem L. Cuniberti Mohlberg, I. Roma:
Edizioni Liturgiche, 1948. Pp. 231-257.

Delahaye, Karl. Erneuerung des Seelsorgsformen aus der Sicht der frühen
Patristik. Freiburg: Herder, 1958. French: Ecclesia Mater chez
les Pères des trois premiers siècles. Pour un renouvellement de la
pastorale d'aujourd'hui. Unam Sanctam, XLVI. Paris: Les Editions
du Cerf, 1964. Pp. 100-108.

Deléani, Simone. Christum sequi. Etude d'un thème dans l'oeuvre de saint
Cyprien. Paris: Etudes Augustiniennes, 1979.

_____. "'Gentiles viae'. Contribution à l'étude du style de saint
Cyprien," Revue des Etudes Augustiniennes, XXIII (1977), 221-244.

Delehaye, Hippolyte. Les origines du culte des martyrs. Subsidia
Hagiographica XX. Bruxelles: Societe des Bollandistes, 1912; 2nd
revised ed., 1933.

Demoustier, Adrien. "Episcopat et Union à Rome selon saint Cyprien,"
Recherches de Science Religieuse, LII (1964), 337-369.

_____. "L'ontologie de l'Église selon saint Cyprien," Recherches de
Science Religieuse, LII (1964), 554-588.

Diepen, H. M. "L''Assumptus Homo' patristique," Revue Thomiste, LXIII
(1963), 225-245.

Dölger, F. J. "Öl der Eucharistie. Zum Schreiben der Synode von
Karthago im Frühjahre 255," Antike und Christentum, II (1930),
184-189.

244

Dugmore, C. W. "Sacrament and Sacrifice in the Early Fathers," Journal of Ecclesiastical History, II (1951), 24-37.

Dumont, Charles. "Lectio divina. La lecture et la parole de Dieu d'après saint Cyprien," Bible et vie chrétienne, XXII (1958), 23-33.

Dürig, Walter. Imago. Ein Beitrag zur Terminologie und Theologie der Römischen Liturgie. Münchener Theologische Studien, V. München: Karl Zink Verlag, 1952. "Tertullian," pp. 22-27.

van den Eynde, Damien. Les normes de l'enseignement chrétien dans la littérature patristique des trois premiers siècles. Paris: Gabalda, 1933.

Fahey, Michael A. Cyprian and the Bible. A Study in Third-Century Exegesis. Beiträge zur Geschichte der Biblischen Hermeneutik, IX. Tübingen: J. C. B. Mohr, 1971.

_____. Book Review of Sacramentum Unitatis by Ulrich Wickert. Journal of Biblical Literature, XCI (1972), 582-583.

Faivre, Alexandre. "Les Fonctions Ecclésiales dans les écrits pseudo-clémentins," Revue des Sciences Religieuses, L (1976), 97-111.

_____. Naissance d'une Hierarchie: Les Premières Étapes du Cursus Clérical. Théologie Historique, XL. Paris: Beauchesne, 1977.

Feld, Helmut. Das Verständnis des Abendmahls. Darmstadt: Wissenschaft-liche Buchgesellschaft, 1976. Pp. 88-89.

Finkenzeller, Josef. Die Lehre von den Sakramenten im allgemeinen von der Schrift bis zur Scholastik. Handbuch der Dogmengeschichte, IV, 1a. Edited by Michael Schmaus, et al. Freiburg: Herder, 1980.

Fischer, Joseph A. "Die Konzilien zu Karthago und Rom im Jahr 251," Annuarium Historiae Conciliorum, XL (1979), 263-286.

Fraenkel, P. "Solus dominus misereri potest: Saint Cyprian, De lapsis, ch. XVII, et le problème de son interpretation," Texte und Unter-suchungen, CVII (Studia Patristica X). Berlin: Akademie-Verlag, 1970. Pp. 71-76.

Frend, W.H.C. The Donatist Church. Oxford: Clarendon Press, 1952.

_____. "The 'seniores laici' and the Origins of the Church in North Africa," The Journal of Theological Studies, XII (1961), 280-284.

Fluck, R. "La vie de la communauté chrétienne au IIIe siècle à travers la correspondance de saint Cyprien," Jeunesse de l'Eglise, IV (1945), 89-124.

de Gaiffier, B. "Réflections sur les origines du culte des martyrs," La Maison-Dieu, 52 (1957), 19-43.

Gallicet, Ezio. "Cipriano e la Bibbia: 'Fortis et sublimis vox'," Forma Futuri: Studi in onore del Cardinale Michele Pellegrino. Torino: Bottega d'Efrasfo, 1975. Pp. 43-52.

Gamber, Klaus. "Das Eucharistiegebet in der frühen nordafrikanischen Kirche," Liturgica, III. Scripta et Documenta, XVII. Abadia de Montserrat, 1966. Pp. 51-65.

Gaudette, Pierre. "Baptéme et Vie Chrétienne chez saint Cyprien de Carthage," Laval Théologique et Philosophique, XXVII (1971), 163-190; 251-279.

van der Geest, J. E. L. Le Christ et l'Ancien Testament chez Tertullien. Latinitas Christianorum Primaeva, XXII. Nijmegen: Dekker and van de Vegt, 1972.

Gerhardsson, Birger. "The Seven Parables in Matthew XIII," New Testament Studies, XIX (1972), 16-27.

Gerken, Alexander. Theologie der Eucharistie. München: Kösel-Verlag, 1973.

Glaue, P. "Die Vorlesung heiliger Schriften bei Cyprian," Zeitschrift für die Neutestamentiliche Wissenschaft, XXIII (1924), 141-152.

Granfield, P. "Consilium and Consensus: Decision Making in Cyprian," Jurist, XXXV (1975), 397-408.

_____. "Episcopal Elections in Cyprian: Clerical and Lay Participation," Theological Studies, XXXVII (1976), 41-52.

Grass, H. "Abendmahl - II. Dogmengeschichtlich," Die Religion in Geschichte und Gegenwart. Handbuch für Theologie und Religionswissenschaft, Dritte Auflage. Edited by Kurt Galling. Tübingen: J. C. B. Mohr, 1957. I: 21-34.

Greenslade, S. L. "The Apostolic Ministry - II," Theology, L (1947), 134-138.

_____. "Scripture and Other Norms in Early Theories of the Ministry," The Journal of Theological Studies, XLIV (1943), 171-176.

Grelot, Pierre. Sens chrétien de l'Ancien Testament. Esquisse d'un traité dogmatique. Tournai: Desclée, 1962.

Gribomont, Jean. "Le lien des Deux Testaments selon la Theologie de S. Thomas," Ephemerides Theologicae Lovanienses, XXII (1946), 70-89.

246

Gribomont, Jean. "Sens plenier, typique et littéral," Ephemerides Theologicae Lovanienses, XXV (1949), 577-587.

_____. "Ecclesiam adunare. Un écho de l'Eucharistie africaine et de la Didachè," Recherches de théologie ancienne et médiévale, XXVII (1960), 20-28.

Griffe, E. "De l'Église des Apôtres à l'Église des presbytres," Bulletin de Littérature Ecclésiastique, II (1977), 81-102.

Groh, Dennis E. "Tertullian's Polemic Against Social Co-optation," Church History, XL (1971), 7-14.

Gülzow, H. Cyprian und Novatian. Der Briefwechsel zwischen den Gemeinden in Rom und Karthago zur Zeit der Verfolgung des Kaisers Decius. Beitrage zur Historischen Theologie, XLVIII. Tübingen: J. C. B. Mohr, 1975.

Gurrieri, John A. "Sacramental Validity: The Origins and Use of a Vocabulary," The Jurist, XLI (1981), 21-58.

Gy, Pierre-Marie. "'Eucharistie' et 'Ecclesia' dans le premier vocabulaire de la liturgie chrétienne," La Maison-Dieu, 130 (1977), 19-34.

_____. "Remarques sur le vocabulaire antique du sacerdoce chrétien," Études sur le sacrement de l'ordre. Edited by J. Guyot. Lex Orandi XXII. Paris: Les Editions du Cerf, 1957. Pp. 125-145. ET: in The Sacrament of Holy Orders. Collegeville: The Liturgical Press, 1962, 98-115.

Hammerich, Holger. "Der tägliche Empfang der Eucharistie im 3. Jahrhundert," Zeitschrift für Kirchengeschichte, LXXXIV (1973), 93-95.

Hamp, Vinzenz. "Melchisedech als Typus," Pro Mundi Vita: Festschrift zum eucharistischen Weltkongress 1960. Edited by the Theological Faculty of Ludwig-Maximilian Universität, Munchen. Munchen: Max Hüber Verlag, 1960. Pp. 7-20.

Hanson, Anthony Tyrrell. Jesus Christ in the Old Testament. London: S.P.C.K., 1965.

Harnack, Adolf. "Cyprian als Enthusiast," Zeitschrift für die Neutestamentliche Wissenschaft, III (1902), 177-191.

_____. History of Dogma, vol. II. Translated by Neil Buchanan. Orig. German: 1900. New York: Dover, 1961.

_____. "Das Leben Cyprians von Pontius: die erste christliche Bio-graphie," Texte und Untersuchungen, XXXIX, 3. Leipzig, 1913.

Harnack, Adolf. Militia Christi. Tübingen, 1905; Darmstadt: Wissenschaftliche Buchgesellschaft, 1963. ET: Militia Christi: The Christian Religion and the Military in the First Three Centuries. Translated by David McInnes Gracie. Philadelphia: Fortress Press, 1981.

Hebert, A. G. "Imagerie et Doctrine," La Maison-Dieu, 22 (1950), 69-84.

Hefele, Charles Joseph. Histoire des Conciles, I. Paris, 1855; Paris: Letouzey et Ané, 1907. Pp. 154-156, 165-191. ET: A History of the Christian Councils, I. Translated by William R. Clark. Edinburgh: T & T Clark, 1872. Pp. 86-116.

Hein, Kenneth. Eucharist and Excommunication. A Study in Early Christian Doctrine and Discipline. 2nd and revised edition. European University Papers, XIX. Frankfurt: Peter Lang, 1973. Pp. 365-410.

Hinchliff, Peter. Cyprian of Carthage and the Unity of the Christian Church. London: Geoffrey Chapman, 1974.

Hoppenbrouwers, H. A. M. Recherches sur la terminologie du martyre de Tertullian à Lactance. Latinitas Christianorum Primaeva XIV. Nijmegen: Dekker & van de Vegt, 1961.

Hübner, Siegfried. "Kirchenbusse und Exkommunikation bei Cyprian," Zeitschrift für katholische Theologie, LXXXIV (1962), 49-84; 171-215.

Hummel, Edelhard L. The Concept of Martyrdom According to St. Cyprian of Carthage. Studies in Christian Antiquity, vol. IX. Washington, D.C.: The Catholic University of America Press, 1946.

Janssen, Harry. Kultur und Sprache. Zur Geschichte der alten Kirche im Spiegel der Sprachentwicklung. Von Tertullian bis Cyprian. Latinitas Christiana Primaeva VIII. Nijmegen: Dekker & van de Vegt, 1938.

Jay, Pierre. "Saint Cyprien et la doctrine du Purgatoire," Rechercheres de Théologie ancienne et mediévale, XXVII (1960), 133-136.

Jourjon, Maurice. "Les premiers emplois du mot laïc dans la littérature patristique," Lumière et Vie, LXV (1963), 37-42.

Kelsey, David H. The Uses of Scripture in Recent Theology. Philadelphia: Fortress Press, 1975. Ch. 4: "Event and Expression."

Kilmartin, Edward J. "Apostolic Office: Sacrament of Christ," Theological Studies, XXXVI (1975), 243-264.

_____. "Eucharist: Nourishment for Communion," Populus Dei. II: Ecclesia. Edited by Giuseppe D'Ercole. Communio XI. Rome, 1969. Pp. 1043-1085.

248

Kilmartin, Edward J. "Ministry and Ordination in Early Christianity against a Jewish Background," Studia Liturgica, XIII (1979), 42-69.

_____. "Patristic Views of Sacramental Sanctification," Readings in Sacramental Theology. Edited by C. Stephen Sullivan, F.S.C. Englewood Cliffs, N.J.: Prentice-Hall, 1964. Pp. 144-164.

Klein, Gunter. "Die hermeneutische Struktur des Kirchengedankens bei Cyprian," Zeitschrift für Kirchengeschichte, LXVIII (1957), 48-68.

Kneller, C. A. "Sacramentum Unitatis. Zu Cyprians Schrift ad Donatum," Zeitschrift für katholische Theologie, XL (1916), 676-703.

Koch, H. Cyprianische Untersuchungen. Arbeiten zur Kirchengeschichte IV. Bonn: Marcus und Weber, 1926.

_____. "Die Didache bei Cyprian?" Zeitschrift fur die Neutestamentliche Wissenschaft, VIII (1907), 69-70.

Kolping, Adolf. Sacramentum Tertullianeum. Bottrop i. W.: Wilhelm Postberg, 1948.

Kottje, Raymund. "Das Aufkommen der täglichen Eucharistiefeier in der Westkirche und die Zölibatsforderung," Zeitschrift für Kirchengeschichte, LXXXII (1971), 218-228.

Kötting, Bernhard. "Zur Frage der 'successio apostolica' in frühchristlicher Sicht," Catholica, XXVII (1973), 234-247.

_____. "Die Stellung der Konfessors in der Alten Kirche," Jahrbuch für Antike und Christentum, XIX (1976), 7-23.

Laminski, A. "War das altkirchliche Episkopat wirklich monarchisch? Gemeinde und Bishof bei Cyprian," Theologische Versuche, VIII. Edited by J. Rogge and G. Schille. Berlin: Evangelische Verlagsanstalt, 1977. Pp. 85-96.

Lang-Hinrichsen, Dietrich. "Die Lehre von der Geduld in der Patristik und bei Thomas von Aquin," Geist und Leben, XXIV (1951), 209-222; 284-299. Esp. 220-222.

Legrand, Hervé, M. "La présidence de l'Eucharistie selon la tradition ancienne," Spiritus, XVIII (1977), 409-431. ET: Worship, LIII (1979), 413-438.

_____. "Recherches sur le presbyterat et l'épiscopat," Revue des Sciences philosophiques et théologiques, LIX (1975), 645-724.

Lehaut, A. "Aquariens," Dictionnaire d'Histoire et de Geographie Ecclesiastiques, III. Edited by Alfred Boudrillart. Paris: Librairie Letouzey et Ané, 1924. Col. 1102-1103.

Lemaire, André. "Ministères aux origines de l'Église," Spiritus, XVIII (1977), 386-408.

Lepin, Marius. L'Idée du Sacrifice de la Messe d'après les théologiens depuis l'origine jusqu'à nos jours. Paris: G. Beauchesne, 1926.

Lods, Marc. Confesseurs et martyrs. Successeurs des prophètes dans L'Église des trois premiers siècles. Cahiers théologiques XLI. Neuchâtel-Paris: Delachaux & Niestlé S.A., 1958.

Loi, Vincenzo. "Il Termine 'Mysterium' nella Literatura Latina cristiana prenicena," Virgiliae Christianae, XIX (1965), 210-232.

de Lubac, Henri. "A propos de l'Allégorie chrétienne," Recherches de Science Religieuse, XLVII (1959), 5-43.

_____. "Corpus Mysticum. L'Eucharistie et L'Église au Moyen Age. 2nd Edition. Paris: Aubier, Éditions Montaigne, 1949. "Note B: Sur l'Eucharistie 'anti-type'," pp. 351-357.

_____. L'Ecriture dans la tradition. Paris: Aubier, 1967. ET: The Sources of Revelation. New York: Herder and Herder, 1968.

_____. "'Typologie' et 'Allégorisme'," Recherches de Science Religieuse, XXXIV (1947), 180-226.

Luneau, Auguste. "Moïse et les Pères latins," Cahiers Sidniens, VIII (1954), 401-421.

Lutzenberger, George. "The priest as a member of a ministerial college. The development of the Church's ministerial structure from 9? to c.300 AD.," Recherches de Theologie ancienne et medievale, XLIII (1976), 3-63.

de Margerie, Bertrand. "L'intérét théologique du "De Mortalitate' de saint Cyprien," Sciences Ecclésiastiques, XV (1963), 199-212.

Marliangeas, B. -D. Clés pour une théologie du ministère: In persona Christi, In persona Ecclesiae. Theologie Historique, LI. Paris: Editions Beauchesne, 1978.

Marliangeas, B. -D. "'In Persona Christi' 'In Persona Ecclesiae': Note sur les origines et le développement de l'usage de ces expressions dans la théologie latine.' Vatican II: La Liturgie après Vatican II. Unam Sanctam LXVI. Paris: Les Éditions du Cerf, 1967. Pp. 283-288.

_____. "In Persona Christi - In Persona Ecclesiae," Spiritus, XIX (1978), 19-33.

250

Marrou, H. I. "'Doctrina' et 'disciplina' dans la langue des Pères de l'Eglise," Archivum latinitatis medii aevi (Bulletin du Cange), IX (1934), 5-25.

Martin, Jochen. Die Genese des Amtspriestertums in der frühen Kirche. Questiones Disputatae XLVIII. Freiburg: Herder, 1972. Pp. 87-119.

Mayer, Cornelius Petrus. Die Zeichen in der geistigen Entwicklung und in der Theologie des jungen Augustinus. Cassiciacum XXIV, I. Würzburg: Augustinus-Verlag, 1969. Pp. 284-297.

Meslin, M. "Institutiones ecclesiastiques et clericalization dans l'Eglise (II-Ve S.)," Concilium, XLVII (1969), 41-52. ET: "Ecclesiastical Institutions and Clericalization from 100 to 500 A.D.," Concilium, XLVII (1959), 39-54.

Michaélidès, Dimitri. Sacramentum chez Tertullien. Paris: Études Augustiniennes, 1970.

Michel, G. A. "Firmilian and Eucharistic Consecration," The Journal of Theological Studies, V (1954), 215-220.

Mohrmann, Christine. "Episkopos-Speculator," Études sur le latin des Chrétiens, IV. Storia e Letteratura CXLIII. Roma: Edizioni di Storia e Letteratura, 1977. Pp. 231-252.

_____. "Pascha - Passio - Transitus," Ephemerides Liturgicae, LXVI (1952), 37-52. Also in: Études sur le latin des Chrétiens, I. Storia e Letteratura LXV. Roma: Edizioni di Storia e Letteratura, 1958. Pp. 205-222.

_____. "Praedicare - Tractare - Sermo," Études sur le latin des Chrétiens, II. Storia e Letteratura LXXXVII. Roma: Edizioni di Storia e Letteratura, 1961. Pp. 63-72.

_____. "Quelques observations sur 'sacramentum' chez Tertullien," Romantias et Christianitas. Festschrift: Iano Henrico Waszink. Edited by W. den Boer et al. Amsterdam-London: North-Holland Publishing Company, 1973. Pp. 233-242.

_____. "Sacramentum dans les plus anciens textes chrétiens," Harvard Theological Review, XLVII (1954), 141-152. Also in: Études sur le latin des Chrétiens, I. Storia e Letteratura LXV. Roma: Edizioni di Storia e Letteratura, 1958. Pp. 233-244.

_____. "Statio," Études sur le latin des Chrétiens, III. Storia e Letteratura CIII. Roma: Edizioni di Storia e Letteratura, 1965. Pp. 307-333. Originally in: Vigiliae Christianae, VII (1953), 221-245.

Mohrmann, Christine. "Word-Play in the Letters of St. Cyprian," Études sur le latin des Chrétiens, I. Storia e Letteratura LXV. Roma: Edizioni di Storia e Letteratura, 1958. Pp. 280-298.

Montiminy, Jean-Paul. "L'offrande sacrificielle dans l'anamnèse des liturgies anciennes," Revue des Sciences philosophiques et théologiques, L (1966), 385-406.

_____. "La Participation des laïcs à l'Eucharistie du IIIe au VIe siècle," Sciences Ecclésiastiques, XIX (1967), 351-372.

Morel, Valentin. "Le développement de la 'discipline' sous l'action du Saint-Esprit chez Tertullien," Revue d'Histoire Ecclesiastique, XXXV (1939), 243-265.

Navickas, John Cyprian. The Doctrine of St. Cyprian on the Sacraments. Würzburg: C. J. Becker, 1924.

Neunheuser, Burkhard. Taufe und Firmung. Handbuch der Dogmengeschichte, IV, 2. Edited by Michael Schmaus et al. Freiburg im Breisgau: Herder, 1964. ET: Baptism and Confirmation. Translated by John Jay Hughes. New York: Herder and Herder, 1964. Esp. pp. 92-106.

Nock, Arthur Darby. "Hellenistic Mysteries and Christian Sacraments," Mnemosyne, IV, V (1952), 177-213. Also in: Essays on Religion and the Ancient World. Cambridge, Mass.: Harvard University Press, 1972. Pp. 791-820.

O'Malley, T. P. Tertullian and the Bible: Language - Imagery - Exegesis. Latinitas Christianorum Primaeva XXI. Nijmegen: Dekker & van de Vegt, 1967.

Osborn, E. F. "Cyprian's Imagery," Antichthon, VII (1973), 65-79.

Pellegrino, Michele. "Eucaristia e martirio in San Cipriano," Convivium Dominicum. Studi sull' Eucaristia nei Padri della Chiesa antica e Miscellanea patristica. Catane: Centro di Studi Sull' Antico Cristianesimo, Università di Catania, 1959. Pp. 133-150.

_____. "Le sens ecclésial du martyre," Revue des Sciences Religieuses, XXXV (1961), 151-175.

Pepin, Jean. Mythe et Allégorie: Les Origines greques et les Contestations judeo-chrétiennes. Paris: Aubier, Editions Montaigne, 1958.

_____. "Stilla aquae modicae multo infusa vino," Divinitas, XI (1967), 365-369.

Perler, Othmar. "L'Évêque, représentant du Christ, selon les documents des premiers siècles," L'Episcopat et l'Eglise universelle. Edited by Yves Congar et B. D. Dupuy. Unam Sanctam XXXIX. Paris: Les Éditions du Cerf, 1962. Pp. 49-53.

_____, ed. Méliton de Sardes: Sur La Pâque; et Fragments. Sources Chretiennes CXXIII. Paris: Les Éditions du Cerf, 1966. "La Typologie," pp. 29-32.

Pétré, Hélène. Caritas. Étude sur le vocabulaire latin de la charité chrétienne. Louvain: "Spicilegium Sacrum Lovaniense," 1948.

Plummer, A. "Sacraments," A Dictionary of the Bible, Vol. 4. Edited by A. Hastings. Edinburgh: T. & T. Clark, 1902. Pp. 327-329.

Plumpe, Joseph C. Mater Ecclesia: An Inquiry into the Concept of the Church as Mother in Early Christianity. Washington, D.C.: The Catholic University of America Press, 1943. "Tertullian:" pp. 45-62; "Cyprian:" pp. 81-108.

de la Potterie, Ignatius. "L'origine et le sens primitif du mot 'laïc'," Nouvelle Revue theologique, LXXX (1958), 840-853.

Poukens, J. B. "Cyprian et ses contemporaines," Pour l'Hisdu mot "Sacramentum," I. Les Anténiceens. Edited by J. de Ghellinck et al. Louvain: "Spicilegium Sacrum Lovaniense," 1924. Pp. 153-220.

Probst, Ferdinand. Liturgie der drei ersten christlichen Jahrhunderte. Tübingen, 1870. Pp. 183-207, 215-230.

Rahner, Karl. "History of the World and Salvation History," Theological Investigations, V. London: Darton, Longman & Todd, 1966. Pp. 97-114.

_____. "One Mediator and Many Mediations," Theological Investigations, IX. London: Darton, Longman & Todd, 1968. Pp. 169-184.

Ratzinger, J. Volk und Haus Gottes in Augustins Lehre von der Kirche. Münchener Tehologische Studien VII. München: Karl Zink Verlag, 1954. Pp. 92ff.

Renaud, Bruno. "L'Église comme assemblée liturgique selon saint Cyprien," Recherches de Théologie ancienne et medievale, XXXVIII (1971), 5-68.

_____. "Eucharistie et culte eucharistique selon saint Cyprien." Université Catholique de Louvain: Unpublished Dissertation, 1967.

Réveillaud, Michel. "Note pour une Pneumatologie Cyprienne," Texte und Untersuchungen, LXXXI (Studia Patristica VI). Berlin: Akademie-Verlag, 1962. Pp. 181-187.

253

Ring, Thomas G. _Auctoritas bei Tertullian, Cyprian and Ambrosius_. Cassiciacum XXIX. Würzburg: Augustinus-Verlag, 1975.

Rordorf, Willi et al., edd. _L'Eucharistie des Premiers Chrétiens_. Le Point Théologique XVII. Paris: Beauchesne, 1976. ET: _The Eucharist of the Early Christians_. Translated by M. J. O'Connell. New York: Pueblo, 1978. "Tertullian," by Victor Saxer, pp. 132-155. "Cyprian of Carthage," by Raymond Johanny, pp. 156-182.

_____. "La théologie du ministère dans l'Eglise ancienne," _Verbum Caro_, XVIII (1964), 84-104.

Ruch, C. "La Messe d'après les Pères jusqu'à saint Cyprien," _Dictionnaire de Théologie Catholique_, X, I^e. Paris: Librarie Letouzey et Ané, 1928. Col. 864-964.

Rusche, Helga. "Die Gestalt des Melchisedek," _Münchener Theologischer Zeitschrift_, VI (1955), 230-252.

Ruwet, Jean. "Lecture liturgique et livres saints du Nouveau Testament," _Biblica_, XXI (1940), 378-405.

Sage, Michael M. _Cyprian_. Patristic Monograph Series I. Cambridge, Mass.: The Philadelphia Patristic Foundation, Ltd., 1975.

Saumagne, Charles. _Saint Cyprien, Evêque de Carthage, "Pape" d'Afrique (248-258). Contribution à l'étude des "persécutions" de Dèce et de Valérien_. Paris: Editions du Centre National de la Recherche Scientifique, 1975.

Saxer, Victor. Book Review of _La Condition Collégiale des Prêtres au IIIe Siècle_ by A. Vilela (Paris: Beauchesne, 1971), _Vetera Christianorum_, IX (1972), 108-115.

_____. "Figura Corporis et Sanguinis Domini: une formule eucharistique des premiers siècles chez Tertullien, Hippolyte et Ambrose," _Rivista di Archeologia Cristiana_, XLVII (1971), 65-89.

_____. _Morts, Martyrs, Reliques en Afrique Chrétienne aux Premiers Siècles. Les témoignages de Tertullien, Cyprien, et Augustin à la lumière de l'archeologie africaine_. Théologie Historique LV. Paris: Beauchesne, 1980.

_____. _La vie liturgique et quotidienne à Carthage vers le milieu du IIIe siècle. Le témoignage de S. Cyprien et ses contemporains d'Afrique_. Studi di Antichità Cristiana XXIX. Cité du Vatican: Pontificio Istituto di Archeologia Cristiana, 1969.

Schrijner, Joseph et Christine Mohrmann. _Studien zur Syntax der Briefs des hl. Cyprian, I & II_. Latinitas Christianorum Primaeva V & VI. Nijmegen: Dekker & van de Vegt, 1936-1937.

Schweitzer, Erich. "Fragen der Liturgie in Nordafrika zur Zeit Cyprians," Archiv für Liturgiewissenschaft, XII (1970), 69-84.

Simonis, Walter. Ecclesia Visibilis et Invisibilis. Untersuchungen zur Ekklesiologie und Sakramentenlehre in der afrikanischen Tradition von Cyprian bis Augustinus. Frankfurt am Main: Joseph Knecht, 1970.

von Soden, Hans. "MUSTERION und sacramentum in den ersten Jahrhunderten der Kirche," Zeitschrift für die Neutestamentliche Wissenschaft, XII (1911), 188-227.

Stanley, David M. "Become Imitators of Me: The Pauline Conception of Apostolic Tradition," Biblica , XL (1959), 859-877.

Stommel, E. "Die bischöfliche Kathedra im christlichen Altertum," Münchener Theologische Zeitschrift, III (1952), 17-32.

Struckmann, Adolf. Die Gegenwart Christi in der hl. Eucharistie nach den schriftlichen Quellen der vornicänischen Zeit. Vienna: Verlag von Mayer, 1905.

Swann, William. "The Relationship Between Penance, Reconciliation with the Church and Admission to the Eucharist in the Letters and De Lapsis of Cyprian of Carthage." Catholic University of America: Unpublished Dissertation, 1981.

Swete, H. B. "Eucharistic belief in the second and third centuries," The Journal of Theological Studies, III (1902), 161-177.

Taft, Robert. "Historicism Revisited," Studie Liturgica, XIV (1982), 97-109. French: "Historicisme: Une Conception à Revoir," La Maison-Dieu, 146 (1981), 61-83.

de la Taille, Maurice. "Le sens du mot 'Passio' dans la lettre LXIII de saint Cyprien," Recherches de Science Religieuse, XXI (1931), 576-581.

Taylor, John H. "St. Cyprian and the Reconciliation of Apostates," Theological Studies, III (L1942), 27-46.

Thani Nayagam, X. S. The Carthaginian Clergy. A Short Documentary Chronology of St. Cyprian's Life and Writings, together with a Study of the Carthaginian Clergy during the Period 248-258. Tuticorin: Tamil Literature Society, 1960.

Thornton, Lionel S. The Form of the Servant, II: The Dominion of Christ. London: Dacre Press, 1952.

Tigcheler, Jo. Didyme L'Aveugle et L'Exégèse Allégorique. Nijmegen: Dekker & van de Vegt, 1977. Pp. 15-50.

Tixeront, J. History of Dogmas, I: The Antenicene Theology. ET: St. Louis: B. Herder, 1930. Ch. XI: "St. Cyprian and the Baptismal Controversy," pp. 355-376.